English Unlimited

Coursebook · A2+
HTL
1

Alex Tilbury
Theresa Clementson
Leslie Anne Hendra
David Rea

Barry Jenkins
Brian Lott
Andrea Zimpernik
Liselotte Pope-Hoffmann
Susanna Häring
Waltraud Donath
Bernd Mayr

With contributions by Maggie Baigent, Chris Cavey & Nick Robinson
Course consultant: Adrian Doff

www.oebv.at

Contents

Unit 0 — About you
p. 7

Goals
- Introduce yourself
- Say what you can do
- Fill in an online form
- Ask for and give personal information
- Talk about your school career / ideal school day

Vocabulary
- Countries and languages
- Introducing yourself
- Letters, numbers, addresses
- Personal information

Grammar
- Subject pronouns and possessive adjectives

Listening
- Introducing yourself
- Clara enrolling in a course

Unit 1 — People in your life
p. 12

Goals
- Introduce people, say who they are
- Ask questions to check information
- Talk about present and past schools / school experiences
- Describe people's personality
- Describe relationships
- Write short profiles about people

Vocabulary
- People you know
- Talking about schools
- How you know people
- Personality

Grammar
- Possessive 's
- be past: was, were
- Adjectives and adverbs

Listening
- Open day at school
- Michael and Donna's friends
- Greetings

Unit 2 — Away from home
p. 22

Goals
- Say what you want to do
- Say what your interests are
- Make and respond to offers and requests
- Write an email requesting something

Vocabulary
- Interests and wants
- Offers and requests
- Taking care of a guest

Grammar
- a, an or some
- Present simple

Listening
- What do you miss?
- Talking about free time activities
- Gwen asking for things
- Melek's guest

p. 34 **Competence check: Units 1–2**

Unit 3 — Your time, your space!
p. 38

Goals
- Talk about your free time, likes and dislikes
- Talk about habits and customs
- Make and respond to invitations
- Talk about cities, neighbourhoods and homes
- Find information in adverts for rooms
- Take a phone message, ask people to repeat
- Write a blog entry

Vocabulary
- Free time activities
- Adverbs of frequency
- Invitations
- Describing places / homes
- Things in the home
- Prepositions of place
- An environmentally-friendly home
- Adverts for rooms

Grammar
- Subject / Object pronouns
- Adverbs
- Sentence structure

Listening
- Invitations
- My favourite room
- Alicja looking for a room

Unit 4 — Changes
p. 50

Goals
- Talk about past events
- Talk about first times
- Talk about technical innovations
- Talk about new experiences
- Write a personal letter / email giving news

Vocabulary
- Good and bad experiences

Grammar
- Past simple verbs
- Past simple

Listening
- Yoko's technology firsts
- From Nigeria to Scotland
- Andrew's first swimming experience

Unit 5 — What would you like?
p. 60

Goals
- Buy things in shops
- Talk about preferences and give reasons
- Talk about shopping and food
- Order a meal
- Write short practical requests and reminders

Vocabulary
- Shops and shopping
- Preferences and giving reasons
- Buying things
- Food
- Describing food

Grammar
- Countable and uncountable nouns

Listening
- Interview with the manager of a new shopping mall
- Jason in the shopping centre
- Ordering in a restaurant

p. 70 **Competence check: Units 3–5**

2

Speaking	Reading	Writing	Extras	
- Enrolling in a course - Talking about your school career / ideal school day	- School careers	- Introducing yourself - Creating an ideal school day	- **Independent learning:** How to use this book	

Speaking	Reading	Writing	Extras	Explore p. 19
- Introductions, relationships - Talking about your old school / a person you know well - Talking about famous people	- What was your old school like?	- Introductions / Relationships - Describing your old school	- **Keyword:** *OK* - **Across cultures:** Greetings	- **Writing:** A profile about yourself - **Reading:** Emails and profiles from abroad

Speaking	Reading	Writing	Extras	Explore p. 30
- Interviewing a person - Asking for something - Taking care of a guest	- Sofasurfing.com - Melek's guest	- A profile for a website - Writing an email from a business trip	- **Keyword:** *in* - **Across cultures:** Breakfasts	- **Reading:** Leaflets for language holidays - **Writing:** An email requesting something - **Listening:** Sightseeing in London

Speaking	Reading	Writing	Extras	Explore p. 48
- How often do you …? - Free time / special occasions - Inviting someone out - Describing places / homes / famous landmarks - Renting a room	- Interviews from the online magazine *Leisure Exhibition* - Place to place - DublinCapitalRentals.com	- Having a good time to me means … - Describing your home - Planning activities for a weekend with colleagues	- **Keyword:** *on*	**Speaking:** A phone message **Writing:** A blog entry

Speaking	Reading	Writing	Extras	Explore p. 58
- Accidental inventions - Talking about useful inventions - Talking about your experiences	- Things that changed the world	- Writing about Susan's last weekend	- **Keyword:** *have* - **Independent lerarning:** Self-study - **Info point:** Shapes and drawings	- **Reading:** Forest park adventure - **Writing:** A personal letter / email giving news

Speaking	Reading	Writing	Extras	Explore p. 67
- Talking about preferences - Buying things in shops - Talking about food - Ordering a meal - Describing different dishes	- Food myths	- Describing food	- **Keyword:** *this, that, …* - **Independent learning:** Using a dictionary	- **Writing:** Short requests and reminders - **Listening:** Ordering a takeaway on the phone - **Speaking:** In the shopping mall - **Reading:** A takeaway menu

Unit 6 — Work and leisure
p. 74

Goals
- Talk about work and school
- Describe present activities
- Say why you can't do things
- Say you're not sure about facts and numbers

Vocabulary
- Work and school 1
- *Make* and *do*
- Work and school 2
- Saying you're busy

Grammar
- Present progressive

Listening
- Working hard
- Liam and Melanie talking at a club
- Julie on the phone

Unit 7 — Getting around
p. 86

Goals
- Make arrangements, talk about timetables
- Buy a travel ticket
- Check in and board a flight
- Tell a story
- Talk about a journey
- Write invitations and give directions

Vocabulary
- Using transport
- Things for a trip
- Prepositions of movement
- Buying a ticket
- Airports
- Storytelling expressions

Grammar
- Present tense: arrangements and timetables
- Articles

Listening
- Mary on the phone
- Charlie buying a ticket
- Belinda at the airport
- Patrick's journey

Unit 8 — Getting together
p. 98

Goals
- Find information in a cinema programme
- Talk about films
- Make and respond to suggestions
- Make arrangements to meet
- Talk about hopes and plans
- Planning a weekend break
- Write and reply to an invitation
- Write a thank-you note

Vocabulary
- Films
- Suggestions
- Talking about films

Grammar
- Comparatives and superlatives
- Passive

Listening
- John and Rachel's phone call
- A film night
- Weekend in La Mauricie

p. 112 **Competence check: Units 6–8**

Unit 9 — Are you OK?
p. 116

Goals
- Talk about health
- Buy things in a pharmacy
- Understand instructions on medicines
- Give advice
- Write an email apologising

Vocabulary
- The body and health
- Giving advice
- Giving reasons for advice

Grammar
- Giving advice with *if*

Listening
- Marc at the pharmacy
- Talking about remedies

Unit 10 — Experiences
p. 128

Goals
- Talk about experiences
- Say what you've never done and always wanted to do
- Talk about places you've been to
- Find out information about things
- Start and finish conversations

Vocabulary
- Sights
- Safety signs
- Getting information

Grammar
- Present perfect verbs
- Present perfect
- Past perfect

Listening
- I've always wanted to …
- Advice about day trip destinations

p. 140 **Competence check: Units 9–10**

- p. 144 — **Activities**
- p. 150 — **Grammar reference and practice / Irregular verbs**
- p. 169 — **Vocabulary**
- p. 186 — **Key Competence checks**
- p. 189 — **Maps**

Speaking	Reading	Writing	Extras	Explore p. 84
- What's happening right now? - Your typical week - Sorry, we're just having dinner - Saying you're busy	- What do you do all day? - Working as a travel agent	- What are people doing? - What are your tasks at work?	- **Keyword:** *spend* - **Across cultures:** School life - **Info point:** Calculating	- **Listening:** American high schools - **Speaking:** Expressing uncertainty

Speaking	Reading	Writing	Extras	Explore p. 96
- Talking about arrangements - Getting around - A journey you like - Buying a ticket - At an airport - Telling a story - Describing a journey	- How do you get there? - One-wheeled wonder - Help! A traveller's tale	- A journey you like - Your story	- **Keyword:** *get* - **Across cultures:** Saying sorry	- **Writing:** Giving directions - **Listening:** A trip to Cambodia

Speaking	Reading	Writing	Extras	Explore p. 109

- Making comparisons
- Choosing a film to see
- Arranging to meet
- Planning a film night
	- A cinema programme
	- John and Rachel's messages
		- Describing a film	- **Keyword:** *about*	- **Writing:**
				  – Invitations and replies
				  – A review of your favourite film
				- **Speaking:** Presenting your favourite film
				- **Reading:** A festival programme

Speaking	Reading	Writing	Extras	Explore p. 125
- At a pharmacy - Remedies for a cold - If I have a cold, …	- Medicine packages - Home remedies - Stay healthy at school	- Home remedies – giving your opinion - A blog entry giving advice	- **Keyword:** *of* - **Info point:** Measuring	- **Writing:** An email apologising - **Listening:** Staying healthy

Speaking	Reading	Writing	Extras	Explore p. 137
- Have you ever …? - I've always wanted to … - Places you've been to	- Grandpa Frank's story - Great places	- Things you've never done - An article about a famous Austrian sight - An article about a fascinating place	- **Keyword:** *at, take* - **Across cultures:** Your experiences	- **Listening:** World travellers - **Speaking 1:** A famous place - **Speaking 2:** Starting / Finishing conversations

Each unit of this book is designed to help you achieve specific communicative **GOALS**. These goals are listed at the beginning of each unit. They are based on the language-learning goals stated in the Common European Framework of Reference for Languages (CEFR).

The first pages of each unit help you develop your language skills and knowledge. These pages include **SPEAKING**, **LISTENING**, **READING**, **WRITING**, **GRAMMAR** and **VOCABULARY**, with key language highlighted in blue. They are followed by a communicative speaking or writing task which will help you activate what you have learned.

The **Extras** section of each unit begins with a **Keyword**, which looks at one of the most common and useful words in English. This is sometimes followed by an **Across cultures** or an **Independent learning** section. At selected points in the coursebook, Extras also includes an **Info point** with *HTL*-relevant information and terminology. The Extras section is modular in nature and doesn't have to be dealt with at the point where it occurs in the unit.

The **Explore** section provides additional language and skills work, aiming to help you become a better communicator in English. In this section, you are also introduced to the task formats which you will encounter in the **Standardisierte Reife- und Diplomprüfung**.

The unit concludes with a **Self-assessment** grid in which you are encouraged to measure your progress against the unit goals set out at the beginning. You can complete this grid either in class or at home.

After every third unit, a **Competence check** section of four pages gives you the opportunity to revise the topics and language from the previous three units.

At the back of the book, there is a **Grammar reference** with extra practice exercises, a **Picture dictionary** and a **Vocabulary** with English sample sentences and German translations.

 638j3i Go to www.oebv.at and type in the code for additional online materials.

 The **Writing coach** gives you information about text types and tips for writing good texts. The different text types are relevant for the **Standardisierte Reife- und Diplomprüfung**.

 Media tasks are tasks which train your digital competence.

 Business training are tasks which train business communication and competence.

 This audio is on the teacher's CD.

 This audio is available online. Go to www.oebv.at and enter the code.

 Certain exercises have been marked this way to indicate that they are more challenging and/or are an optional consolidation exercise. These exercises may go beyond A2+ level.

Goals
- introduce yourself
- say what you can do
- fill in an online form
- ask for and give personal information
- talk about your school career / ideal school day

Hi, my name's Andrew

Vocabulary **1**

Countries and languages

1 qp49hp

a Listen to the introductions. Number them in the order you hear them.

Hi, my name's Sean and I'm from a small town in Wales. I can speak English, some French, some Japanese and some Hungarian. My older sister taught me to snowboard last winter. I practise very often, so I can do it pretty well now.

Hello, I'm Ina. I'm from Slovakia. We live close to the Austrian border, so I can speak some German, Slovak, of course, English and Russian. Our house is quite big, so I have a great, old piano in my room. I can play it very well and sometimes, when our aunt, uncle and cousins come over, we sing the latest songs together. This is a lot of fun.

Hello my name's Valery. I'm from the United States. My family lives in a small house near the coast in San Francisco. My first language is English, but I also speak Spanish and some Chinese. My brother and I like surfing. We go surfing every day after school. I can even do it with my dog in front of me on the board.

Hi, my name's George. I'm from Australia. My parents and I live in a cool new flat in Sydney. From my bedroom, I can see the famous Opera House. English is my mother tongue, but I also speak a little French. My grandma lived in Hong Kong for five years, so she showed me how to write my name in Chinese.

Hi, I'm Anna. I'm from Austria. I live in an old farmhouse in Salzburg with my mother, my brother and our cats Suzie and Tommy. I speak German, of course, English, and I can read Arabic letters, but I can't speak Arabic. Every Saturday I go to dance classes with my friends. I like it a lot. Our instructor is very good and always makes us laugh.

Hi, I'm Umut. I'm from Turkey. My hometown is Istanbul, where my parents own a large hotel. We also live there on the top floor. My two little brothers and I often play hide and seek in the hotel at night. We meet a lot of people from different countries, so I speak Turkish, German, English, and some Arabic. I can greet people in Japanese.

b Read the introductions in 1a. Find and list in abbreviations:

1 five countries: _____
2 11 languages: _____
3 who lives in a house: _____
4 who speaks some Arabic: _____
5 who can dance: _____
6 who can't speak French: _____
7 who doesn't have brothers and / or sisters: _____

About you

c Think of five more countries. What languages do people speak there? What do you know about these countries?

Example: In Canada, they speak English and French. It's a country with a lot of forests and clean rivers.

Writing & Speaking **2** Write your own paragraph about yourself. Then talk in groups. Introduce yourselves and find out what languages you can speak.

Listening **3** Listen to Clara's phone call to the holiday exchange programme manager and write down her personal details in the form below.

2 ni29a3

```
http://www.holidayexchange.ie
```

Martello House   11 Strand Promenade, Bray, Co. Wicklow, Ireland
                                    +353 404 284 2155

| Type of programme | About us | Community | International |

Holiday exchange programme

Programme / code	Outdoor activity advanced OA6
Title	☐ Mr ☐ Ms
First name(s)	(1) Clara
Surname	(2)
Address	(3) 14/4, Graz
Postcode	(4)
Telephone – mobile	(5) 043 699
Email	(6) @kmail.com
Skype	(7)
Nationality	Austrian
Language(s)	(8) German, English,

Vocabulary **4** How do you say these letters? Test each other.

Letters, numbers addresses

Example: A: *What's this?* B: *H.*

| Aa | Bb | Cc | Dd | Ee | Ff | Gg | Hh | Ii | Jj | Kk | Ll | Mm |
| Nn | Oo | Pp | Qq | Rr | Ss | Tt | Uu | Vv | Ww | Xx | Yy | Zz |

5 a How do you say:

1 these addresses?   25 Gore Street   113 Station Road   84 First Avenue
2 these postcodes?   M1 3AQ   T5S 3X2   CA 90501
3 these phone numbers? 0161 264 4600   780 452 1111   022 258 6491

b How do you say these email and website addresses? Can you guess the countries from the addresses?

1 www.bbc.co.uk   4 sport.indiatimes.com
2 robsilva@airnet.br   5 www.cambridge.org
3 msuzuki@spaceblue.jp

8

About you

Vocabulary

Asking for personal information

3 d6nc8k

6 a Nina is asking for personal details. Write down your answers.

- What's your name?
- How do you spell that?
- What's your home address?
- And what's your phone number?
- What's your email address, please?
- What's your nationality?
- What languages do you speak?
- Do you have Skype? I would need your Skype name as well, please.
- Please also tell me what your favourite hobbies are.

b *Role play*. Interview your partner. Cover the questions and look at your neighbour's answers. Say the questions.

Grammar refresher

Possessive adjectives

→ Grammar reference and practice, p. 150

7 Complete the table below.

Subject pronouns	Possessive adjectives
I	
	your
he	
	her
	its
we	
	their

8 Look at the table above. Complete the sentences with the words in brackets.

1 How do *you* spell *your* surname? (you, your)

2 A: What's _____ email address? B: Sorry, _____ aren't on the internet. (they, their)

3 A: Where's _____ from? B: He's Irish, but _____ father's from the USA. (he, his)

4 A: What's _____ name? B: Karen. _____'s John's mother. (she, her)

5 A: Do _____ speak English? B: Yes, but _____ mother tongue is German. (you, my)

6 A: Do _____ need our passports? B: No, only _____ student cards. (we, our)

Reading

Picture dictionary, *Study subjects*, p. 168

9 a Read Anna and Philipp's profiles. What schools do they go to now?

Name: Anna Berger
Age: 15
School now:
College of electronics, TGM, Wien
Old schools:
New secondary school: KMS Neubaugasse, Wien
Primary school: VS Neustiftgasse, Wien
Nursery school: Privatkindergarten Neustiftgasse, Wien
Favourite subjects:
Maths, electronics, P. E.

Name: Philipp Schwarz
Age: 14
School now:
College of I–IT[1] HTBLA, Weiz
Old schools:
Academic secondary school: BG/RG Oberschützen, Burgenland
Primary school: VS Oberwart
Nursery school: Städtischer Kindergarten, Oberwart
Favourite subjects:
Programming, English, management

[1] I–IT: industrial information technology

About you

b Write your own profile using the ones in 9a as models. Complete it with a photo.

Speaking **10 a** Work in pairs. Tell each other about your school careers so far and your favourite subjects in your new school.

Talk about:
- the kind of schools you went to.
- the subjects you had and liked or did not like.
- your favourite subjects in the new school.

> Use phrases like:
> From 2015 to 2018, I went to …
> I had …
> I liked / didn't like … because …
> Now, my favourite subjects are …
> because …

b Look at Anna and Philipp's timetables. They show typical days at a vocational college.

Find the answers to these questions:

1. When do they start and finish school?
2. How many lessons do they have?
3. How long are their lessons?
4. What subjects do they have?

Anna	Monday
8.00–8.50	Hardware design
8.50–9.40	Hardware design
9.50–10.40	Maths
10.40–11.30	Maths
11.30–12.20	Science
12.20–13.20	Lunch break
13.20–14.10	Prototyping electronic systems
14.20–16.00	Personal and social studies

Philipp	Wednesday
8.00–10.40	Programming
10.50–11.40	English
11.40–12.30	Maths
12.30–13.20	Maths
13.20–13.50	Lunch Break
13.50–14.40	Science
14.45–15.35	German
15.40–16.30	IT practice

c Fill in your own timetable. What is your week like? Work in pairs, choose different days and describe your timetables.

Example: *On Monday from 08.00 to 08.50 we have …* ▪ *Lunch is from …* ▪ *School ends at …*

Time	Monday	T____	W____	T____	F____

Writing & Speaking

11 a An ideal school day. Create the best day at school you can imagine. What does a day with all your favourite subjects look like?

Time	Subject
8.00 a.m.	
4.00 p.m.	

b Work in pairs and talk about your ideal days.

Example: *On my ideal day I have P.E. in the morning and we play football for two hours. What is your first lesson?*

Independent learning: How to use this book

12 a Do the quiz in groups. Where in this book can you find:

1 a plan of the book?
2 a list of the irregular verbs?
3 a chart of English sounds?
4 a picture dictionary?
5 a grammar reference and practice?
6 maps of English-speaking countries?
7 vocabulary of all the units?

b Continue the quiz and find answers to these questions.

1 What colour do the grammar boxes have?
2 What is the title of the section that gives you information about people and traditions in other countries?
3 If you want to prepare for the exams or tests, which section do you go to?
4 If you want to know how to use a specific word like "in" or "of", where do you look?
5 Look at the self-assessment. At the end of each unit in this book, you will be asked similar questions to check your progress. Now complete the self-assessment. Choose the symbol that is true for you.

Self-assessment	I can do this well. ✓✓	I can do this most of the time. ✓	I still need to work on this. !!
introduce yourself			
say what you can do			
fill in an online form			
ask for and give personal information			
talk about your school career / ideal school day			

Goals
- introduce people, say who they are
- ask questions to check information
- talk about present and past schools / school experiences
- describe people's personality
- describe relationships
- write short profiles about people

Listening 1

a Manuel is at his new school's open day event with his older sister Mona, who explains to her brother who is who. Listen to the conversation twice. Put the people's names into the picture.

b Manuel, James and Alina talk at the party. Complete the conversation with these expressions.

| Nice to meet you | what's your name again? | Aren't you | that you are | was elected | this is |
| are both | please call me | can you say that again | Actually, I am | Is that right? | He is | Isn't |

Manuel: Hello, I'm Manuel
Alina: Hi, I'm Alina.

Manuel: (1) _____ . And (2) _____ James, my classmate.

James: Sorry, (3) _____ ?

Alina: It's Alina. But (4) _____ Ally.

James: Hello, Ally. (5) _____ one of George's classmates?

Alina: No, I'm not. (6) _____ a year ahead, in the third form. What form are you in?

Manuel: We (7) _____ in the first form. My sister told me

(8) _____ our student representative. (9) _____ ?

Alina: Yeah, I (10) _____ last year. (11) _____ Mr Larkins your English teacher this year? You're lucky, he's so much fun.

James: Sorry, (12) _____ ? It's so loud here, I couldn't hear what you were saying.

Alina: Sure, I said Mr Larkins is a really good English teacher. You are lucky to have him.

James: Really? Cool. (13) _____ from Scotland, right?

Alina: Yes, I really like his accent.

People in your life

Vocabulary 2 — People you know

Complete the sentences about the people in the picture on p. 12.

1 Jakob's baseball team is last year's local _____. He is from _____.
2 Mr Larkins is Mona's English _____. He was born in _____.
3 The _____'s name is George. He is in the second form.
4 Rob is Sally's _____.
5 Sally is Manuel's old _____.
6 Alexandra is _____. She is also in Manuel's class.
7 The _____ is called Alina. She is in the third form.
8 Erkan's _____ are from Turkey.
9 Ms Robson is standing next to Alina. She is Mona's _____.
10 Erkan is Michelle's _____. Her _____ is French.
11 The woman with the long, dark hair is the head of the _____.

Grammar refresher 3 — Possessive 's

Look at the open day picture on p. 12 again and talk to your partner. Check if your answers in 2 are correct. Write down six sentences.

Example: *Isn't Mr Larkins the maths teacher? No, he is the English teacher.*

→ Grammar reference and practice, p. 150

> ⊕ Don't forget the possessive 's when talking about people's relationships.
> Example: *Alexandra is Manuel's classmate.*
>
> ⊖ When you want to check information, you can also ask negative questions.
> Example: *Isn't Erkan Michelle's boyfriend?*

Grammar refresher 4 — *be* in the past

Read what Manuel says about the open day. Complete the gaps with was, were, wasn't and weren't.

→ Grammar reference and practice, p. 151

Nora Newfield (1) _____ a kindergarten nurse before she moved here, so she handles all the pupils', teachers' and parents' requests very well. Rob and Sally, the twins, (2) _____ always together at our old school. They also organised the charity cinema evening last May. They (3) _____ the ones who chose that interesting film about the teenagers who wanted to break out of their boring life. That (4) _____ great, (5) _____ it? Alina, the new student representative, (6) _____ elected four months ago. Alexandra (7) _____ in the fitness centre last Saturday when we went swimming there. We talked about Mona's French teacher. Her marks (8) _____ so good, and she (9) _____ happy about this.

People in your life

Speaking 5 a Work in groups of four. You all meet at the open day event. Individually decide who you would like to be.
- Are you Manuel's classmate or already a bit older, a teacher or even the headteacher?
- Take two minutes to write down a few ideas about your identity.

My identity

Name: _____

From: _____

Friends: _____

Teacher(s) I know: _____

Hobbies: _____

Likes: _____

Dislikes: _____

b Introduce yourself to the other group members and find out who they are. Make notes.

Name:	Name:	Name:

Writing 6 a Write at least five sentences about the other group members.

Example: *I met Dora. She is Alina's classmate and best friend.*

b Compare your texts in class and draw a chart with all the people from Manuel's school.

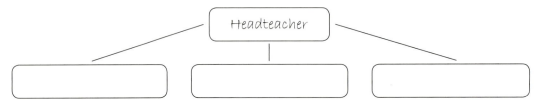

14

People in your life

What was your old school like?

Reading 7 a Read the four short interviews with Austrian pupils for an English youth magazine. Did they like their old schools?

1

How was your old school different to this one?
My old school was in a small village, and it was only ten minutes from my home. I could easily get there in ten minutes. There weren't many pupils, only about 100. It was a new type of secondary school. It was OK. This school's ten times bigger than my old school and it's a modern building. I go to school by train, which is terribly slow. It takes me an hour in the morning and an hour in the afternoon, but I still think my new school's cool. And my classmates are cool too. (Felix, 15)

What was your first school like?
I was already eight years old when I came to Austria. First I went to a really modern primary school with laptops for every pupil. There were twenty-four pupils in my class, and our teacher was a young woman. She wasn't very strict. School was boring. It was the same every day. We were at school from eight to half past twelve from Monday to Friday. In the afternoons I often had German lessons, but they were difficult. I wasn't good at German and always wrote extremely slowly to get the endings of the words right. (Ayse, 15)

2

3

What was your old school like?
It was great! It was an old-fashioned secondary school, but with extra sports lessons. We were in the classroom in the morning, but in the afternoons we were always in the gym or on the football field. I like sports. We were allowed to warm up for 10 minutes at the beginning. Often we just ran around. While some of us were screaming at each other really loudly to let our frustration out, others were quietly walking around or chatting. Everything was allowed. My favourite sport is football – I was the goalkeeper for the school team. I was very happy at that school. (Martin, 14)

What was your former school like?
Well, I was at an academic secondary school for four years. The subjects were mostly interesting and on the whole I found school pretty easy and my marks were very good. But I'm a practical person, and so my parents and I looked for a school that also teaches you practical skills. I like the cooking lessons very much. They're fun! (Jessica, 14)

4

b Are the statements true (T) or false (F)?

	T	F			T	F
1 Felix's old school was near his home.			4 Martin spent all day on the football field.			
2 Felix misses his old school.			5 Jessica was good at school.			
3 Ayse's German lessons were easy.						

Vocabulary 8 Look at the expressions for talking about schools. Match them with their opposites in the boxes.

Talking about schools

~~old-fashioned~~   terrible   boring   different every day   easy

1 modern _____ old-fashioned _____   4 great _____

2 the same every day _____   5 interesting _____

3 difficult _____

15

People in your life

Grammar
Adjectives and adverbs
→ Grammar reference and practice, p. 151

9 a Read the explanation and fill in the correct form of the word *calm*.

Adjectives give information about a noun: THE THING IS IMPORTANT

| Article | Adjective | Noun | the _____ teacher |

Adverbs are formed with -ly and give information about a verb: THE ACTION IS IMPORTANT

| Subject | Verb | Adverb | Place | The teacher speaks _____ in class. |

b Read Manuel's and Mona's conversation on p. 144. Work in pairs and look at the highlighted words. Which ones are adverbs, which ones are adjectives? What do the words describe? Compare your answers in class.

Writing

10 a Look at the short interviews on p. 15 again and write your own text about your old school. Use adjectives and adverbs to make your text interesting. You can use a dictionary to find new words.

b Compare your stories in class. Who used new adjectives / adverbs correctly?

Personal characteristics

Vocabulary
Personality

11 a Read through the descriptions of the different signs of the zodiac.

- What signs do your family members have?
- What are they like?

Aries ♈ Aries are adventurous and creative, but can also be temperamental.	**SCORPIO ♏** Scorpios are enthusiastic and practical, but can also be impatient.
LIBRA ♎ Librans are kind and protective, but can also be possessive.	**CAPRICORN ♑** Capricorns are analytical and witty, but can also be nervous.
TAURUS ♉ Taureans are funny and outgoing, but can also be irritable.	**Sagittarius ♐** Sagittarians are reliable and friendly, but can also be jealous.
PISCES ♓ Pisces are dependable and supportive, but can also be indecisive.	**AQUARIUS ♒** Aquarians are entertaining and charming, but can also be moody.
GEMINI ♊ Geminis are caring and adaptable, but can also be anxious.	**LEO ♌** Leos are independent and ambitious, but can also be hot-headed.
CANCER ♋ Cancerians are hard-working and loyal, but can also be unforgiving.	**VIRGO ♍** Virgos are intelligent and optimistic, but can also be stubborn.

b Read the descriptions again and highlight all the adjectives. Use a dictionary to check their meaning.

c What are you like? Describe yourself and complete the sentence by using adjectives from 11a.

"I'm _____ and _____, but I can also be _____."

12 Work in A/B pairs. A, ask B "What are you like?" Can you guess B's star sign from the answer or is it completely different? Then change roles.

13 Work alone. Write a description of a person (80–100 words). If possible, add a photo.

People in your life

We're interested in the same things

Listening **14** Listen to Michael talking about Roberto. How do they know each other?

15 a Complete the profiles with the missing words.

Name: Roberto

Nationality: (1) _____   Age: 19

How you know the person: We were together on (2) _____

Relationship now: (3) _____

Past school: the International School in Rome

Present occupation: student of mathematics at (4) _____

occupation [ˌɒkjəˈpeɪʃən]: *noun* a person's job or regular activity. *What's your occupation? Actually, I'm a student.*

Roberto

b Listen again. What else does Michael say about Roberto?

1 He   is / isn't   very outgoing.

2 He loves   cross-country hiking / swimming in the sea .

3 He has already hiked   along the coast of Cornwall / across Sicily .

4 His   mother / father   told him about Cambridge University.

5 He is intelligent, but also   lucky / hard-working .

Michael

Vocabulary **16** Look at sentences A–I. Which is about:

Relationships

1 how often you see or contact each other? _____

2 how close your relationship is? _____

3 how similar your interests are? _____

A We don't see each other a lot.
B We get on really well.
C We're interested in the same things.
D We can talk about everything together.
E We get in touch maybe twice a year.
F We like different things.
G We spend a lot of time together.
H We're very close.
I We don't know each other very well.

Speaking **17 a** *Media task*. Go online and find information about a famous person.

Think about:
- **person:** nationality, age, why you like him / her
- **person's past:** school career, occupation(s)
- **person's present:** occupation, private life (married? / children? …)

b Prepare to talk about this person for two minutes. Don't forget to use adjectives and adverbs.

c Work in pairs. Tell each other about the people you have chosen and why.

People in your life

Keyword: OK

18 a Read the conversations and decide what OK means in each conversation.

- A OK = I understand
- B OK = all right / good
- C OK = no problem
- D OK = yes, you can

1 A: Can I use your mobile phone?
   B: OK. Here it is.
2 A: I'm sorry I'm late.
   B: That's OK. Take a seat.
3 A: My name's Lesley – with a 'y'.
   B: L-E-S-L-E-Y. OK.
4 A: Hi. How are you?
   B: I'm OK, thanks. And you?

b Practise the conversations in pairs.

19 Work in pairs. Think of answers to 1–6 using OK.

1 How was your weekend?
2 Can I use your computer?
3 How's your girlfriend?
4 Sorry, I can't remember your name.
5 My address is 143, not 134!
6 Can I open the window, please?

Across cultures: Greetings

20 Match the words and expressions with the pictures.

bow ☐   kiss ☐   exchange cards ☐   hug ☐   shake hands ☐   say hello / hi ☐

1   2   3   4   5   6

6   73p9y8

21 a Seung-wan talks about how people greet each other in South Korea. What does he say? Make notes.

1 Two male friends usually _____.
2 Two female friends usually _____.
3 Male and female friends usually _____.

b Paul talks about greetings in England. How does he say they are different?

22 What do you do when you meet people? What do people usually do in your country?

Example: *At a party, friends usually hug.*

Talk about:
- two friends at a party.
- two classmates at school.
- a young and an old person at a friend's home.
- two strangers at a friend's home.
- a student and a teacher.
- two business people meeting.

23 *Media task.* Do you know anything about greetings in other cultures? Go online, choose a country you are interested in and find out how people greet each other there.

Example: *In Japan, I think, friends usually …*

People in your life

Explore writing: A profile about yourself

 24 a Look at the writing coach tips and read Susi's message in Mailpals. What is Susi's message about?

Writing coach

Layout:
State your name & contact details.

Greetings:
- No need to be very formal: *Hi, Hello everybody* – are fine.
- Don't use exclamation marks. This could sound rude in English.

Purpose of the post:
State why you are posting your profile: use *I'd like to, I want to, I'm interested in + -ing* form.

Introduce yourself:
State your hobbies to find others who like the same things.

---

http://www.m@ilpals.net/profile_025

Name: Susanne   Email: susi_99@kmail.com
Date: 15 September   From: Austria
Age: 17   Hobbies: Reading, swimming, animals, nature

Hi,

I'm Susi, and I'd like to write to people from all over the world. I want to find out about different countries and cultures and write about my hobbies and my country.

I'm from Salzburg, a famous town in Austria, so I speak German. I have already had English for several years at school and want to learn the language really well. I can also speak a little Italian.

Thank you for your emails.

Susi

Closing:
Thank your readers in advance for their reply. Alternative phrase: *I look forward to your emails.*

Description:
- Describe your hometown.
- Say what languages you can speak.

---

b Answer the questions.

1 Who wrote this message?

2 When was the message written?

3 Why does Susi write the message?

4 Write down the email address.

5 Write down the greeting and the closing.

6 What languages does she speak?

7 Where does Susi come from?

Language skills | Extras | Explore

People in your life

25 a Read Mariella's answer. Tick (✓) the information she gives.

☐ her age ☐ her parents ☐ her brothers and sisters
☐ her friends ☐ her hobbies ☐ where she lives
☐ where she's from ☐ her current school

Writing coach

Tenses:
- Write about your friends and hobbies using the present tense.
- Remember to use the past tense for past experiences.

Showing interest:
Ask questions to show your interest in the other person.

Emojis:
You can use emojis in informal emails and online conversations.

b Now write a short profile about yourself.

c Work in pairs. Swap profiles with your partner and write an email reply, using the texts as examples.

http://www.m@ilpals.net/email

Hi Susi,

My name's Mariella. I'm from Madrid, the capital of Spain, but now I live in Barcelona. This is me in the photo with my best friends, Ana and Pedro. We're all 16 years old. We went to the same primary school. Ana still lives in Madrid, but Pedro and I live in Barcelona and go to the same school. The school is very strict and we have to work hard to pass all the exams. In our free time we both do in-line skating, our favourite hobby, or we sometimes go to the cinema.

I don't speak English very well, but can we be email friends? Are you interested?

Would love to hear from you, please write back.

Mariella :-)

Explore reading: Emails and profiles from abroad

26 Read Mariella's email, then choose the correct answer (A, B, C or D) for questions 1–3. Put a cross (☒) in the correct box. The first one (0) has been done for you.

TIP: Before you start reading a text, always read the instructions and the questions carefully.

0 Mariella
- A lives in Madrid. ☐
- B moved to Barcelona. ☒
- C left Barcelona. ☐
- D stayed in Madrid. ☐

1 Mariella, Ana and Pedro
- A were at nursery school together. ☐
- B go to the same school. ☐
- C are not at the same school anymore. ☐
- D were not at primary school together. ☐

2 Mariella and Pedro
- A attended different schools. ☐
- B do not take any exams. ☐
- C study a lot. ☐
- D never study. ☐

3 Mariella and Pedro
- A hardly ever go in-line skating. ☐
- B never go to the cinema. ☐
- C don't have a favourite hobby. ☐
- D often spend their free time together. ☐

People in your life

27 Read Matilda's post. First decide whether the statements (1–4) are true (T) or false (F) and put a cross (☒) in the correct box. Then identify the sentence in the text which supports your decision. Write the first four words of this sentence in the space provided. There may be more than one correct answer; write down only one. The first one (0) has been done for you.

TIP 1: Note that the sentence beginning ('the first four words') may not contain the answer.

http://www.m@ilpals.net/profile_026

Name: Matilda
Date: 28 September
Age: 26
Email: matilda@kmail.com
Hobbies: reading, meeting friends
From: Italy

My name's Matilda and I live in Rome, the capital city of Italy. I'm a teacher in an international school, where I teach maths – but in English. All the other lessons are in English too, except Italian language and literature. Most of our students are Italian, but they like to speak English and they watch a lot of TV in English. So their English is very good. I speak English with most of my colleagues at school. I also have some American friends in Rome who can't speak Italian. That's why they enjoy doing the tourist city walks with me.

TIP 2: Contracted forms like *I'm, you're, don't* … count as one word.

	Statements	True	False	First four words
0	Matilda works in a big city.	☒		*My name's Matilda and*
1	She teaches English.			
2	There are lessons in Italian too.			
3	Her students are English and American.			
4	All her friends speak Italian.			

Self-assessment ✓✓ ✓ !!

- introduce people, say who they are
- ask questions to check information
- talk about present and past schools / school experiences
- describing people's personality
- describing relationsships
- write short profiles about people

Goals
- say what you want to do
- say what your interests are
- make and respond to offers and requests
- write an email requesting something

I miss my friends

Listening 1

a Are you ever away from home for a long time? What do you miss when you are away?

Example: When I'm away from home, I really miss Austrian bread.

b Listen to four people talking about things they miss when they are away from home. Fill in the missing words.

I'm from Austria but I go to school in England. When I'm away from home, I really miss the (1) _skiing_ in winter and my (2) _brother_, Christoph. In Austria I always drink a (3) _a glass of hot milk_ at breakfast, but here I usually have some (4) _black tea_. I could also drink (5) _orange juice_ but I don't like anything (6) _fruity_ in the morning. (Lisa, from Austria)

When I'm away from home, I really miss my (7) _mother_ and my sister. I also miss the (8) _food_. Sudanese cuisine is really nice. Do you know what my all-time favourite (9) _sweet snack_ is? – Sesame seed (10) _candy_. There is nothing like it anywhere. I don't miss the (11) _weather_, though. Sudan can be too hot in summer. While I am away, I always try to read (12) _some Sudanese newspaper_ online because they are really hard to find here. (Khalid, from Sudan)

When I'm not at home, I really miss my (13) _best friend_. I try to text them every day. Of course, I also miss my (14) _family_. I always call my (15) _grandma_ at least once a week because she looks after my dog while I am away. I like to take some of my favourite (16) _magazines_ to read with me to remind me of home. (Paul, from the US)

When I'm away from home, I really miss my (17) _family_, my (18) _rabbits_ and the food. You just don't get the same quality (19) _chocolate & cheese_ outside of Switzerland. Well, actually, the cheddar (20) _cheese_ here in England is quite good, too. I would really like to learn how to make it, but I don't know if I have time to do a (21) _course_. (Angela, from Switzerland)

Away from home

Grammar 2

Present simple

→ Grammar reference and practice, p. 152

Complete the sentences in the table with these verbs. Sometimes you need two verbs to make negative forms.

~~miss~~   doesn't   call   don't   misses   does   read   text   are   gets   eats   do   travel

I / you / we /they
1 Lisa: I _miss_ skiing in winter.
2 You _just don't_ get the same quality cheese outside of Switzerland.
3 We _text_ our friends every day.
4 Sudanese newspapers _are_ available online.
5 _Do_ Khalid's parents _travel_ with him?

he / she / it
6 Khalid _misses_ his mother and sister.
7 Angela _eats_ Cheddar cheese in England.
8 Paul _doesn't_ his grandma every day.
9 It _gets_ very hot in Sudan in summer.
10 _Does_ Paul _read_ his favourite magazines?

3

a Khalid wrote Lisa an email and asked about Viennese attractions. Read Lisa's reply to his email. Complete the email with the verbs in brackets.

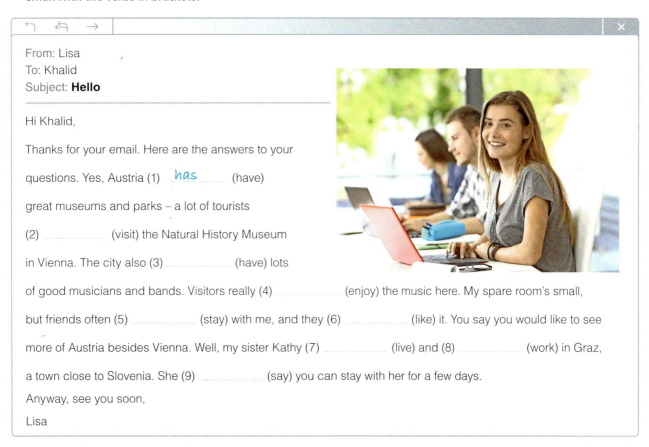

From: Lisa
To: Khalid
Subject: **Hello**

Hi Khalid,

Thanks for your email. Here are the answers to your questions. Yes, Austria (1) _has_ (have) great museums and parks – a lot of tourists (2) _____ (visit) the Natural History Museum in Vienna. The city also (3) _____ (have) lots of good musicians and bands. Visitors really (4) _____ (enjoy) the music here. My spare room's small, but friends often (5) _____ (stay) with me, and they (6) _____ (like) it. You say you would like to see more of Austria besides Vienna. Well, my sister Kathy (7) _____ (live) and (8) _____ (work) in Graz, a town close to Slovenia. She (9) _____ (say) you can stay with her for a few days.
Anyway, see you soon,
Lisa

b Complete these sentences using **don't** or **doesn't**.

1 Angela's sister _____ like chocolate.
2 My friends and I _____ usually go out during the week.
3 His brother _____ eat meat.
4 You _____ call me every day.
5 Our grandparents _____ use social media at all.

c Make questions, so that the sentences above are the negative answers.

Example: *Does Angela's sister like chocolate? No, Angela's sister doesn't like chocolate.*

23

Away from home

Listening 4 a Listen to Moira and Sam talking about their free time. Tick (✓) the things they do.

8 7jm8ut

1 reads books and newspapers ☐
2 reads magazines ☐
3 watches TV ☐
4 cooks ☐
5 goes to restaurants ☐

6 plays football ☐
7 goes sailing ☐
8 drives to the mountains ☐
9 plays tennis ☐
10 goes to the gym ☐

b Think about things you do and things you don't do in your free time. Talk to your classmates. Find out who does similar things.

I'm interested in

Reading 5 a Discuss in pairs and take notes. When you travel, do you stay:

- in hotels ? _____
- with friends ? _____
- on campsites ? _____
- somewhere else ? _____

b Read the introduction to the website Sofasurfing.com and (circle) the correct answer. Is it for people who:

1 want to   travel / stay at home ?
2 have / don't have   a lot of money?
3 want to   stay with old friends / make new friends   ?

 Home   My profile   Search   Sign Up   Links

http://www.sofasurfing.com/home

Would you like to meet people from different cultures? Do you want to see different parts of the world? On Sofasurfing.com you can read people's profiles, email them and go and stay in their homes. You can sleep on a sofa or spare bed for one or two nights or weeks and it's free. Join Sofasurfing.com, make friends around the world and start your adventure today.

c Read Melek and Fiona's profiles. What do they have in common, and what are their differences?

Melek
Female, 16

I'm a student.
I'm from Turkey.
I speak Turkish, English and a bit of German.
I'm interested in music, football and cinema.
I'd like to go to Cuba and Ireland.
I want to learn languages.
I live in a small house with my family. We have a nice living room with a big, comfortable sofa.
My hometown is Istanbul. It's beautiful and it has lots of things to see and do. We live near the centre.
My family is very friendly. My brother Erkan speaks English too. My mother works full-time, but she cooks dinner for us at the weekend.
No smokers, please.
Email me.

Fiona
Female, 21

I'm a music student.
I'm from Ireland.
I speak English and French.
I'm interested in music, dance and meeting people from other cultures.
I'd like to go to China, Sweden, Turkey and the USA.
I want to get a good job and learn salsa.
I live in a flat on my own. It has a spare room with a spare bed, so friends often stay with me.
My hometown is Dublin. It's a great place and it has lots of nice cafés and clubs.
My family lives in Galway, but my father often comes here for work. He stays with me and takes me to nice restaurants.
Phone or email first.

Write notes about:

1 what they do.

2 their languages.

3 their interests.

4 their travel plans.

d Compare your ideas with a partner.

Vocabulary
Interests and wants

6 a What can you remember about Melek and Fiona? Cover their profiles and make sentences.

Melek Fiona	is interested in would like to go to wants to	music • cinema • dance • football Cuba • China • Sweden • Ireland • the USA learn salsa • get a good job • learn languages

b Look at the profiles again to check.

Speaking & Writing

7 a Interview your partner about their profile and their travel plans. What do you have in common and what are your differences? Ask and answer about:

- things you are interested in.
- things you want to do / would like to do.

b Write a profile of your partner, like Melek's or Fiona's, for the Sofasurfing website.

Away from home

Would you like … ?

Listening

8 a Listen to Lisa and Gwen on the phone. Tick (✓) the things they talk about.

Lisa

Gwen

1 newspapers
2 chocolate
3 biscuits
4 apples

5 a camera
6 a rucksack
7 books
8 bread

b Listen again and make notes. What is Lisa happy to bring? What is she not happy to bring?

Happy to bring	Not happy to bring

Grammar refresher

A, an, some

9 a Write a, an or some under the pictures.

1 *a*
cup of coffee

2 *some*
books

3
glass of apple juice

4
apple

5
magazine

6
sandwich

7
newspaper

8
orange

9
oranges

10
clothes

b Complete the rules in the box: a, an and some.

→ Grammar reference and practice, p. 154

a or an = 1

_____ = 2, 3, 4, …

Use _____ before a vowel (a, e, i, o, u) or when you hear a vowel (e.g. an hour).

Use _____ before a consonant (b, c, d, …).

Use _____ when talking about more than one thing (countable: e.g. some apples) or a small amount of something (uncountable: e.g. some apple juice).

Away from home

Vocabulary 10 — Offers and requests

a Answer the questions below and complete the offers and requests. Then make short conversations.

A Which answers can you use with offers? _____

B Which answers can you use with requests? _____

Offers		Answers
Would	_____ sweets?	1 OK. / All right.
	_____ from Austria?	2 No, sorry. / No, thanks.
Requests		
Can I	bring them next time?	3 Yes, of course. / Yes, please.
		4 No problem.
	bring _____ Austrian newspapers?	5 No, I'm afraid not.
Could you		

b Make more short conversations. Use the words from the boxes below.

Example: A: *Can I use your dictionary?* B: *Yes, of course.* A: *Thanks.*

Offers	Requests
some books	use your dictionary
something to eat	spell your name
a newspaper	have your email address
a drink	open the window

Speaking 11

a Work in A/B pairs. Read the situations below and role-play the two conversations.

Conversation 1

Desert island show: A, you are taking part in this show. A helicopter has dropped you on a desert island. B can be there in 3 days. B, ask A what he/she wants. A, tell B what you want.

Conversation 2

B, you have won a competition and been given $1000 to spend in New York. As A is your friend, you have decided to spend $500 on him/her. Ask B what he/she would like. A, tell B what you would like.

b Talk to another pair of students and compare your answers. Which is the most interesting answer? Report back to the rest of the class.

Away from home

Taking care of a guest

Reading & Listening

12 a Read the email and answer the questions.

1. Where does Liam live?
2. Speculate: How do Melek and Fiona know each other? What about Fiona and Liam?

From: Fiona
To: Melek
Subject: **Hello**

Hi Melek,

Hope you're OK! I'm fine, but I really miss Istanbul and all the people I met – Dublin is grey and boring at the minute. Could I ask you a favour? One of my colleagues, Liam, will be in Istanbul next month, and he doesn't know anybody there. Is there any chance you could meet him and show him around the city one day?
He's a lovely guy and he'd really appreciate it. Also, could you please send me some more almond biscuits? They are my favourite food in the world!

Thank you,

Fiona

---

10   yk654h

b Liam arrives at Melek's home in Istanbul. Listen and tick (✓) the things Melek asks him about:

- his family.
- things to do.
- food.
- a drink.
- sports.
- places to go.

Vocabulary

Taking care of a guest

13 Match the questions and answers. There are two extra answers that you should not use.

1. Would you like something to drink?
2. Do you want something to eat?
3. Are you interested in seeing some sights?
4. And would you like to take a boat trip on the Bosporus?
5. What else would you like to do?

A Yes, I am. I'm really interested in architecture.
B Oh yeah, please. I like boat trips.
C Well, I'd like to eat some real Turkish food later.
D No, I'm fine, thank you. The hotel food is very good.
E Er, just a glass of water, please.
F No thanks, the hotel has one I can use.
G Oh, that would be great. I've read about the market.

Speaking

14 You have a guest in your home. In pairs, take turns to be the guest. Have two conversations.

Ask about how to:

- offer your guest something to eat and drink.
- find out what your guest is interested in.
- find out what your guest would like to do and see.

Writing

15 *Business training.* You are travelling for a business meeting in Milan, Italy. Write an email to your colleague back home and:

- tell him / her where you are and what it is like there.
- ask if he / she would like anything from Italy.
- inform him / her that Lucia, the marketing assistant from the Milan office, will be at your office soon. Ask your colleague to meet Lucia for you and suggest some things she would like to do in your town.

Keyword: *in*

16 What do the highlighted expressions mean? Add P(lace), T(imes) or L(anguages) next to the correct sentence.

1 I'm from Austria but I go to school in England.
2 My mother's office is in the same street.
3 We were in the same office.
4 When I was at primary school in 2007, …
5 How do you say this phrase in English?

17 a Add *in* to these sentences.

1 My birthday is ˅*in* October.
2 I live a small village.
3 I was Athens in the summer of 2017.
4 My friend and I were in Spain together 2018.
5 I can say 'I love you' French.
6 I'm bad-tempered the morning.

b Change the sentences in 17a so they are true for you. Compare your sentences.

Example: *My birthday is in ~~October~~ March.*

Across cultures: Breakfasts

18 a Read the description of two typical breakfasts. How different are they from your experiences?

Full breakfast in England

Famous worldwide, the full breakfast remains a well-loved British tradition. It is not eaten every day but often saved for weekends and holidays. The term "full" comes from the fact that this meal includes many different foods. It was traditionally served at breakfast time, but it may also replace lunch.

Breakfast may begin with orange juice, cereals, stewed or fresh fruits, but the heart of the full breakfast is bacon and eggs, variously accompanied by sausages, grilled tomatoes, mushrooms, tea, buttered toast and marmalade.

Each country in the UK and Ireland also have their choice of accompaniments. You may find, for example black pudding, baked beans and fried bread. Nowadays there is also a variety of vegetarian choices, such as tofu sausages.

The origins of the full breakfast are unclear and believed to originate in rural England as a rich meal to carry workers through a long morning.

Egyptian breakfast

A popular, ancient Egyptian breakfast dish is called *ful medames*, which is usually eaten on Fridays. To make the dish, the Arabic word *fūl* or beans are cooked with cumin, onion, tomato, garlic and parsley. These beans are often accompanied by a selection of sides: flat breads, tahini sauce with lemon, hard boiled eggs and chopped tomato and cucumber salads.

Ful medames is an Egyptian breakfast recipe which goes as far back as the fourth century where the beans were buried over hot coals to slow cook – *medames* means "buried" in Egyptian. Today people enjoy it throughout the Middle East, from Sudan to Syria, Israel and Yemen.

Tahini is very often served as a side dish or dip. It is made from toasted, ground sesame seeds, water and lemon and is usually an ingredient in the famous chickpea paste called hummus. It is great with many other Middle Eastern dishes.

Many Egyptians drink black tea with milk or mint leaves – with or after breakfast.

b Discuss in groups of four. Compare your experiences. What breakfast do you like best? Why?

Away from home

Language skills | Extras | Explore

Explore reading: Leaflets for language holidays

19 Read the three leaflets for language holidays. Which three countries can you study in?

20 Read the language holiday leaflets. Some parts are missing. Choose the correct part (A–I) for each gap (1–6). There are two extra parts that you should not use. Write your answers in the boxes provided. The first one (0) has been done for you.

TIP: Make sure you check which kind of word goes before and comes after the gap.

Learn English in Ireland with (0) ____

A

- Live with your teacher's family
- Study one-to-one with your teacher

Flexible study courses for adults (over 18):
- 10–25 hours a week
- 2–10 weeks

Our homestay courses include visits to places of interest. You can add activities to your course – golf, tennis and watersports are available. Some of our teachers have specialised knowledge of subjects like (1) ____ . We can offer English courses based on the vocabulary of these subjects.

B

(2) ____ Cape Town, South Africa.

Good Hope Studies was one of the first English-language schools in Cape Town, South Africa, and offers junior language courses from 14 to 16 years and adult classes from 17 plus.

You can study the following English language courses at this school:
- standard courses
- intensive courses
- Cambridge Exam preparation courses

The courses are offered all year round. Last year, students from 50 different countries learned (3) ____ .

We hope to see you here soon!

C

Study English at Bell Malta Language Centre if you want to combine (4) ____ .

Malta is a major centre for English-language teaching. English is an official language, and (5) ____ . Malta is the perfect choice if you want to study English while enjoying a holiday in the Mediterranean. Bell Malta is a modern building situated in St Julian's. It is close to the beach and numerous restaurants, cafés and bars.

Top courses

- English Pathways: 21 hours a week of intensive general English
- Summer English: (6) ____ aged 16–22 years
- Business English: 25 hours a week of intensive business English

Accommodation available with local families.

A sport and cookery course
B language learning with watersports
C English at our language school
D Homestay English
E for children and pensioners
F Learn English in
G for young adults
H medicine, marketing, graphic design, etc.
I people speak it everywhere on the island

0	1	2	3	4	5	6
D						

30

Away from home

21 Look at the leaflets on p. 30 again. Which course does the following email confirmation refer to: A, B or C?

From: Placement office
To: student002
Subject: **Confirmation**

Dear Student,

We are pleased to confirm your place on an intensive general English course (Ref. EP53) from 15–30 August. Your accommodation is with Mrs Vicky Ferro and family. She will contact you with more information.
We look forward to welcoming you to our island.

Kind regards,

Placement office

22 Which of the language holidays would you choose? Give reasons for your choice.

Language holiday:

Reasons:

Explore writing: An email requesting something

23 Read the emails in 24 and (circle) the correct answer.

1 Tim is in   Istanbul / Australia / (Croatia) .
2 He wants to   stay with Erkan in Turkey / return to Australia / meet Erkan in Croatia .
3 He offers Erkan   information about museums / a gift from Zagreb / some food .

24 Look at the highlighted expressions in the emails. Which are greetings? Which are goodbyes?

From: Tim
To: Erkan
Subject: **Visit**

Dear Erkan,

My name's Tim and I'm from Australia. You can check my profile on Sofasurfing.com. I'm in Croatia now and would like to come to Istanbul. Could I stay with you on August 1 and 2?
A couple of questions: if I stay, can I use your kitchen? Also, could you tell me about museums in Istanbul?

Thanks and bye,

Tim

From: Erkan
To: Tim
Subject: **Re: Visit**

Hi Tim,

August 1–2 is no problem for my family and me. Of course, you can use our kitchen. I have lots of information about museums.
You can read it when you're here. Looking forward to meeting you.

Best wishes,

Erkan

From: Tim
To: Erkan
Subject: **Re: Re: Visit**

Hi again,

Thanks very much, Erkan. Would you like something from Zagreb?

See you soon.

Tim

Away from home

25 a Read the emails and compare the informal and the more formal requests.

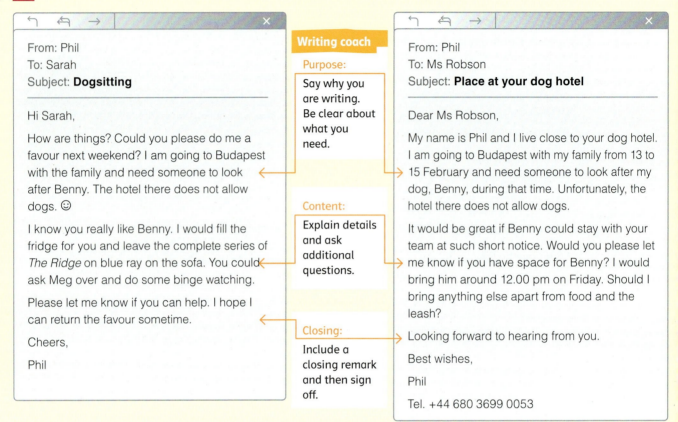

b Write the informal and more formal expressions from the emails under the correct heading.

	informal	more formal
Greeting phrases	Hi	Dear Ms / Mr
Introduction		
Requested favour		
Details		
Closing remark		
Sign off		

26 a You decide to use Sofasurfing.com to find a place to stay in another country. Write an email to your host.
- Give information about yourself.
- Ask two or three questions.
- Check your email. Are the capital letters correct?

b Read another student's email and write a reply. Read the reply to your email. Did they answer all your questions?

Away from home

Explore listening: Sightseeing in London

27 Answer the questions below.

- Have you ever been to London? When were you there? For how long? What did you do? Which sights can you remember?
- If you have not been to London, would you like to go? Why? / Why not?

28 You are going to listen to a tour guide on a bus tour through London. First you will have 45 seconds to study the task below, then you will hear the recording twice. While listening, answer the questions (1–8) using a maximum of four words. Write your answers in the spaces provided. The first one (0) has been done for you.

After the second listening, you will have 45 seconds to check your answers.

TIP: You may leave out articles and contract words: do not = don't.

0	How many people live in London?	*more than / over eight million*
1	Where are many important sights located?	
2	How much are tickets for the city's museums and galleries?	
3	In which park can you find people giving speeches?	
4	What is the name of the famous department store in London?	
5	How much does an Oyster Card cost?	
6	What is Soho famous for?	
7	Why is Notting Hill so well known?	
8	What can you get in the area around Leicester Square?	

29 *Media task.* Use your smartphone and record yourself talking about your favourite place. Now write down five questions about your favourite place and ask your partner these questions. Can he/she answer them correctly when listening to your recording?

Self-assessment

- say what you want to do
- say what your interests are
- make and respond to offers and requests
- write an email requesting something

First of all, think about what you have learned up to now. Are you close to "I can do this well" or closer to "I need to work on this"?

Put a mark where you think you are at the moment. Then do the tasks and check your answers with the key on p. 186. Put another mark in a different colour where you see yourself after you've done the task.

Reading

- I can understand an email about how people know each other.
- I can understand an email about their likes and dislikes.
- I can understand an email about planning activities.

Reading 1 Read Deborah's email to her friend Amr. What's the email about?

From: Deborah@mail.com
To: amr@mail.com
Date: May 12
Subject: **Holiday trip**

Hi Amr,

I hope you're doing OK in your mountaineering camp? Can you please help me decide on our holiday next July? As promised, I'm trying to plan some activities, but I'm not sure who likes what kind of sport. You enjoy cycling, don't you? The two options I like most offer a great variety of activities, but I want to make sure everybody is happy and has a good time. You and I like water sports, but I can't remember if Mona does. Somehow, I remember that she did not like our swimming course. She often had an excuse not to join us, and Sue is afraid of extreme heights, if I remember correctly. She tried to avoid the rope-climbing exercises in our PE classes, so we should not plan anything that scares her. One thing I'm sure of, however, we all like running around and discovering new stuff together, so some kind of team challenge would be great. Are you interested in going to Ashcombe, an adventure centre, or would you rather spend a few days in the forest adventure park in Scotland? I'm fine with both options, as all my favourite activities are outside, no matter what we do.

Thanks for letting me know.

Cheers,

Deborah

---

2 Read Deborah's email again. First decide whether the statements (1–5) are true (T) or false (F) and put a cross (☒) in the correct box. Then identify the sentence in the text which supports your decision. Write the first four words of this sentence in the space provided. There may be more than one correct answer; write down only one. The first one (0) has been done for you.

	Statements	True	False	First four words
0	Deborah loves being outdoors.	☒		I'm fine with both
1	Amr goes climbing in his free time.			
2	Deborah thinks Amr does not like cycling.			
3	Mona does not like swimming.			
4	Sue has always avoided running.			
5	Deborah prefers Scotland.			

Reading

- I can understand a leaflet about outdoor activities.

Reading 3 Read the Ashcombe Adventure Centre leaflet. Some parts are missing. Choose the correct part (A–I) for each gap (1–6). There are two extra parts that you should not use. Write your answers in the boxes provided. The first one (0) has been done for you.

Welcome to Ashcombe Adventure Centre! If you're (0) _____ to experience some fun outdoor activities, you have found the right place. If you like to get active or maybe you like putting your mind to the test, we have a range of fun activities to suit your needs. Are you 14+ years? If so we'd love to help you to book an exciting event here in a beautiful South Devon Valley. We take bookings (1) _____ programmes which can include a stay in our on-site accommodation with an evening meal in our dining and bar area. Most activities are for groups of 6 or more, although the clay shooting can be for individuals.

How about clay shooting, archery or raft building and quad bike safari just to get started? After lunch, it's the paintball games in our action-packed wooded site and if you've still got the energy, go for a quick descent over the trees on the hyperslide and (2) _____ the restaurant and lounge.

The introductory archery experience starts with a few practice arrows with tuition[1] to warm you up. Following the warm up, your teams will compete in a variety of challenging games. Sessions can be both indoors and outdoors – weather-dependent. All skills and abilities welcome with experience or none at all, this activity is all about staying calm under pressure and hitting (3) _____ !

Raft building: Within a given timeslot, your teams must build a raft with the equipment provided and then head down (4) _____ to test your creations. If you have done a good job, your team should be able to complete the race around the buoy[2] at the far end of the lake, competing against the other team/s.

Team challenges:
We have created three challenging activities for you, from (5) _____ physically demanding tasks. Aggravator puzzles and activator puzzles are a series of mentally challenging, logic based, team-orientated puzzles. Each puzzle requires a different skill. In the treasure hunt, your teams will follow a series of challenging clues around the Ashcombe Adventure Centre grounds, finding answers to the questions & riddles, and (6) _____ en route.

Source: adapted and abridged from ASHCOMBE ADVENTURE CENTRE www.ashcombeadventure.co.uk

A to the lake
B that yellow mark as many times as possible
C that wall as often as you can
D the mind bending to the more
E looking for an exciting place
F collecting items of local flora & fauna
G well-earned refreshments in
H on the lake
I for individual activities or whole

0	E
1	I
2	G
3	B
4	A
5	D
6	F

[1] **tuition**: guidance [2] **buoy**: an object floating in water

Writing

- I can write an email responding to requests.
- I can write an email speaking about my free time activities and how I know people.

Writing 4

Look at Deborah's email on p. 34 again. Amr writes his reply. He knows all the group members very well and can help Deborah make a decision on their planned holiday.

In his email Amr should:

- present his preferences (e.g. he loves the mountaineering camp, misses toast and homemade jam for breakfast, loves the indoor climbing classes in the morning but does not like balance exercises on the ground)
- point out the preferences of others (Deborah is right about Sue and Mona: Pete went to primary school with Amr, loves logical puzzles and his favourite subjects are maths and physics, Ben went to secondary school with Sue, helped her overcome her fear of heights; he is Mona's brother and likes Sue very much)
- suggest his favourite place for the holiday and explain why

Write Amr's email in reply to Deborah's (around 150 words).

Writing

- I can write an email requesting information.

Writing 5

You and your friend are planning to go on language holidays this summer. Scotland is the ideal destination for you and your friend. You write an email to the local agency *Speak Scotland* asking for information about language courses, accommodation and spare time activities.

You should:

- introduce yourself.
- ask for information about language courses, accommodation and spare time activities.
- point out your reasons for making language holidays.

Write about 150 words.

From: _____
Sent: _____

Dear Sir or Madam,

Listening

- I can understand a clearly spoken description of green living with specific technical vocabulary.

Listening 6

You are going to listen to an interview about an environmentally friendly home. First you will have 45 seconds to study the task below, then you will hear the recording twice. While listening, answer the questions (1–8) using a maximum of four words. Write your answers in the spaces provided. The first one (0) has been done for you.

After the second listening, you will have 45 seconds to check your answers.

0 What does green living do? — *reduce carbon footprint*
1 Whose negative effect should a green house reduce?
2 What building materials can you produce with a minimum carbon footprint?
3 What is important for an efficient green home?
4 How can you provide optimal insulation?
5 What energy generating features can you use in green houses?
6 What do solar panels convert into energy?
7 How can you save water?
8 How much more efficient are modern washing machines compared to old ones?

Language

- I can form sentences about free time activities with more than one adverb.
- I know where to put adverbs of frequency in a sentence.

Language 7

Put these words in the correct order to form sentences.

1 really / away / miss / I / from home / am / my sister / when.
2 from / I'm / but / Madrid / I / now / live / in Barcelona.
3 We / both / in-line skating / do / our / free time / in.
4 name's / Andrew / my / and / from / I'm / a small / in / town / Wales.
5 I / every / Saturday / go to / with / dance classes / my friends.
6 I / from / my bedroom / can / see / the / Opera House / famous.

Goals
- talk about your free time, likes and dislikes
- talk about habits and customs
- make and respond to invitations
- talk about cities, neighbourhoods and homes
- find information in adverts for rooms
- take a phone message, ask people to repeat
- write a blog entry

Reading 1 Read the interviews taken from the online magazine *Leisure Exhibition*. Which of the pictures A – F match the interviews?

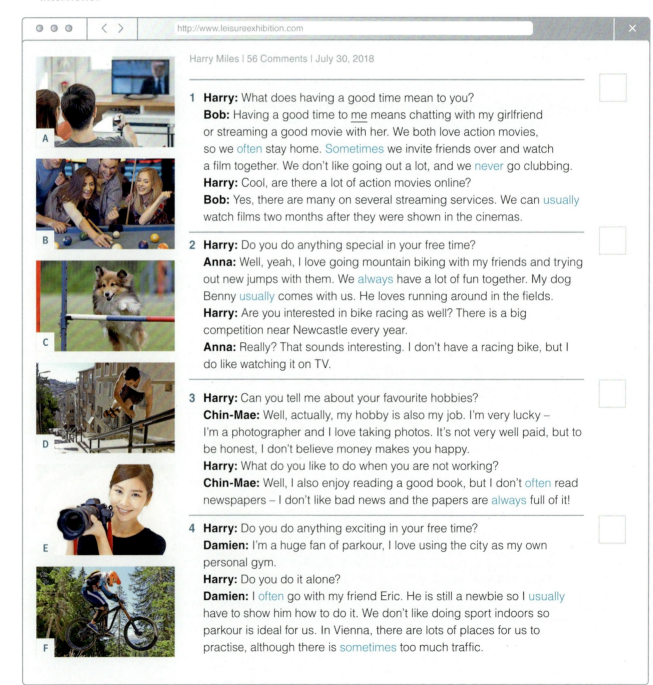

Harry Miles | 56 Comments | July 30, 2018

1 **Harry:** What does having a good time mean to you?
   Bob: Having a good time to me means chatting with my girlfriend or streaming a good movie with her. We both love action movies, so we often stay home. Sometimes we invite friends over and watch a film together. We don't like going out a lot, and we never go clubbing.
   Harry: Cool, are there a lot of action movies online?
   Bob: Yes, there are many on several streaming services. We can usually watch films two months after they were shown in the cinemas.

2 **Harry:** Do you do anything special in your free time?
   Anna: Well, yeah, I love going mountain biking with my friends and trying out new jumps with them. We always have a lot of fun together. My dog Benny usually comes with us. He loves running around in the fields.
   Harry: Are you interested in bike racing as well? There is a big competition near Newcastle every year.
   Anna: Really? That sounds interesting. I don't have a racing bike, but I do like watching it on TV.

3 **Harry:** Can you tell me about your favourite hobbies?
   Chin-Mae: Well, actually, my hobby is also my job. I'm very lucky – I'm a photographer and I love taking photos. It's not very well paid, but to be honest, I don't believe money makes you happy.
   Harry: What do you like to do when you are not working?
   Chin-Mae: Well, I also enjoy reading a good book, but I don't often read newspapers – I don't like bad news and the papers are always full of it!

4 **Harry:** Do you do anything exciting in your free time?
   Damien: I'm a huge fan of parkour, I love using the city as my own personal gym.
   Harry: Do you do it alone?
   Damien: I often go with my friend Eric. He is still a newbie so I usually have to show him how to do it. We don't like doing sport indoors so parkour is ideal for us. In Vienna, there are lots of places for us to practise, although there is sometimes too much traffic.

38

Your time, your space!

Grammar 2

Subject and object pronouns
→ Grammar reference and practice, p. 154

a Read through the interviews on p. 38 again, and underline all the pronouns.

b Complete the pronouns table with the words you have just underlined.

Subject	Object
I	me
you	
he	
she	
it	
we	
they	

Grammar 3

Adverbs of frequency

a Look at the highlighted words in the interviews on p. 38, and fill in the gaps in the correct order below.

How often?

never 0% → 1 → 2 → 3 → always 100%

b Look at your timetable on p. 10, and write five sentences using adverbs of frequency.

Example: *School always starts at 8:15.*

c Complete the grammar rules with these words.

after   in the middle   the beginning   between

→ Grammar reference and practice, p. 155

Subject   Adverb   Verb   Object

Adverbs of frequency are (1) _____ the subject and the verb:
Chin-Mae often takes photos.

If the verb is "am, is, are, was, were", the adverbs of frequency are placed (2) _____ the verb:
Anna is usually outdoors with her dog Benny.

If there are more verbs forming the verb phrase, put the adverbs of frequency (3) _____:
Bob can often meet his friends because they all live in the same area.

Adverbs of frequency can also be put at (4) _____.
Sometimes we invite friends over and play board games.

Speaking 4

Work in pairs. Interview each other about how often you:
- invite friends over to your home.
- go to the cinema.
- go clubbing.
- play ball games.
- read newspapers.

Example: A: *How often do you practise the guitar?* B: *Well, I usually practise at the weekend, but I never play the guitar when my friends are around.*

Your time, your space!

What do you usually do?

Grammar — Sentence structure

5 a Adverbs in sentences. Fill in the gaps.

1 Adverbs of manner answer the question: H_____?
2 Adverbs of place answer the question: W_____?
3 Adverbs of time answer the question: W_____?
4 Adverbs of frequency answer the question: H_____ o_____?

→ Grammar reference and practice, p. 155

Adverb	Subject	Adverb of frequency	Verb	Object	Adverbs
Every morning	Tom	usually	meets	his friends	at the bus station.

b Put the words into the correct order. Can you identify: subject, verb, adverbs of frequency, manner, place, time?

1 birthday parties / Do / go to / you / usually / ?   *Do you usually go to birthday parties?*
2 do / What / usually / in / you / do / the morning / ?
3 never / anything / John / sweet / eats / in the evening / .
4 go to / My / at weekends / the cinema / parents / often / I / and / together / .
5 don't / forget / birthdays / I / usually / friends' / .
6 family / on / does / do / usually / What / your / Sunday afternoons / ?
7 goes / often / her flat / Claire / in the evening / to the gym / near / .
8 sometimes / tennis / Mario / in the local / sports club / plays / with his cousin / .

Speaking

6 a What do you usually do? Choose a day or time that you enjoy, for example:
- your birthday - Christmas - Saturday - New Year's Eve

b In pairs, ask each other about your days. Talk about what you do, how you do things, how often you do them, where and when.

Example: A: *What do you usually do for your birthday?* B: *Well, in the morning, I usually go …* - *I sometimes meet …* - *We always eat …*

Writing

7 a How do you spend your free time? How often and where do you do your favourite activities? What does having a good time mean to you?

b Write six sentences with the highlighted words and give them to your teacher.

Having a good time to me means playing football in the park with my friends.
I like / enjoy taking photos of people.
I love dancing.

c Listen to what the other students wrote. Can you guess whose sentences they are?

Inviting someone out

Ellen and Janine

Listening 8

874a53

🔊 13

a Do you often invite people to your home? Who do you invite? What do you invite them for?

Example: *I sometimes invite friends to a film night.*

b Listen to Ellen and Léon inviting friends out.
1 Where do they invite them?
2 Can the friends go?

Vocabulary 9
Invitations

Complete the sentences with these words.

~~free~~   like   Yes   want   Are   sorry

Checking 1 Are you *free* on Saturday evening?

2 _____ you interested in football, Robert?

Inviting 3 Do you _____ to come to my place for a sleepover?

4 Would you _____ to come with me?

Answering 5 _____ , please. That sounds great.

6 Oh no, I'm _____ I can't.

Léon and Robert

Speaking 10

a Think of three things you'd like to invite a friend to. For example:
- a sports event
- a sleepover
- a video games night
- a concert
- a party
- a film night

b Decide the date and time of each thing and other details.

For example:
- **sports event**: What sport? Which teams?
- **concert**: Who? Where?
- **sleepover**: When? Who else?
- **party**: Where? What for? Dress code?
- **video games night**: Where? What time? Which games?
- **film night**: Where? What films?

11 Invite different people to your three places. Find someone to go to each place.

Example: *Hi, Manuel. Are you free on Sunday?*

Writing 12

a *Business training.* A delegation of business partners from Las Vegas are visiting your company. You are planning three activities for the weekend. Write an email to Jim, Tom and Laura inviting them to join you and your team. Think of interesting and fun activities.

b Compare your invitations in class and vote on the most interesting weekend programme for your American business partners.

Your time, your space!

Your space

Vocabulary 13 What can you see in the photos? Check the picture dictionary on p. 166.

Places
→ Picture dictionary, *Places*, p. 166

A

B

C

Reading 14 a Read the article about Lisa and Lawrence. Where do they live and go to school / work?

Place to place

Lisa, aged 16, lives in Vienna, the capital of Austria, but goes to a boarding school in Berkshire, UK, more than 1,000 kilometres away.

"I grew up in Vienna and I love it here, but my parents want me to go to boarding school in England," she says. "At the beginning of term, three times a year, I have to travel for almost a day to get there, by plane and then by train, but it's OK. My school is in Crowthorne, Berkshire, in southwest England near the town of Reading. I don't want to live in the English countryside forever. It's nice and green and a great place to study, but it's very quiet. Vienna is an exciting place with lots of places to go out, shops and museums, but it's quite polluted compared to Crowthorne."

There are more and more people like Lisa all over the world. Many people now live and work or study in very different places as people become more mobile. Lawrence Wood, an English businessman, works in London but lives in another country because the city is too expensive. He flies to London on Monday mornings and flies back to Malta on Thursday evenings, where his wife Samantha and his two young children live in a family apartment in Paceville.

"Our new place in Malta is next to the sea. It's safe, and our apartment is big and cheap," says Lawrence. "We have a beautiful view of the Mediterranean. It's five minutes from the kids' school and seven kilometres from the airport. The flying's OK. It's three or four hours, but I only do it twice a week."

b Which place(s) mentioned in the article can you see in pictures A–C?

15 Read the article in 14 again. Answer the questions about Lisa and Lawrence.

1. How long are their journeys?
2. How often do they travel?
3. How do they travel?
4. What do they like about the places where they live / study?
5. Who do they live with?
6. Why do they live and work / study in different places?

Vocabulary 16 Find the opposites of the adjectives in the article.

Describing places

1. boring / *exciting*
2. ugly / _____
3. expensive / _____
4. noisy / _____
5. dangerous / _____
6. _____ / clean

Speaking 17 Think of places you really like or do not like. Why do you like or dislike them?

- Give your opinions about places you know and discuss in small groups. Use the words in 16.
Example: *I really like Oxford Street in London … because …*

Where I live

Vocabulary 18 Prepositions of place

Complete the sentences with the prepositions.

| in | on | from (500 metres) | next to | near |

1 Lisa lives _____ Vienna, _____ the east of Austria.
2 The city is _____ the Danube.
3 The boarding school is _____ the English countryside, _____ the town of Reading.
4 Lawrence's new place in Malta is _____ the sea.
5 It's five minutes _____ the kids' school.

19 Which groups of expressions go with *in*? Which expressions go with *on*?

I live …
1 _____ a village • a town • a city • the city centre • the country • the countryside
2 _____ the north / south of England • the east / west of the city
3 _____ the road to Reading • a river • the metro / underground line
4 _____ a flat • an apartment • a house
5 _____ the ground floor • the tenth floor

Writing 20 Write five or six sentences about where you live.

Speaking 21 *Media task.* Choose a famous landmark and use the internet (English websites only) to find out where it is and when and why it was built.

- Work in pairs and interview each other. A, describe your landmark without saying its name. B, ask questions to find out more about the landmark.
- Can you guess what landmark your partner has chosen?

Your time, your space!

In a flat

Vocabulary 22 a Nicola and her mother, Carole, share a flat. Look at the pictures. What rooms can you see?

Things in the home

- a bathroom
- a bedroom
- a dining room
- a kitchen
- a living room
- a bedroom and study

b Match the things with a–w in the pictures.

a bath	a chair	a drawer	plates	a tea towel
bedclothes	a computer	a fridge	pots and pans	towels
a bedside table	a cooker	a kitchen bin	a rug	a wardrobe
a book shelf	cutlery	a mirror	a sofa	a washing machine
a bunk bed	a desk	a plant		

Listening 23 Listen to Nicola and make notes.

- What is her favourite room? _____
- What does it look like? _____
- What does she do there? _____

14 33b5nf

44

Your time, your space!

Speaking 24 Discuss the following questions with a partner.
- What rooms do you have in your home?
- What is your favourite room? Why?

Vocabulary 25 a Look at the pictures of an environmentally friendly home and write the words in the boxes. You can use the picture dictionary on p. 166 for help.

An environmentally friendly home
→ Picture dictionary, *Homes*, p. 166

balcony   triple glazed window   sliding door   green roof   video games   blinds   solar panels
conservatory   energy efficient windows   tree   bushes   pond   waste separation unit   insulation
computer   Wi-Fi internet   TV set   sound system

b Describe the two pictures to a partner.

Examples: *There is a sliding door on the ground floor. There are trees next to the house. There is wi-fi internet access.*

Speaking 26 a You are going to house-sit for a friend. Decide what questions you want to ask.

Examples: *Is there a … ? ▪ Are there any … ? ▪ Where's … ? ▪ Where are … ? ▪ Can I … ?*

house-sit ['haʊs sɪt] verb to stay in someone's home when they are away to keep it safe: *My friend always house-sits for us when we're on holiday.*

b Talk in A/B pairs. You're both in A's home. B is the house-sitter. Then change roles and talk again.

- B, ask questions about the house. A, show him/her the house.
- Use words from 22 and 25.

Extras   Explore

Your time, your space!

Renting a room

Reading 27 Read the adverts. Which place is best for someone who:

1 doesn't smoke and has a car? ☐
2 doesn't like noisy places and doesn't have a car? ☐
3 doesn't have furniture? ☐

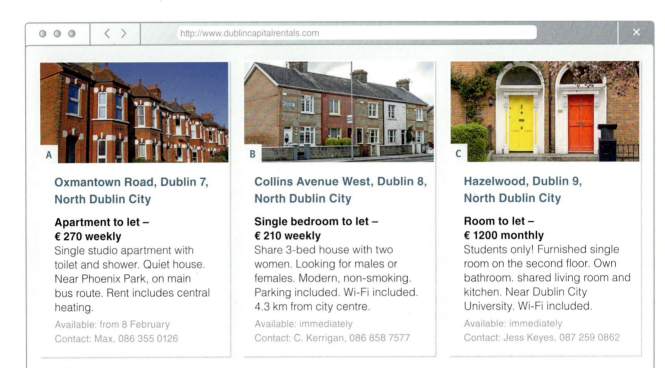

http://www.dublincapitalrentals.com

A Oxmantown Road, Dublin 7, North Dublin City

Apartment to let –
€ 270 weekly
Single studio apartment with toilet and shower. Quiet house. Near Phoenix Park, on main bus route. Rent includes central heating.
Available: from 8 February
Contact: Max, 086 355 0126

B Collins Avenue West, Dublin 8, North Dublin City

Single bedroom to let –
€ 210 weekly
Share 3-bed house with two women. Looking for males or females. Modern, non-smoking. Parking included. Wi-Fi included. 4.3 km from city centre.
Available: immediately
Contact: C. Kerrigan, 086 858 7577

C Hazelwood, Dublin 9, North Dublin City

Room to let –
€ 1200 monthly
Students only! Furnished single room on the second floor. Own bathroom. shared living room and kitchen. Near Dublin City University. Wi-Fi included.
Available: immediately
Contact: Jess Keyes, 087 259 0862

Vocabulary 28 *Adverts for rooms* Find words or expressions in adverts A–C which mean:

1 money you pay to live somewhere – r _ent_
2 for one person – s _____
3 system for making a place warm – c _____ h _____
4 men / women – m _____ / f _____
5 ready to live in – a _____
6 now, without waiting – i _____
7 with bed, wardrobe, chairs, etc. – f _____
8 only for you – o _____
9 for you and other people – s _____

Listening 29 Listen to Alicja calling about one of the rooms. Which one is she interested in?

 15 s6wv4k

30 Match the questions and answers.

1 Does the room have its own bathroom and kitchen?
2 Is there a washing machine?
3 Is it near a bus stop for the city centre?
4 Is heating included in the rent?
5 Can I see the room this evening?

A Yes, it's five minutes from the bus stop.
B Yes, any time after six.
C It has a bathroom with a shower, but you'll share the kitchen.
D Yes, it's in the kitchen, and there's a dishwasher.
E Yes, it's two hundred and ten euros a week for everything, except the telephone.

Extras **Explore**

Your time, your space!

Speaking **31** **a** Work in A/B pairs. Think of four questions you want to ask about the flat or apartment.
- A, you're interested in the apartment on Oxmantown Road.
- B, you're interested in the room in Hazelwood.

b A, phone B. B, look at p. 149 and answer A's questions.

c Change roles. B, phone A. A, look at p. 147 and answer B's questions.

Keyword: on

32 Add the highlighted expressions to the table.
1 Plates and mugs and stuff are up here on the shelf.
2 Please use the wardrobe on the left.
3 I like talking to my girlfriend and watching something good on TV with her.
4 All Saints Day is on 1 November.
5 And can he come on Friday?
6 On Sofasurfing.com, you can read people's profiles, email them and go and stay in their homes.
7 You can sleep on a sofa or spare bed for one or two nights.
8 Managers are often on planes or trains and in hotels and offices around the world.

Places	Days, dates	Transport	Media, communication
on the second floor	on 23 March	on the bus	on the phone

33 **a** Add on to the questions.
1 What did you do ∨ Friday evening? *(on)*
2 How often do you go the internet?
3 What's your favourite programme TV?
4 What do you listen to the radio?
5 When was your first trip a plane?
6 Do you always work Mondays?

b Write five more questions with on.

c Walk around and ask three different people each question. Make notes of what your friends answered. Sum up your findings and report in class.

34 **a** On also forms special phrases. Can you find the correct explanation in English and add the German translation?

Phrase		Explanation	German translation
1 on second thought	A	with a limited amount of money	
2 on a budget	B	independently	
3 on principle	C	at work	
4 do something on purpose	D	after thinking about it again	
5 be on duty	E	only if …	
6 on condition that	F	do something intentionally	
7 do something on your own	G	as a rule	

b Work in pairs and use each phrase in a sentence.

47

Explore speaking: A phone message

35 **a** Listen to Maria talking to Paul about a room she wants to rent through *roomtrip.com*. Complete Paul's note.

> Dad,
> Maria _____ rang. She wants to book the _____ but couldn't find out if it is _____ .
> Ring her back on _____
> or email her at _____ .
> Paul

Paul: Hello?
Maria: Hello, this is Maria Gilberto. I'm calling about the double room advertised on *roomtrip.com*. Can I speak to Mr Robertson, please?
Paul: Sorry, you need to talk to my father about this. He's not in at the moment.
Maria: Oh, I see.
Paul: Can I take a message?
Maria: Yes, please. It's Maria Gilberto, and I'd like to …
Paul: Sorry, can you say that again?
Maria: Maria Gilberto. G-I-L-B-E-R-T-O.
Paul: G-I-L-B-E-R-T-O. OK, thanks. And what's the message?
Maria: Erm, I'd like to book your double room on the second floor from 15 to 22 August and want to know if it's still available. There was a problem when I tried to find out online.
Paul: Right. I'll tell my dad.
Maria: Could he call me back please or email me?
Paul: Sure. Could you give me your number and email address?
Maria: OK. My mobile number is 0039778 944 6532.
Paul: Sorry, can you slow down a bit, please?
Maria: Sorry, it's 0039778 944 6532. I'm in Italy.
Paul: OK, and your email?
Maria: It's m.gilberto@zmail.com
Paul: OK, any capital letters?
Maria: No, everything in lower case.
Paul: Thanks. I'll tell my dad to contact you.
Maria: Thanks a lot, that's very kind. I look forward to hearing from him. Bye.
Paul: Bye.

b Read the conversation to check.

36 Look at the highlighted expressions in the conversation. Which can you use:

1 when you want to talk to someone?
2 when the person is not there?
3 when you offer to take a message?
4 when someone speaks too fast?
5 when you want someone to repeat?
6 to say you understand?

37 **a** Work in pairs. A, use these role cards. B, use the cards on p. 145. Have two conversations. A, you start the first conversation and B, you start the second conversation.

Student A

Conversation 1

Your name: Bogdan (or Bogdana) Gabrovec
Nationality: Slovenian
Your phone number: 00386 614 573 1246
email: b_gabrovec@kmail.com
You want to book a holiday bungalow in Cornwall advertised on www.bythesea.com

Student A

Conversation 2

Student B wants to book your unique tree house hotel that you advertised on: www.natureretreat.uk.
Your mother has all the information, she will be back in 2 hours. Take a message.

b Check each other's messages. Is all the information correct?

Explore writing: A blog entry

38 a Read Jakob's blog entry on www.breakadviceforyou.co.uk about his stay in San Gimignano, Italy. What was his stay like?

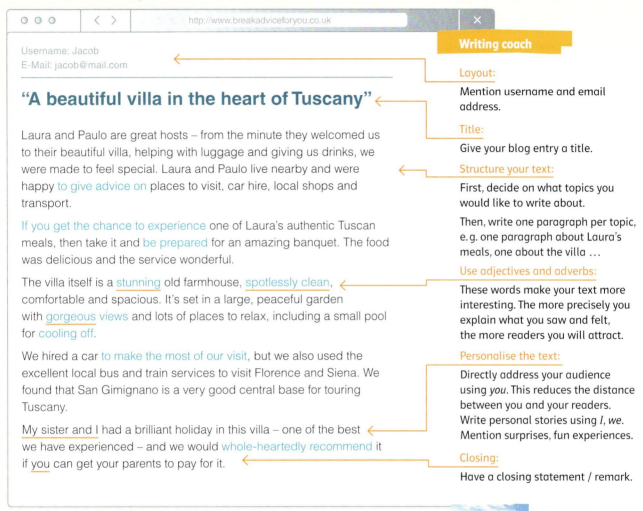

Username: Jacob
E-Mail: jacob@mail.com

"A beautiful villa in the heart of Tuscany"

Laura and Paulo are great hosts – from the minute they welcomed us to their beautiful villa, helping with luggage and giving us drinks, we were made to feel special. Laura and Paulo live nearby and were happy to give advice on places to visit, car hire, local shops and transport.

If you get the chance to experience one of Laura's authentic Tuscan meals, then take it and be prepared for an amazing banquet. The food was delicious and the service wonderful.

The villa itself is a stunning old farmhouse, spotlessly clean, comfortable and spacious. It's set in a large, peaceful garden with gorgeous views and lots of places to relax, including a small pool for cooling off.

We hired a car to make the most of our visit, but we also used the excellent local bus and train services to visit Florence and Siena. We found that San Gimignano is a very good central base for touring Tuscany.

My sister and I had a brilliant holiday in this villa – one of the best we have experienced – and we would whole-heartedly recommend it if you can get your parents to pay for it.

Writing coach

Layout:
Mention username and email address.

Title:
Give your blog entry a title.

Structure your text:
First, decide on what topics you would like to write about.
Then, write one paragraph per topic, e.g. one paragraph about Laura's meals, one about the villa …

Use adjectives and adverbs:
These words make your text more interesting. The more precisely you explain what you saw and felt, the more readers you will attract.

Personalise the text:
Directly address your audience using *you*. This reduces the distance between you and your readers. Write personal stories using *I, we*. Mention surprises, fun experiences.

Closing:
Have a closing statement / remark.

b Analyse this text.
- Underline all words that describe places.
- Write a heading for each paragraph.

39 *Media task.* Use an online dictionary to make sure you understand the highlighted words and phrases above.

- Find a picture of a holiday home or destination you would like to visit.
- Write a blog entry similar to the one above about your destination.

Write around 200 words.

Self-assessment

- talk about your free time, likes and dislikes
- talk about habits and customs
- make and respond to invitations
- talk about cities, neighbourhoods and homes
- find information in adverts for rooms
- take a phone message, ask people to repeat
- write a blog entry

Goals
- talk about past events
- talk about first times
- talk about technical innovations
- talk about new experiences
- write a personal letter / email giving news

Technology – talking about the past

Reading 1 a Read the article. What is it about?

http://thingsthatchangedtheworld.com

Things that changed the world

The web

Sir Tim Berners-Lee is a British computer scientist. He grew up in London in the late 1950s, and as a boy he was interested in trains. He recalls: "I made some electronic gadgets to control the trains. Then I ended up getting more interested in electronics than trains. Later on, when I was in college, I made a computer out of an old television set." After graduating from Oxford University, Berners-Lee became a software engineer at CERN, the large particle physics laboratory near Geneva, Switzerland. Scientists come from all over the world to use its accelerators, but Sir Tim noticed that they were having difficulty sharing information. Tim saw that millions of computers were already connected through the internet and realised they could share information by using a technology called hypertext. He began work using a NeXT computer, one of Steve Jobs' early products. In 1990, Tim wrote the three fundamental technologies that remain the foundation of today's web:

- HTML: Hypertext Markup Language. The markup (formatting) language for the web.
- URI: Uniform Resource Identifier. A kind of "address" that is unique and used to identify each resource on the web. It is also commonly called a URL.
- HTTP: Hypertext Transfer Protocol. Allows for the retrieval of linked resources from across the web.

In 1991 people outside of CERN were invited to join this new web community. As the web began to grow, Tim realized that anyone anywhere should be able to use it without paying a fee or having to ask for permission. CERN announced this in April 1993, which sparked a global wave of creativity, collaboration and innovation never seen before. In 2003, the companies developing new web standards committed to a Royalty Free Policy for their work. In 2014 almost two in five people around the world used the internet.

Tim founded the World Wide Web Consortium (W3C), an international community devoted to developing open web standards and became its director. In 2009, Sir Tim established the World Wide Web Foundation, whose target is to build a just and successful society by connecting everyone and supporting participation.

Two gadgets

The first personal music player

A German-Brazilian, Andreas Pavel, made the Stereobelt in 1972. It had headphones and used cassettes. Pavel wanted people to have music everywhere they went. He met directors of electronics companies and they listened to the Stereobelt but said, "People don't want to wear headphones and listen to music in public." So Pavel never sold his idea, but his personal music player was the first. Sony's Walkman was the second, and people loved it.

The first laptop

The first real laptop was the GRID Compass. A British man, William Moggridge, made it in 1979 for GRID Systems Corporation. It was 5 kg and had a 340-kilobyte memory. It was very expensive, about $9,000, but the US government liked the small computer and bought a lot of them. NASA used a GRID Compass on the Space Shuttle in the early 1980s.

b Read the article again and answer the questions.

1. In what decades were the technical inventions created?
2. Which inventions were created by Europeans?
3. What was the second personal music player called?
4. What technical innovation was used on the Space Shuttle?
5. Where did Sir Tim work in the late 1980s/early 1990s? What do they do there?
6. How does Sir Tim believe the internet should be used?

c Discuss with your partner. What do you use to listen to music, to call people and to surf the internet?

Grammar

Past simple verbs
→ Irregular verbs, p. 165

2 a Read the article on p. 50 again and <u>underline</u> all verbs in the past tense.

b Put the verbs from the article into the correct section of the table. Add the infinitive form of the verbs.

Past (regular -ed)	Infinitive	Past (irregular)	Infinitive
ended	end	grew	grow

3 Complete the paragraphs with the past forms of these verbs. There are two extra words you should not use.

use   work (2×)   start   want   join   listen   help   go   cost   have
think   make (2×)   write   buy   meet

A Moggridge (1) _____ for GRID Systems Corporation.

His laptops (2) _____ about $9,000, but the American government (3) _____ them and (4) _____ them on the Space Shuttle.

B Pavel (5) _____ the Stereobelt in 1972.

He (6) _____ to some electronics companies and he (7) _____ the directors. They (8) _____ to the personal stereo but said it was a bad idea because it (9) _____ headphones. They said no one (10) _____ to listen to music with headphones.

C After graduation, Tim Berners-Lee (11) _____ as an engineer at the telecommunications company Plessey in Poole, Dorset. In 1978, he (12) _____ D. G. Nash in Ferndown, Dorset, where he (13) _____ type-setting software for printers. Berners-Lee worked as an independent contractor at CERN from June to December 1980. While in Geneva, he (14) _____ the first hypertext code, which he (15) _____ would help researchers to share information.

51

Changes

Grammar — **4 a** Note the word order in past simple questions and statements. What do you notice?

Past simple

→ Grammar reference and practice, p. 156

Questions	Statements
Where did Sir Tim work?	➕ He worked at CERN in Switzerland.
Was the inventor of the Stereobelt an American?	❌ No, he was a German-Brazilian.
Did the first mobile phone cost more than $3,000?	✅ Yes, it did. It cost $9,000.

b Create your own quiz. Look at the article in 1 again (p. 50) and write questions and the correct answers about the texts. Then test your partner's knowledge and ask your questions. Take turns asking and answering questions.

Listening — **5 a** Listen to Yoko. How does she feel about new technology?

17 zc8kg2

b Listen again. Answer the questions with expressions from the boxes. There are two extra phrases you should not use.

when she was 7 years old   in 2002   in 2005   in 2007   about 14 or 15 years ago   two months ago

about 12 years ago   by the end of kindergarten   by the end of 2005   when she was 11 years old

last summer   last year

When did Yoko:

1 get her first mobile phone? _____
2 check a transport timetable on her phone? _____
3 use a laptop properly for the first time? _____
4 play a game online? _____
5 buy something online? _____
6 win an online competition? _____

c Tell each other when you did the things Yoko was talking about. Use in, last and ago.

Speaking — **6** Accidental inventions. Work in pairs. Student A reads about an invention on this page, student B reads the text on p. 145. Tell your partner:

1 name of invention   2 function of invention   3 name of inventor   4 date / place of invention

> **Velcro**
>
> Swiss engineer George de Mestral was on a hunting trip with his dog in the Swiss Alps when he noticed how seeds would stick to its fur. He published his invention in 1951 but it wasn't until NASA came along that the technology was really popularized. In the 1960s, Apollo astronauts used it to stop pens and equipment flying away.

7 *Media task*. Go online and find out about a famous or useful invention for yourself. Only use English websites! Use the information to prepare a short presentation about the history of your invention. Use words like in, ago, and last and use the past simple. Make sure you use your own words.

52

Talking about new experiences

Writing 8 Read through the notes (1–3) about Susan's last weekend. Use the past simple to complete the story.

1 Friday evening

café with friends
old stories about school life
a really good time
a lot of laughs
home very late

2 Saturday

long lie-in
new book very exciting
cinema with Lucy
an Austrian restaurant with parents
Wiener schnitzel – first time – great
very tired
bed at 11 p.m.

3 Sunday

early breakfast
dogs for walk
with Tom and his sister to the zoo
work-out at the gym
very hungry
huge bowl of pasta for dinner – brother sushi
homework for Monday
very tired – bed at 10 p.m.

Last weekend

On Friday night Susan met her friends and they went to a cafe …

Speaking 9 What did you do last weekend? Tell your partner about it.

Listening 10 a Read about Onyinye and look at the photos. What differences between Nigeria and Scotland do you think she will talk about?

Onyinye was born in Nigeria but grew up in the UK. She talks about her memories of moving to Scotland when she was a child.

Changes

b Listen to Onyinye and (circle) the right words.

1 Onyinye moved when she was   five / fifteen   years old.
2 She says everything was   difficult / different .
3 She   remembers / doesn't remember   the first time she saw snow.
4 She   enjoyed / didn't enjoy   playing in the snow.

Vocabulary | **11**
Good and bad experiences

Which expressions are about good experiences? Which are about bad experiences? Which can be about both? Put the expressions in the correct columns. You can also add some of your own.

It was really   exciting   difficult   strange
                       interesting   boring
It was very

I had   ~~a great time~~   lots of fun   a terrible time   a lovely time   a very bad time

Good experiences	Bad experiences	Both
I had a great time		

Listening | **12 a** Listen to Andrew talking about an important event in his life – learning to swim.

Answer the questions.

1 When was it?
2 Where was he?
3 Who was he with?
4 How did he feel?

b What do you think about Andrew's story?

- Do you remember how you learned to swim?

Writing & Speaking | **13 a** Write down one or two important events in your life.

For example, when you:

- started going to school.
- got a baby sister / brother.
- moved into a new house or flat.
- met an important new person.
- went on a trip.
- started going to your new school.

b Think about each event.

- **When did it happen?** *last month, many years ago …*
- **Where did it happen?** *at work, in Innsbruck, in a club …*
- **What happened?** *We had a car accident, I met …*
- **How was it?** *It was exciting, I had a terrible time …*

c In pairs, ask and answer questions about each other's events.

Example: A: *So, when did you learn to snowboard?* B: *That was three years ago.* A: *And where was that?*

Keyword: *have*

14 Put the words in the correct group.

a baby   breakfast   lunch   a bath   a cat   a meal   a break   a drink   two brothers   a shower   something to eat   a digital camera   a sandwich   a lot of friends   a nice flat   a meeting   a coffee   a lesson   a conversation

Possessions	Activities	Food and drink	Relationships
have a new car,	have a party,	have dinner,	have a big family,

15 Talk to other people in the class and find someone who:

1 has a big family.
2 never has breakfast.
3 had a conversation online yesterday.
4 still has a digital camera.
5 has a cat.
6 often has English tutoring.

Example: *Do you have a big family? What time do you have breakfast?*

Independent learning: Self-study

16 a Which media do you use most often?

b Independent learning quiz. Answer these questions.

A

B

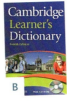
C

D

E

	Learning English independently
1	Do you read in English outside school? If so, what?
2	What media do you use for learning English? (e.g. How do you learn and practise new words?)
3	Have you ever watched a film in English? If so, which one?
4	Do you have any English-speaking friends?
5	What social media do you use in English?
6	Do you read or even write blogs in English?
7	Do you listen to podcasts in English?
8	Do you read about your favourite sports or music stars in English? If so, what websites do you use?

c Compare your answers with a partner.

Changes

Info point: Shapes and drawings

Shapes

A line has only one dimension – the length. It has a beginning and an end. It is the only 1-D shape.
A 2-D shape has length and width, but no depth. It can have edges and corners, but only in one plane.
A 3-D shape has length, width and depth. Most of them have faces, edges and corners. All 3-D shapes are solids.

17 a Study the table below.

b Work in A/B pairs. Cover the text in the table with a sheet of paper so that you can only see the pictures. A, point at a picture, B, identify and describe the shape. Then change roles.

Example: *This is a football field. It has the shape of a rectangle. / It is rectangular / of rectangular shape.*

Two-dimensional shapes			Three-dimensional objects		
	A square has four equal sides.	The three overlapping shapes in this picture are square.		A cube has a surface of six equal squares. They are called 'faces'.	A dice is a cubic object often used in board games.
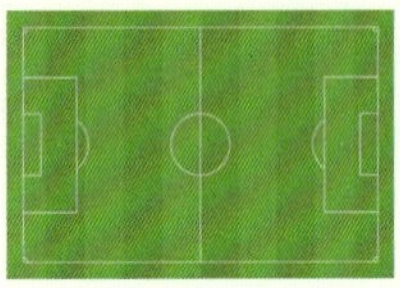	A rectangle also has four sides.	The opposite sides of a rectangular field have the same lengths.		A cylinder can be solid or hollow.	A drum is a quite loud cylindrical object.
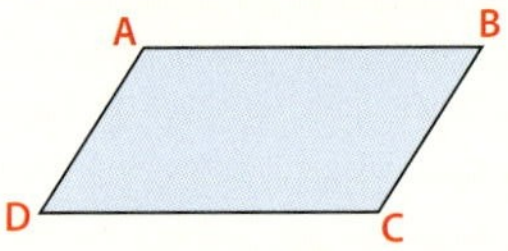	A parallelogram is closely related to a rectangle, but its sides are shifted either to the right or to the left. So it has no right angles.			A prism can be built on a triangular or a rectangular base.	
	The triangle is one of the basic geometric shapes.	The chequered flag is triangular.		A cone is a curved 3-D object with a circular base that narrows toward a point.	An icecream cone is a sweet conical object.
	A regular pentagon has five sides.	There is a pentagonal building in Washington, DC. What is it?		A pyramid has a square base.	The main entrance to the Louvre is pyramidal.
	This illustration shows circles in a circle. Looking at it can make you dizzy.	A ring is circular. You can draw a circle with a drawing compass.		A sphere is often also called ball or globe.	Marbles are spherical objects made of glass or stone.
	A spiral is a fascinating geometric shape.	London City Hall has a spiral staircase.		The earth has two hemispheres: the northern and the southern hemisphere.	

Changes

18 Work in pairs. List and discuss real-life objects that look like the shapes on p. 56.

Example: *A bowling ball is a heavy, spherical object made of plastic.*

Drawings

Technical drawings are usually scale drawings. They show the object in a specific ratio to the actual size of the object. A scale like 1:10 (say: "one to ten") shows objects 10 times smaller than they really are (10 mm in the drawing represents 100 mm in reality). The first number always refers to the length of the drawing on paper and the second number refers to the length of the real-life object.

19 Complete the sentences with the words in the boxes.

wide   high   depth   length   width   height   deep   long

1 The table is 160 cm long. — Its *length* is 160 cm.
2 The dimensions of the cupboard are: length 80 cm, width 40 cm, height 180 cm. — It is 80 cm _____, 40 cm _____ and 180 cm _____.
3 The lake is 80 m deep. — Its _____ is 80 m.
4 The shirt has 1-cm-wide blue stripes. — The _____ of the stripes is 1 cm.
5 Aeroplanes fly very high. They fly at 30,000 feet. — They fly at a _____ of 30,000 feet.
6 The depth of the box is 20 cm. — It is 20 cm _____.

20 Listen and answer the questions.

1 How would you describe an equilateral triangle?
   A It has two equal sides and angles.
   B It has three equal sides and angles.
   C It has no equal sides or angles.
   D It has one angle that is a right angle.

2 The angles of a triangle always add up to
   A 90 degrees.
   B 160 degrees.
   C 180 degrees.
   D 360 degrees.

3 Which statement describes a square?
   A It is diamond-shaped.
   B It has two pairs of equal sides and four right angles.
   C It has four equal sides.
   D It has depth.

4 Which statement describes a parallelogram?
   A It looks like a square.
   B It looks like a shifted rectangle.
   C Its opposite angles aren't equal.
   D Its opposite sides aren't parallel.

5 Which statement is true?
   A A circle has a central point.
   B A circle has a beginning.
   C A circle has two diameters.
   D A circle doesn't have a radius.

5 How many rings make up the Olympic logo?
   A Three rings
   B Four rings
   C Five rings
   D Six rings

21 Listen to the instructions and draw the shapes.

22 a Now think of your own drawing and draw it. Include shapes and objects from p. 56.

b Work in A/B pairs. A, describe your drawing to B. (If you need more language to describe your drawing, look at the conversation on p. 144) B, listen to A and draw.

c B, check with A if your drawing is correct. Then change roles.

Changes | Language skills | Extras | Explore

Explore writing: A personal letter / email giving news

 23 a Read Carrie's email below. Informal phrases are highlighted in blue. What's the email about?

TIP: You should use language like in the email when writing to a friend.

From: Carrie
Sent: 27 August
To: Hannah
Subject: **My first trip alone**

Hi Hannah,

How are you? Hope all's well at home? I'm doing great. This summer I was allowed to go on my first trip abroad alone. My mum's friend, who lives in southern Italy, invited me to join her and her children at their summer residence near Naples. When Mum told me, I was so excited! Yeah, ok, I was really nervous, too. ;-)

I booked my train ticket to the airport online; it was really easy. Mum helped me find a flight to Naples. I even chose my seat on the plane on the computer. Of course, I booked a window seat ☺. Got a new super-light suitcase in that cool shopping centre we went to in June – remember?

Flying alone is fantastic! It's like you're discovering the world yourself.

Naples was cool, too. And Emilia and Lauro are fun! They are 14 and 16. And, yes, Lauro looks great … You've got to see the pics when we meet next week.

Got so much to tell you! I even learned standup paddleboarding in the sea. I ate fresh seafood, went to a party and met Lauro's friends and we hiked up the slopes of Mount Vesuvius. You know, that volcano we read about in Latin class.

I plan to visit them again next year. We are now linked on sharepictures.com. You really HAVE to see the pics!

How about your summer? Any news? I'm dying to know …

That's all for now, got to go,

Love, Carrie

Writing coach

Greetings:
Informal greeting: *Hi, Hello* and person's name.

Contractions:
- Informal writing includes contractions: *all's, I'm, it's.*
- You can also abbreviate words: *pics.*
- Incomplete sentences are OK.

Closing:
Informal ending: *love, yours, best, take care, cheers.*

Paragraphing:
Put one main idea into one paragraph → new idea = new paragraph.

Closing:
Close the email with a phrase. Alternatives would be: *Hope to hear from you again soon. / Write soon. / Best of luck with … / Hope all goes well with …*

b Work in pairs. What was your last holiday like?
- Where were you?
- What did you do?
- Did you meet new people? Who?
- Are you still in contact? Do you write each other?

c Make sentences and write them down.

1	How	A	from you.
2	I hope	B	for now.
3	I'm	C	from you soon.
4	Good to hear	D	are you?
5	That's all	E	you're well.
6	Hope to hear	F	fine.

24 a Make a list of things you did in the last few weeks. Then write an email to a friend, telling him / her about them.

Things I did …

b Read each other's emails, then ask questions to find out more.

Example: *Oh, you bought a new computer. What kind?*

Self-assessment

- talk about past events
- talk about first times
- talk about technical innovations
- talk about new experiences
- write a personal letter / email giving news

Goals
- buy things in shops
- talk about preferences and give reasons
- talk about shopping and food
- order a meal
- write short practical requests and reminders

Listening 1 a Talk together. Find out about each other's shopping habits.

1 Do you like shopping? Why? / Why not?
2 What do you enjoy buying? What don't you enjoy buying?
3 Do you use the internet for shopping? What do you usually buy?

b Listen to the radio interview with the manager of a new shopping mall, and tick (✓) the things that are mentioned.

sports shop ☐	escalators ☐	pharmacy ☐
lifts ☐	bank / cash machine ☐	jewellery ☐
shoe shop ☐	music ☐	luggage ☐
video games ☐	toilets ☐	newsagent ☐
clothes shop ☐	sales assistants ☐	Indian restaurant ☐
supermarket ☐		

Vocabulary 2 a In the shopping centre. Where do you go to do these things?

Shops and shopping
1 buy boots?
2 buy maps?
3 get money?
4 buy trousers?
5 buy a football?
6 wash your hands?
7 buy medicine?
8 buy a magazine?

b What other things can you buy in each shop?

Example: *In a sports shop, you can buy baseball caps.*

c What are your favourite shops to buy the above things?

Grammar 3 a Which of the following can you count? These are countable nouns.

Countable and uncountable nouns
Which can you not count? These are uncountable nouns.

A milk   B glass of milk   C T-shirt   D cotton   E carrot   F rice

What would you like?

→ Grammar reference and practice, p. 157

b Match pictures A–F (p. 60) to sentences 1–6 in the table.

Countable	Uncountable
How many carrots do you want?	How much rice do we need?
1 I'm wearing a T-shirt.	4 I prefer cotton to polyester.
2 I'd like a glass of milk, please.	5 Have some milk if you like.
3 I eat a lot of carrots.	6 I eat lots of rice.

c Read through Katie's interview on p. 146 and underline the nouns after much, many, some, lots of and a lot of. Put the expressions in the columns. Which are countable and which are uncountable?

Many	Much	Some	A lot of/lots of
suitcases	luggage	information	light

4 Make three rules.

1 You can use many, a / an and numbers with
2 You can use much with
3 You can use some and a lot of with

A countable and uncountable nouns.
B countable nouns.
C uncountable nouns.

5 Circle the correct words.

1 How many / much tomatoes would you like?
2 How many / much milk do you have in your tea?
3 Would you like a / some rice?
4 I'd like an / some apple, please.
5 I buy a lot of / a bread every week.
6 Can you buy some banana / bananas ?
7 I'd like some lettuce / lettuces in my sandwich.
8 I need six tomato / tomatoes .

Vocabulary
Talking about preferences and giving reasons

6 Match 1–4 with A–D.

1 I prefer
2 I'd rather
3 I like them
4 I don't like DVDs.

A because they aren't so sweet.
B Vietnamese to Thai.
C have a Ferrari than a Lada.
D I think streaming is easier.

Speaking

7 Look at the choices below, and talk to your partner about which you prefer.

- 3D or 2D video games
- action films vs comedy
- skateboarding vs skiing
- swimming pools vs the beach
- shopping online vs going shopping
- classical music vs pop music

What would you like?

Shopping trip

Listening **8** a Listen to Jason shopping. Which three shops does he go to? Make notes.

1 _____
2 _____
3 _____

b What does he buy? Listen again to check.

Vocabulary **9** a Who asks questions 1–7? Write J (Jason) or A (the shop assistant).

Buying things

1 Do you need some help?
2 How much is this one?
3 How much are they?
4 How many would you like?
5 Is that everything?
6 Do you have any hiking maps?
7 Would you like anything else?

b Match questions 1–7 with these answers.

A Yes, they're over there.
B It's 9.99.
C I'd like a new outdoor jacket.
D They're 79.95.
E Yes, I think so.
F I'll have six, please.
G No, that's fine, thanks.

10 Look at how much and how many in the conversations. Which expression do you use to ask about the price of something? Which expression do you use to ask about the number of things?

Speaking **11** Work in pairs. Choose a shop and think of three things you want to buy. Take turns to be the shop assistant and the customer. Role-play the conversations.

Example: A: *Can I help you?* B: *Yes, please. I'm looking for a map of San Francisco.*

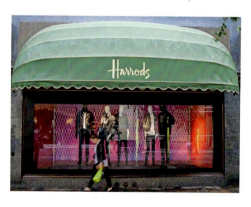

What would you like?

Vocabulary **12** Which of the foods on the shopping list do you like? Tell each other.

Food
→ Picture dictionary, Food, p. 167

13 a Find one more food in the list that:

is *sweet*: bananas,

is *good for you*: carrots,

has a *skin*: onions,

is *round*: watermelon,

is good if you're *on a diet*: chicken,

is *high in carbohydrates*: potatoes,

is *low in carbohydrates*: lettuce,

is *a dairy product*: yoghurt,

bananas   prawns
lettuce   lemons
rice   yoghurt
lamb   apples
chocolate carrots
cheese   watermelon
beef   broccoli
chicken   potatoes
butter   onions
bread   salmon

b Compare your ideas. Do you agree?

Example: A: *Potatoes are good for you.* B: *No, they're not because they are high in carbohydrates.*

Reading **14 a** In an interview Anthony Warner, 'The Angry Chef', claims to show the "lies and stupidity" in the food world, especially around new diets, wellness and detox. Here are five of his opinions – match them to the pictures.

A

Myth 1 – Detoxing

When people say, "I'm detoxing," what they're saying is, "I'm not eating for two days." It's just an extreme weight-loss diet, but you make up toxins that aren't there and say, "I'm doing this to get rid of these toxins" – which your body will do naturally anyway. It creates fear around food.

Myth 2 – Eat like a caveman

The paleo diet is just a low-carb diet given a non-scientific justification. We've been eating carbohydrates for a very long time, but they just say, "Well, caveman ate meat." They have this idea from *The Flintstones*, but anyone who works in anthropology will say, "No, they're obviously wrong."

B

Myth 3 – Home-cooked food is always best

It's linked to wanting women to get back into the kitchen: "Natural home-cooked meals are the only way to be healthy … Things were better before women went to work." Underlying the demonisation of convenience food, there is a lot of sexism. "Things were better in our grandmother's day" – were they?

Myth 4 – Sugar is 'toxic'

Sugar has an enormous amount of energy and is one of the most important building blocks for life. But they say, "It has no nutritional value." That makes absolutely no sense.

Myth 5 – Don't eat processed food

People will have a ready-meal from the supermarket and say, "I'm too busy to cook." Then they'll say poor people should just stop buying hamburgers. Nonsense.

D

E
C

b Sum up Anthony's opinion about the five myths in your own words.

Example: *Anthony thinks that detoxing does not work because your body gets rid of the toxins anyway.*

Speaking **15** *Media task.* In pairs, choose one of Anthony's 'myths' and research facts about one of the myths online. Prepare a short statement agreeing / disagreeing with him and present it in class.

What would you like?

Ordering a meal

Speaking 16 a Talk about the questions in pairs.

1. Do you like eating out in cafés or restaurants? Why? / Why not?
2. Where do you usually eat during the week / at weekends?

b Kim is going for a meal at Nicol's in London, but she doesn't eat meat. What can she order from the menu? What would you choose?

Nicol's ALE & GIN Establishments Since 1875

SANDWICHES – SERVED UNTIL 5 P.M.

All our sandwiches are served with the choice of fries, mixed salad or home-cooked crisps.

SMOKED BACON, JUICY PLUM TOMATO & CHEDDAR CHEESE
OPEN SANDWICH £7.75
Served on salty toasted ciabatta.

SMASHED AVOCADO & GRILLED PEPPER
OPEN SANDWICH (V) £7.75
With soft mozzarella, Batavia lettuce and olives.
Served on crunchy toasted sourdough.

CHARGRILLED RUMP STEAK SANDWICH £7.75
With caramelized onions served on toasted ciabatta bread

FISH FINGER SANDWICH £7.75
Hand-battered cod goujons with creamy tartare sauce.
Served on savoury farmhouse bread.

CHICKEN & AVOCADO SANDWICH £7.75
Hand-pulled Shropshire chicken, avocado and lemon herb oil served on toasted ciabatta bread.

NICOL'S CLUB SANDWICH £7.75
Hand-pulled Shropshire chicken, crispy smoked bacon, lettuce, tomato and mild mayonnaise served on farm-house bread.

SAUSAGE SANDWICH £7.50
3 Gloucester Old Spot sausages with spicy English mustard, served on toasted sourdough.
Vegetarian option also available (V)

SIDES

Fries (V) • £3.50
Chips (V) • £3.50
Macaroni cheese (V) • £3.95

Marinated olives (V) • £3.25
Cauliflower cheese (V) • £2.95
Mushy peas (V) • 50p
Side salad (V) • £2.95

Garlic bread (V) • £2.50 / With cheese • £2.95
Selection of breads
with English herb oil & butter (V) • £3.00
Hand-battered onion rings with sour cream (V)
Small • £2.75 / Large • £4.75

Listening 17 a Listen to Kim ordering food for her parents and herself. What does Kim order?

b Listen again and complete Kim's sentences.

1. We'd _____ .
2. Is it p _____ ?
3. Could I have _____ ?
4. What's _____ ?
5. Does it _____ ?
6. Can I have a _____ ?

c Work in A/B pairs. You are at Nicol's. A, you are the customer, B, you are the waiter. A, choose one of the following roles. Then change roles and have another conversation.

- You don't like vegetables, but are very hungry.
- You want a dessert with lots of chocolate.
- You're hungry, but on a tight budget.
- You're allergic to garlic.

What would you like?

Vocabulary — Describing food

18 a You probably like certain foods because of their taste or smell. Here are several adjectives that can describe food. Link the words to their meaning.

	Adjektives		Meaning	Food
1	bitter	A	seasoned with a lot of salt	dark chocolate, beer
2	bland	B	crisp, easily breakable	
3	crunchy	C	not stimulating, a bit boring	
4	greasy	D	food that has a sharp taste, like dark chocolate or some kinds of beer	
5	hot / spicy	E	pleasant, slightly salty or with herbs; like crisps	
6	juicy	F	food cooked or flavoured in smoke	
7	mushy	G	fried in oil	
8	salty	H	a lot of flavour, like curry	
9	savoury	I	food that contains a lot of liquid	
10	smoked	J	very soft	
11	sour	K	having an acid taste, like unripe fruit	
12	sugary	L	no flavour	
13	creamy	M	cooked with oil in the oven	
14	tasteless	N	very sweet	
15	roasted	O	soft, smooth food that often contains cream	
16	mild	P	cooked under the grill or on a barbecue	
17	grilled	Q	not very strong	

b Write down two food products in every line of the table above that you think meet the category. There is one example. Use a dictionary to help you.

Speaking & Writing

19 a Work in pairs. Use the table above to ask and answer the questions.

1. What's your favourite food? What's your favourite drink? Why?
2. Do you eat and do other things at the same time? What?
3. Is there something you especially like eating in winter / in summer? What?
4. Is there something you don't eat at all? Explain why not.

Example: *I really like oranges because they are so juicy and sweet when they are ripe.*

b Explain these Austrian dishes to your partner. Use the adjectives above.

A
breadcrumbed and fried veal scallop

B
roast pork

C
sugared pancakes (with raisins)

D
special Viennese chocolate cake (= Sachertorte)

c Some friends from the US visited you. You went for a meal at a traditional Austrian restaurant. Write a blog entry about the food (75–100 words).

Keyword: *this, that, these, those*

20 a Match sentences 1–4 with pictures A–D.

1 How much is *this* one?
2 They're over there, on *that* wall.
3 Could I try *these* shoes on, please?
4 Could I have some of *those* carrots, please?

A   B

C   D

b In pairs, ask each other about the names of things in your classroom. Use *this*, *that*, *these* and *those*.

Example: A: *What are those in English?* B: *They're windows.*

21 Replace the underlined words in the conversations with suitable expressions from the boxes. There are two expressions you should not use.

~~That's right.~~   No, that's fine, thanks.   That's a good idea.   That's all right. / That's OK.   Something like that.   That's great!

1 A: Are you a student?
   B: <u>Yes, I am.</u> *That's right*

2 A: Sorry I'm so late.
   B: <u>No problem.</u> _____

3 A: I passed my maths exam this morning.
   B: Really? <u>You did very well!</u> _____

4 A: Would you like to go for a coffee?
   B: Yes, <u>I'd love to.</u> _____

Independent learning: Using a dictionary

22 What kind of dictionary do you use in class / at home?
- monolingual (in English)
- bilingual (your language and English)
- electronic
- CD-ROM
- internet
- mobile phone

23 a Why do you usually use a dictionary? Tick (✓) the list. Read the dictionary entries for *live*. Match A–E with the reasons below.

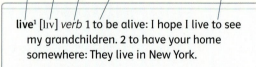
A   B   C   D   E

1 to check the spelling of a word
2 to find out what a word means
3 to find out how to say a word
4 to see an example of the word in a sentence
5 to check the kind of word (noun, adjective, verb)

> **live¹** [lɪv] *verb* 1 to be alive: I hope I live to see my grandchildren. 2 to have your home somewhere: They live in New York.

> **live²** [laɪv] *adj* 1 having life: Millions of live animals are moved around the world each year. 2 A live performance is done with people watching or listening: a live concert ~ live music

b Now answer questions 1–4 about *live*.

1 What kind of word is it?
2 How do you say it?
3 How many meanings does it have?
4 What words often go with it?

24 Work in A/B pairs. A, find the word *book* in your dictionary or on p. 146. B, find the word *match*. Answer the questions in 23b.

25 *Media task.* Do you use any online dictionaries?
- If so, list them here: _____
- Go online and explore all the features the online English dictionary offers. Explain what you have found out in class.

Explore writing: Short requests and reminders

26 a Read the short messages below and underline the phrases to express requests. The first one has been done for you.

> Dear all,
> Change of plan: briefing for sales reps postponed to Monday, 16th, at 6 pm. <u>Pls. make sure you have your iPads with you.</u> See you there.
> Moyra

> Hi Pete,
> Yeah, OK. Pick you up at a quarter to 6 in front of office. Can you bring my laser pointer?
> C U later,
> Anna

> Hi Jim,
> Has Moyra booked a taxi to go to the meeting tonight? Can I join you? Can't reach her. Pls. let me know asap.
> Thx, Andy

> Hi Andy,
> How are you? Can you get back to me on the agenda for the sales reps meeting?
> Howard

> Hi Anna,
> Have you picked up the product samples for Monday evening? They should be downstairs at reception.
> Howard

> Dear all,
> Can anyone bring flipchart paper and markers to the hotel?
> Thx, Pete

> Dear Pete,
> Can you please make an appointment with Greg from Marketing for me? Got to finalise brochures urgently.
> Many thanks, Jim

> Hi Howard,
> Did you bring back the projector this morning? Need to send it to the hotel for Monday …
> Pls, let me know.
> Thx, Jim

> Howard,
> Will mail agenda in approx. 1 hour. Got last minute changes. Your part will be third on the list.
> Thanks, A

> Hi there,
> Got heavy projector to carry; need a lift to hotel for meeting. Is that OK? Could we take Jon, too? Thanks,
> Pete

> Hi there,
> Can you please sort out catering for the meeting on Monday? Have tight schedule.
> Thanks so much, Anna

> Hi Moyra,
> Thanks for the update. Monday's difficult; can't cancel dentist appointment, but will try to make it. I'll be about 30 minutes late. Sorry, Jim

b Complete the team assistant's "Remember" list.

1 Make sure you have your _____ with you.
2 Ask Pete to bring _____ .
3 Check if Moyra has booked _____ tonight.
4 Can Andy join _____ ?
5 Sort out _____ for Monday.
6 Remind Andy to get back to Howard on _____ .
7 Make sure Pete gets a lift _____ .
8 Jim will be about _____ late.
9 Ask Anna about _____ for Monday or go to reception to clarify situation.
10 Make Howard's part point _____ .
11 Ask Howard regarding _____ and notify Jim.
12 Remind Pete to _____ with Greg from Marketing.

27 Look at the phrases you underlined and use them to make your own requests.

Example: *Pls. make sure you have your phone on 'silent' during the meeting.*

28 a *Business training.* Think of a job in a company and decide on a position, e. g. sales rep. Choose three people from different departments to write notes or messages to. Then choose one or two things you want each person to do. For example, write to:

- HR
- accounting
- supply chain manager
- marketing department head

b Read out your messages in class. If any message is directed towards you, write a short reply.

What would you like?

Explore listening: Ordering a takeaway on the phone

29 a Do you ever order takeaway food? • Where? • When? • What kind of food do you order?

b What are the advantages and disadvantages of having a takeaway?

25 5dx6d8

30 You are going to listen to Ms Bradley ordering a takeaway on the phone. First you will have 45 seconds to study the task below, then you will hear the recording twice. While listening, choose the correct answer (A, B, C or D) for each question (1–5). Put a cross (☒) in the correct box. The first one (0) has been done for you.

After the second listening, you will have 45 seconds to check your answers.

TIP: Mark your answer and then move on to the next question.

0 Ms Bradley calls to order
- A lunch.
- B brunch.
- C breakfast.
- D dinner. ☒

1 The takeaway food is for
- A herself.
- B herself and her husband.
- C the people at her office.
- D her family of four.

2 Ms Bradley would like
- A vegetables and rice only.
- B duck, fish, pork and vegetables.
- C chicken, pork, fish and vegetables.
- D beef, pork and fish.

3 She orders
- A two portions of fried rice, one of boiled rice.
- B three portions of fried rice.
- C boiled rice only.
- D one portion of fried, one of boiled rice.

4 The takeaway costs
- A £47.90.
- B £74.90.
- C £49.70.
- D £14.97.

5 The Bradley's address is
- A B-O-W-fort Gardens.
- B B-E-A-U-fort Gardens.
- C B-O-fort Gardens.
- D B-O-U-G-H-fort Gardens.

Explore speaking: In the shopping mall

31 *Role play*. Work in A/B pairs. A, use the role card below. B, go to p. 146 and use the role card there. Use phrases from the box in your conversation.

Student A:

You would like to have coffee and discuss what shop to go to first. You have seen great ankle boots upstairs and would like to get them. Also, you need shower gel and shampoo. If you could find a cool, waterproof sports jacket at a good price, you would also buy it. Later, you would like to check out the new Mexican restaurant close to the entrance to the cinema.

Use phrases like:

I'd really like to … first.
I agree, we should / need …
Please don't forget that …
I don't think (+ -ing form) … is a good idea.
I'd rather (not) have / buy / go …
To be on the safe side, we should …

How much / many … do you think … ?
Let's choose / go for … instead of …, then.
But if we …, we won't have enough …
I think … will be around … euros.
I guess he / she really likes …
This is more than I want to spend on …

68

Explore reading: A takeaway menu

32 Read the takeaway menu. First decide whether the statements (1–5) are true (T) or false (F) and put a cross (☒) in the correct box. Then identify the sentence which supports your decision. Write <u>the first four words</u> of this sentence in the space provided. There may be more than one correct answer; write down <u>only one</u>. The first one (0) has been done for you.

Open 12 p.m. to 2 a.m. every day

Takeaway menu
To place your order, call 3392704. Your takeaway is ready for collection in 15 minutes.

Too busy to leave work?
We have the answer! If you can't come to Mae's Place, we can bring Mae's Place to you. We can arrange special requests for food and drink. Please allow at least 48 hours. For more information, call us on 3392704.

SANDWICHES

Roast beef with mild mustard	£6.00
Roast lamb with hummus and salad	£6.00
Cheese and tomato	£4.50
Cream cheese with smoked salmon	£7.50
Greek sandwich: feta cheese, lettuce, olives, cucumber and tomato	£5.50
Egg mayonnaise	£4.50
Chicken salad	£6.00
Cajun chicken with grilled peppers and spicy mayonnaise	£6.00
Chinese spicy prawns with salad	£6.50
Tuna and spring onion with mayonnaise	£4.50

DESSERTS

Fresh fruit salad with yoghurt	£3.50
Apple pie with cream	£4.50

DRINKS

Bottled water	£2.00
Fresh fruit juices	£3.50

Time to celebrate?
Our party specialists will be happy to organise birthday, Christmas or office parties for you. Complete with plates, glasses and table linen. For parties from 10 to 100.

Food intolerance, allergies?
Our experts can put together meals that will meet your special dietary requirements.

	Statements	True	False	First four words
0	You can order food 24 hours a day.		✗	Open 12 p.m. to
1	You can order food from Mae's Place on the internet.			
2	Mae's Place can deliver food to you at work.			
3	You can ask for food that isn't on the menu.			
4	Mae's Place can organise special events for up to 110 people.			
5	Mae's Place cannot cater for vegetarians.			

Self-assessment ✓✓ ✓ !!

- buy things in shops
- talk about preferences and give reasons
- talk about shopping and food
- order a meal
- write short practical requests and reminders

First of all, think about what you have learned up to now. Are you close to "I can do this well" or closer to "I need to work on this"?

Put a mark where you think you are at the moment. Then do the tasks and check your answers with the key on p. 186. Put another mark in a different colour where you see yourself now you've done the task.

Reading
- I can understand a leaflet about outdoor activities

✓✓   ✓   !!

Reading 1 Read the text about outdoor activities, then choose the correct answer (A, B, C or D) for questions 1–5. Put a cross (☒) in the correct box. The first one (0) has been done for you.

> **TIP:** Only one of the four options is correct, so don't mark more than one.

ABERFOYLE, QUEEN ELIZABETH FOREST PARK
Take the A821 to Aberfoyle and then follow signs to 'The Lodge – Forest Visitor Centre'.

Take in the beautiful surroundings of Queen Elizabeth Forest Park as you fly 46 metres above the ground on two of Britain's longest zip wires. Located in the Trossachs National Park, it's a mecca for Go Ape pilgrims, adventure lovers and those that just want to get out and have some fun in Loch Lomond. Or would you like to spend some days exploring the forest by bike in Queen Forest Park and Britain's largest off-road cycle network?

The stunning[1] scenery around Queen Elizabeth Forest Park in Aberfoyle (Stirlingshire) guarantees a great day out in Scotland. Oh, and let's not forget the course's main attraction: Two of Britain's longest zip wires, each stretching over 400 m, flying customers 150 feet above the ground and over a 90 foot waterfall.

NEW Forest Visitor Centre at Aberfoyle. Forestry Commission Scotland proudly present the state of the art centre, featuring a cafe that offers a spectacular floor to ceiling view of the forest.

We also offer great biking tours as well as forest segway trips. Now – what is forest segway? Take to two wheels with our all-terrain, self-balancing segways and discover more of the forest than ever before. Mastering the green technology takes a matter of minutes – you'll be whizzing[2] through our beautiful woodland trails in no time. Get your friends together for an unforgettable experience in the spectacular local scenery.

Visit goape.co.uk for the most up-to-date information as details differ for each course.

The best fun, of course, is the epic zip wires … step off the platform, sit back and let the wire do the work! Zip trekking adventure is a network of seven tandem zip lines that traverse the skyscraping Douglas Firs, providing you with an exhilarating experience of flying way above the forest floor.

The unforgettable two-hour experience includes:

– A safety demonstration from our experienced team and use of all equipment.
– A 20 minute hike (through one of the most beautiful, dramatic forests out there) to the meeting point.
– A ride off-road where you'll discover winding mountain roads up to the training zip.
– Time in our training zone where you practise landing like a professional.
– Seven zip wires covering a total distance of 3 km – and the certificate to prove you've done it.

HANG OUT WITH US

Source: adapted and abridged from *GoApe*, "HIGH ROPES ADVENTURES IN SCOTLAND", https://goape.co.uk/days-out/scotland/aberfoyle

[1] **stunning**: breath-taking   [2] **whizzing**: driving

0 Aberfoyle can be reached
- A by car driving along the M821.
- B by car taking the exit at Glasgow.
- C by car going through the city of Aberfoyle.
- D by following the signs to "The Lodge – Forest Visitor Centre" on the A821.

1 Aberfoyle Forest Park
- A is perfect for young children.
- B has Britain's second longest zip wire.
- C offers a long zip wire for adventure seekers.
- D is located close to the Trossachs National Park.

2 The zip-wire course
- A offers a great view of the stunning landscape.
- B ends at a 90 foot waterfall.
- C has a length of almost 400 m.
- D takes you 130 m up into the trees.

3 In the Forest Visitor Centre you can
- A eat a 5-course meal.
- B enjoy the most modern facilities.
- C see a picture of the park on the ceiling.
- D look through a glass floor down on the trees below.

4 Going through the forest on a Segway
- A requires some training.
- B enables you to whizz through the forest without trails.
- C you can enjoy rally tracks with your friends.
- D is best done alone so you don't disturb the animals so much.

5 If you book a zip trekking adventure
- A you will be on an unforgettable 20-minute tour.
- B you will get a certificate from Go Ape.
- C you will have to climb up many ropes.
- D you will first walk 3 km to the meeting point.

Listening

- I can understand someone talking about an innovation.
- I can understand a conversation about technical developments in the automotive industry.

Listening 2

You are going to listen to a conversation about technical developments in the automotive industry. First you will have 45 seconds to study the task below, then you will hear the recording twice. While listening, choose the correct answer (A, B, C or D) for each question (1–6). Put a cross (☒) in the correct box. The first one (0) has been done for you.
After the second listening, you will have 45 seconds to check your answers.

0 Robocars …
- A are also known as connected cars. ☒
- B will be manufactured all over the world.
- C can drive without drivers.
- D are completely secure.

1 In the future …
- A 250 million connected cars will be produced.
- B 250 million new connected cars will be registered.
- C a quarter of a billion connected cars will be on the roads.
- D a quarter of a billion cars will have new security measures.

2 Researchers …
- A haven't controlled a Tesla Model X wirelessly.
- B have controlled a Tesla Model X by modifying its engine.
- C were able to make a Tesla Model X completely cyber-proof.
- D were able to control some of the functions of a Tesla Model X.

3 Adding more …
- A technology to cars makes them easier to hack.
- B technology to cars makes it more difficult to hack them.
- C technology to cars doesn't help hackers.
- D technology to cars doesn't provide points of entry for hackers.

4 Carmakers …
- A think it is too costly to separate the car's functions.
- B are unable to separate the car's functions.
- C plan to separate the car's functions.
- D have separated the car's functions.

5 Technology
- A helps to sell cars.
- B is important for the National Safety Council.
- C can help to make cars safer.
- D is important for carmakers.

6 In 2018 …
- A there were fewer traffic deaths than the year before.
- B there were 276.1m cars on the road in the US.
- C the high number of traffic deaths was caused by connected cars.
- D there were 264 000 registered vehicles in the US.

Writing ✓✓ ✓ ！！
- I can write about a shopping experience.
- I can describe shops and products using adjectives.
- I can express an invitation.

Writing 3 Write an email to your friend about a great shopping day you had with your family.
In your email, you should:
- describe the shops you went to.
- point out what you bought.
- suggest to your friend to join you next time.

Write about 150 words.

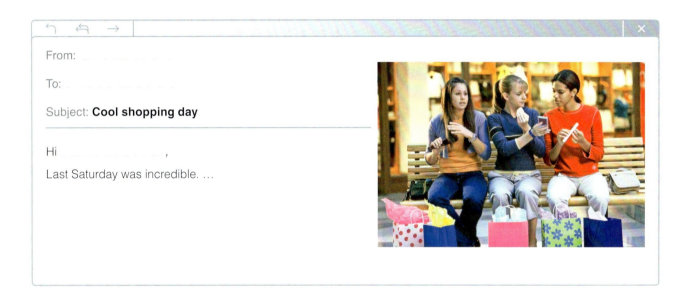

From:
To:
Subject: **Cool shopping day**

Hi _____ ,
Last Saturday was incredible. …

Language ✓✓ ✓ ！！
- I can correctly use *some / a lot of / many / much / a / an*.
- I can differentiate between countable and uncountable nouns.

Language 4 Circle the correct words.
1 How   much / many   luggage do you want to check in?
2 Would you like   a / some   basmati rice with your steak?
3 I prefer   teas / tea   to fruit juice in the morning.
4 I'd like   some / an   orange, please.
5 My dad drinks   many / a lot of   milk every day.
6 She always puts   a / some   lettuce in her sandwich.
7 My little banana tree needs   a lot of / a   light.
8 Eating   a lot of / a   sugar is not good for your body.

Goals
- talk about work and school
- describe present activities
- say why you can't do things
- say you're not sure about facts and numbers

Vocabulary

Work and school 1

1 Work in pairs. Look at the school subjects in the picture dictionary on p. 168. Which ones do you think are useful for these jobs? Write down the correct subjects.

	Occupation	Subject
A	a cook / chef	
B	a fashion designer	
C	a doctor	
D	an accountant	
E	an engineer	
F	a lawyer	

Reading

2 Read the descriptions of the different jobs. What task are they doing right now? Fill in the gaps on the right.

	What do you do for a living?	What are you doing right now?
1	I'm a car mechanic. I repair car engines, check tyres and fix the bodywork after collisions. I do the jobs that are necessary to keep your car on the road. This is not a job where you can make mistakes.	 "I'm checking the tyre."
2	I'm a fashion designer. I create suits and other elegant clothes for men. I especially like to make tailored suits for individual clients. I am proud of my career, and I try to do the best job I can.	 "I _____ a new design."
3	I'm a chef. I cook all night in a five star restaurant, and I'm also responsible for creating the menu. It's a very stressful job because there is always something to do, but it's better than doing the dishes.	 "I _____ a delicious meal. I _____ a lot of spices and herbs to flavour it."
4	I'm unemployed at the moment, so every day I send out applications and make sure my CV is up to date. I always make a copy of any letters I send. Usually, I make about 10 calls a day to ask for interviews. I make myself sandwiches and tea for lunch.	 "I _____ on the computer and _____ out applications."

74

Work and leisure

Grammar — Present progressive

3 a Match 1–4 with A–D.

1 I'm a chef. (present simple)
2 The sun rises in the east. (present simple)
3 I am writing out applications. (present progressive)
4 I'm creating a new design. (present progressive)

A now, at the moment
B permanent / long term situations
C current / temporary situations
D general facts

→ Grammar reference and practice, p. 158

b Complete the sentences.

Present progressive: *be + -ing*

⊕	⊖
I'm checking the tyre.	He isn't writing on the computer.
The chef (1) _____ cooking a delicous meal. She (2) _____ using a lot of spices and herbs to flavour it.	They (5) _____ doing their homework at the moment.
?	
(3) _____ you having a good time? Is he working hard? What (4) _____ you doing right now?	✓ Yes, I am. ✗ No, he (6) _____ .

Speaking

4 a Work in A/B pairs.
- A, look at the picture on the right.
- B, look at the picture on p. 147.
- Write six sentences about your picture.

Think about these questions:
1 Who are the people?
2 Where are they?
3 What are they doing?

Example: *There are six people in an office. A woman is talking to the others …*

b Describe the pictures to each other. How many differences can you find?

Writing

5 Look around the classroom. What are people doing? What is going on outside the window? Write at least six sentences and compare with your partner.

Vocabulary — *Make* and *do*

6 Go through the job descriptions on p. 74 once more, and underline all of the verbs make and do. Now complete the rules using either make or do.

1 _____ is used to create (… a cake) or to produce a result (… a profit, … changes).

2 _____ is used to perform an action (… your homework, … something).

3 Make is also used for communication.

Work and leisure

7 Put the words in the boxes into the correct column: **make** or **do**.

~~dinner~~   ~~an exercise~~   tea   a copy   work   sure   a speech   the dishes   mistakes   the bed   a job   homework   money   your best   the shopping   a phone call   experiments   bread   a shirt   a decision

make	do
dinner	an exercise

8 Complete the sentences with the correct form of **make** or **do**.

1 I'll _____ some shopping on the way home.
2 Teachers never _____ much money.
3 With modern gadgets, you don't need to spend so much time _____ the housework.
4 You need to _____ mistakes in order to learn.
5 When you get back from a holiday there's always a lot of washing to _____ .
6 When do you think you will _____ your decision?
7 Have you got a lot of work to _____ today?
8 Don't _____ a noise, the baby's asleep.
9 Put the kettle on and we'll _____ some tea.

Listening

9 Working hard – explaining what you do.

a Work in pairs. What do you think life is like on an oil rig? Write some ideas in the column below.

	My ideas	Pete's story
work hours		
'me' time / evenings		
sleep		
time off		

27 28tq45

b Listen to Pete, 19, catering assistant, and make notes on his daily life on an oil rig.

c What were the biggest differences between your ideas and Pete's story?

d Do you think Pete has a good 'work-life-balance'? Why (not)?

Work and leisure

Reading 10 a Read the web posting of a travel agent's job profile below. What do travel agents do?

---

https://www.findjobdescriptions.com

Working as a travel agent

Not everyone walks into a travel agency with a clear idea of where they'd like to go on holiday. One of your main roles as a travel agent is to give advice to clients about where and when to travel.
So if they hate hot weather, don't send them to Australia in the summer …

Other duties will include:

- Arranging flights, insurance and accommodation
- Using an online booking system
- Collecting payments
- Advising clients on travel arrangements, e.g. visas and passports
- Sending out tickets to clients
- Keeping clients up to date with any changes
- Dealing with complaints or refunds

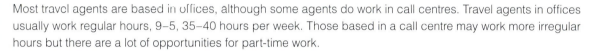

Most travel agents are based in offices, although some agents do work in call centres. Travel agents in offices usually work regular hours, 9–5, 35–40 hours per week. Those based in a call centre may work more irregular hours but there are a lot of opportunities for part-time work.

Travel agents can become a team leader in a call centre or a branch manager. And as you gain more experience, you can find work with bigger tour operators or work with agencies offering more specialised breaks such as adventure or trekking holidays.

How much can you expect to earn as a travel agent? Travel agents starting out can expect to earn around £12k[1] but more seasoned travel agents can earn anything up to £30k. There are often bonuses and incentives to encourage sales.

This job is all about the customer and helping to find and organise their dream holiday. Travel agents need to have customer service skills, a passion for the travel industry and a friendly manner. Other qualities that are needed:

- Paying good attention to detail
- Being well organised
- Having competent IT skills
- Being patient
- Plus, knowledge of another language is always an advantage when working in the travel industry.

---

b Complete the phrases with the correct verbs. You will find similar phrases in the text.

1	_give_	advice to clients	7	_____	on holiday
2	_____	clients _____ visas and passports	8	_____	flights and accommodation
3	_____	with complaints	9	_____	out tickets to clients
4	_____	irregular hours	10	_____	competent IT skills
5	_____	payments	11	_____	in the travel industry
6	_____	more experience	12	_____	attention to detail

[1] **k:** £12 k = 12,000; k = 1,000

Work and leisure

Listening 11 a Listen to Melanie and Liam talking at a club. Complete the sentences with the correct name, Melanie (M) or Liam (L).

1 _____ works at a travel agency.
2 _____ is studying for exams and tests.
3 _____ goes to a vocational college.
4 _____ is putting together a package deal.
5 _____ is preparing lots of presentations right now.

b Look at the sentences again. Which verbs are present simple? Which are present progressive? Why?

Vocabulary 12 Add these expressions to the right groups. Some expressions can be used more than once.

Work and school 2

letters   package deals   the family firm   on trips   clients

1 prepare presentations / _____ / _____
2 work for your exams / _____ / _____
3 put together trips / _____
4 go to school / _____
5 read / write emails / _____

Writing 13 a Work in pairs A/B. Look at the article about working as a travel agent on p. 77 again.

- A, write an email to your colleague Jackie in Vancouver telling her what you are doing in the office today.
- B, write an email to your friend Frank and explain to him why you work as a travel agent. Tell him what you do regularly and what character traits you need for this.

Start like this:

Hi Jackie,
I'm really busy today. I'm already booking the first package deal and it is only 9.00 a.m. …

Hi Frank,
You asked me why I like my job as a travel agent. Well you get to arrange many flights and I often …

b Exchange your stories. <u>Underline</u> all present simple and present progressive phrases in your partner's text. Did he/she use them correctly?

Work and leisure

Sorry, we're just having dinner

Speaking 14 *Role play.* Ask and answer the questions in pairs.

1 How many phone calls do you usually get every day?
2 Who calls you?
3 What kind of calls do you enjoy? Which don't you enjoy?
4 How do you feel when you are busy and get a lot of calls?

Example: *When I'm busy, I don't enjoy …*

Listening 15 a Look at the picture of Julie and her family. How do you think her parents feel? Why?

29 7bm5pt

b Listen to Julie talking to various people on the phone. Number the calls in the order you hear them.

a friend ☐   her employer ☐
her best friend Lynne ☐ a market researcher ☐
a classmate ☐

16 Who does she say these things to?

1 I'm awfully sorry, I can't.
2 Sorry, we're just having dinner.
3 Can I give you a ring later?
4 Sorry, but I've no idea either.
5 Well, actually, I'm quite busy right now.

Vocabulary 17 a Add these expressions to the right group 1–3.

Saying you're busy

studying for an exam   on the internet   busy   writing an essay   making dinner
in a study group   tired   watching a film   not feeling well

Sorry, but I'm I'm afraid I'm Well, actually, I'm Sorry, but we're	(1) *in the middle of* dinner.	+ preposition
	not (2) *interested*.	+ adjective
	(3) *having* a party for my mum's birthday.	+ -ing

b Can you think of more ideas?

Speaking 18 In pairs, plan and practise four short telephone conversations. Say why you cannot do these things.

1 **Your mother asks**: *Can you do the shopping for me?*
2 **Your friend asks:** *I'm going to the gym now. Do you want to come?*
3 **Your teacher says:** *I'd like you to help me carry these books to the library.*
4 **A salesperson says:** *We're having a special sale of trainers. Would you like to buy some?*

Work and leisure

Keyword: *spend*

19 a Add the expressions to the table below.

watching films   at home   with friends   on clothes   working   sleeping   travelling home

on the platform   on video games   with my colleagues   telling stories

I / We	spend / don't spend	45 minutes / two weeks / a lot of time / enough time / a lot of money	**in** the gym / _____ / _____.
			talking / _____ / _____ / _____ / _____ /
			with my family / _____ / _____.
			on sweets / _____ / _____.

b Write five sentences about a typical day in your life. Use *spend*.

c Talk about your typical week.
- How much time do you spend at school / studying?
- How much free time do you have? What do you spend most money on?
- What would you prefer to do more / less of?

Across cultures: School life

20 a Look at the photos below and try to guess where these young people are. Why do you think that?

Work and leisure

b Read what students from different countries say about their school life and make notes. How are their schools different?

1 All my lessons are in different rooms and places around the school. Each room has a three-digit number, and it's very hard for me to remember the numbers. I have different teachers for every subject. I also have a locker where I can keep some of my stuff, but otherwise I have to carry it around with me all day long. I leave home at 7 a.m. and walk 20 minutes to the bus stop. It's a school bus just for our school. The journey on the bus takes nearly an hour because the bus keeps stopping to pick up other kids that go to my school. (Jeremy from Brighton, UK)

2 I live in a small village in Upper Austria, and I have to get up really early as school starts at 8 a.m. I attend a private college of business administration in a nearby town, so I have lots of business-related subjects, like accounting and business studies. My favourite subject is information and office management because I love working on the computer. What I like best of all is the breaks – I can hang out with my classmates. (Nina from Kammer, Austria)

3 I only have to take four or five major subjects every year, but I get assignments every day and have to work really hard because I need excellent grades to get into a good college. My teachers are really nice and helpful, and we only have 10–12 students in each class. The only thing I don't like about school is our school uniform, which looks really nerdy. We usually have lunch in our school cafeteria. The food is quite tasty, and there are lots of different things to choose from. In the afternoon, we always do sport. (Sydney from Bryn Mawr, USA)

4 My school is a co-ed school, which means that there are boys and girls. Each lesson lasts 90 minutes, and the atmosphere is really relaxed. Everybody knows each other, and pupils call their teachers by their first names, as usual in Finland. We have an art and music room, a computer room, a room for textile work, science and language labs, a library, a gymnasium and a swimming pool. I spend most of my afternoons in the room for textile work because I want to be a designer one day. (Mati from Helsinki, Finland)

Jeremy	Nina	Sydney	Mati

c In pairs, talk about the paragraphs above.

Write notes about:

1 something that you already knew.

2 something that surprised you.

3 something you think is a good idea.

4 something you don't like at all.

Info point: Calculating

21 Study the chart and complete it with words from the boxes.

Addition   Division   Extracting the root   Fractions   Multiplication   Raising to a power   ~~Special cases~~   Subtraction

Operation		What you say
1 _____	a + b = c	a plus b is/equals c the sum of a plus b is c one number is added to another one
2 _____	a − b = c	a minus b is/equals c c is the difference between a and b one number is subtracted from another one
3 _____	a × b = c	a multiplied by b is/equals c a times b is/equals c c is the product of a and b
4 _____	a ÷ b = c	a divided by b is/equals c
5 _____	$\frac{x}{y}$; $\frac{x}{y+7}$ $\frac{1}{2}$; $\frac{1}{4}$; $\frac{1}{3}$; $\frac{2}{3}$	x over y; x all over y plus seven x is the numerator, and y is the denominator one half; one fourth/quarter; one third; two thirds
6 _____	a^n; 2^2 4^3; 10^6	a to the power of n; two squared four cubed; ten to the power of six
7 _____	$\sqrt[n]{x}$; $\sqrt{4}$ $\sqrt[3]{27}$	the nth root of x; the square root of four the cube root of twenty-seven
8 _Special cases_	3 × [2 ÷ (4 − 2)] = 3 x < y y > x a ≤ b b ≥ a c ≈ d	three times square bracket two divided by bracket four minus two bracket square bracket equals three x is less than y y is greater than x a is less than or equal to b b is greater than or equal to a c is approximately equal to d

TIP: Remember the order of operations in a calculation. First do any sum in brackets, then divisions and multiplications, lastly additions and subtractions.
- Example: 5 + 4 × 3 =   → Multiplication comes before addition, so 17 is correct.
- Example: 2 × (8 − 4) =   → First calculate the bracket, then do the multiplication. So the correct answer is 8. Or: first you solve the bracket by subtracting 4 from 8 and then you multiply the result by 2.

22 Work in A/B pairs. A, read aloud the calculations below, B, write them in your exercise book and calculate the result. Then B, read aloud the calculations on p. 148 and A, write them down and solve them.

1. 24 − 5 × 4 + 2 × 3 =
2. $\frac{30}{10} + 2^2$ =
3. $\sqrt[3]{(134-9)}$ =
4. [(4 ÷ 2) × 14] ÷ 2 =
5. $\frac{1}{4} + \frac{1}{8}$ =
6. $\frac{(2+3) \times 2}{(5+4) \times 2}$ =

Equations

An equation is the mathematical way of saying: everything on the left of the equals sign is equal to everything on the right of the equals sign.

23 a Match the equations in the box to their descriptions.

1	$Ke = \frac{1}{2}mv^2$	Electrical power equals voltage times current
2	$P = VI$	Distance equals velocity times time
3	$F = ma$	Force equals mass times acceleration
4	$E = mc^2$	Kinetic energy equals half times the mass times velocity squared
5	$s = vt$	Energy = mass times the speed of light squared

TIP: Make sure you use SI units when using these equations. That way the equations will stay consistent and you will get the correct answer. Use the internet to check you know all of the units highlighted in the next exercise.

b Answer the questions by using the equations in 23a.

1 A car of mass 1,500 kg is accelerating at 5 ms^{-2}. What force is being applied? _7,500_ N.

2 A train of mass 18,000 kg has a kinetic energy of 900,000 J. What is its velocity? _____ ms^{-1}.

3 A hairdryer uses 1150 W of power. It is plugged in to the mains (230 V). What current does it draw? _____ A.

4 Assume the speed of light is 3×10^8 ms^{-1}. A star converts 6×10^9 kg of mass into energy every second. How much energy does it produce per second? _____ J.

5 A jogger is running at a steady 16 kmh^{-1}. How many minutes will it take her to run 36 km? _____ mins.

c Write three of your own questions like those in 23b, and ask them to your partner.

24 Solve the following problem. Then explain to a partner how you went about it.

Two people cycle for two days. On the second day they cycle for 2 hours longer and at an average speed of 5 km/h faster than they cycle on the first day. If, during the two days, they cycle a total of 180 kilometres and spend a total of 14 hours cycling, what is their average speed on the first day?

Work and leisure

Explore listening: American high schools

25 You are going to listen to Kerstin, an Austrian exchange student, talking about American high schools. First you will have 45 seconds to study the task below, then you will hear the recording twice. While listening, complete the sentences (1–7) using a maximum of four words. Write your answers in the spaces provided. The first one (0) has been done for you.

After the second listening, you will have 45 seconds to check your answers.

TIP: Make sure your answer doesn't have more than four words.

0 In the morning all students have to show up in their homeroom to _____.
   check attendance / listen to announcements

1 Every student has different subjects, but you have _____.

2 In some schools the dress code doesn't allow students to wear jeans or _____.

3 Having lunch together in the cafeteria is a part of the _____ at school.

4 Taking part in _____ is a good chance to make friends.

5 The best grade you can get is an _____.

6 Whenever a school team plays a match, a lot of students watch, cheer and support _____.

7 Students can buy sweatshirts, T-shirts and sweatpants with the _____ on them.

Explore speaking: Expressing uncertainty

26 a Listen to Andrew talking about how he spends his time.

1 How much time does he spend at school, sleeping, and with his family?
2 What would he like to do more? What would he like to do less?

b You can use these expressions to say you are not sure. Listen again and tick (☒) the expressions Andrew uses.

1 I'm not sure.
2 I don't know.
3 I don't know exactly.
4 I think …

84

Work and leisure

27 a Match the questions with the answers below.

1. How many hours do you spend at school?
2. How much time do you spend at home?
3. How many hours do you spend on homework and studying?
4. How long do you sleep?
5. How much time do you spend with family or friends?
6. How much time do you spend on public transport?

A   I'm not sure. Probably about five hours a week with friends.
B   I don't know exactly. Probably six or seven hours a night.
C   Oh, about eight hours. I leave school at about 5.30.
D   About two or three hours. The buses are slow.
E   I don't know. Maybe about 13 hours a day, and most of that is sleeping.
F   It depends. I would say about one to two hours a day – probably more when I have some tests coming up.

b Tell a partner about a typical day in your life. Choose a weekday or a Sunday. Talk for one to two minutes.

28 a Work alone. Write three more questions like these for other students.

- How many students go to our school?
- How many people live in your home town / village?
- How many people speak your language?
- How far is it from … to … ?
- How old … ?

b Ask and answer all the questions.

Example: A: *How many students go to our school?* B: *I'm not sure. About 250, I think.*

Self-assessment

- talk about work and school
- describe present activities
- say why you can't do things
- say you're not sure about facts and numbers

Goals
- make arrangements, talk about timetables
- buy a travel ticket
- check in and board a flight
- tell a story
- talk about a journey
- write invitations and give directions

Vocabulary

Using transport

1 Unusual ways of transport. Match the words (1–8) with the pictures A–H.

1 Habal-Habal
2 suspension railway
3 hydrofoil
4 sled
5 trolley bus
6 Maglev train
7 terra bus
8 coco taxi

Reading

2 Match the statements to the correct means of transport, and fill in the correct form of the verbs in the gaps.

catch   get   ride   travel   take   go by   get on   leave

1 I'm really excited – I'm meeting my friend Daisy tonight and we haven't seen each other for years. I'll _____ the trolley bus from the town centre.

2 Did you know that in Finland there are as many reindeer as there are people? We're going there for Christmas, and we can _____ a sled every morning.

3 Can you tell me where the train station is, please? My Maglev train _____ at 3.35 p.m. and I'm worried I'll miss it.

4 I'm visiting my cousin in Havana again next month. He has a big flat right in the city centre where I have my own room. So, I'm not taking a lot of luggage with me, that would be a problem anyway, as I usually _____ a coco taxi from the airport to the flat. This is a bit cramped but you get such a cool impression of all the activities in the streets of the city.

5 Look up there – the suspension railway is approaching. This is Chengdu's first elevated monorail. Its carriages look like panda bears. Isn't this cute? We're _____ the one that leaves at 2.15 this afternoon to get to the zoo in the east of the town.

Getting around

6 I'm _____ the next Hydrofoil to Budapest. My aunt is picking me up at the bank in front of the Parliament at 5 p.m. tomorrow. I'm so looking forward to this trip! Hopefully, the weather is warm.

7 My uncle has been to the Philippines several times and he really loves the Habal Habal. He is now creating his own Habal Habal in his garage. You should see the seating he is making out of wood and steel. When he is finished, all the kids in the neighbourhood will be able to _____ a Habal Habal ride with him.

8 "Hi Dad, I'm just _____ north to the Athabasca Glacier. This is so exciting! I'm sitting right at the front behind the driver and can see the snow-covered road ahead of me." … "No, I'm having dinner with Aunt Rose at 8.00 p.m. I won't be there sooner. You know, after refuelling, the terra bus does not leave before 6.00 p.m. and it takes 1.5 hours to her place at least …."

Arrangements

Grammar 3
Present tense: arrangements and timetables

a Look at the statements in 2 (p. 86–87) and underline all the verbs in the present progressive and the present simple.

b Look at sentences 1–10 in the table and answer the questions.

A Which two sentences are about now?

B Which four sentences are about future arrangements?

C Which four sentences are about information in a timetable?

→ Grammar reference and practice, p. 158

1 What are you doing tonight?
2 When does the monorail leave?

3 "I'm sitting right at the front behind the driver and can see the snow-covered road ahead of me."
4 We're taking the train that leaves at 2.15 this afternoon.
5 "Hi Dad, I'm just travelling north to the Athabasca Glacier. …"
6 My maglev train leaves at 3.35 p.m.
7 I'm visiting my cousin in Havana next month again.
8 We're going there in December.

⊖
9 No, I'm not having dinner with Aunt Rose at 6.00 p.m.
10 You know, after refuelling, the terra bus does not leave before 6.00 p.m.

c Look at the underlined future time expressions in the table. Then add these expressions to the correct groups. Some can go in more than one group.

12 March   year   tomorrow   11 o'clock   December   evening

–	at	on	this	next	in
tonight	3.35	Sunday morning	afternoon	month	

Getting around

4 a Work in A/B pairs. A, look at John's arrangements for next week below. B, look at Rachel's diary on p. 147.

Meet Rachel MONDAY Blue Note Café 6.30 p.m.

TUESDAY shopping: chicken, mushrooms, cream, fruit; 8.00 – cook dinner for Mia

Silver Court Dental Practice
Name: John Ellis
Date & time: Thursday 9th Nov, 4 p.m.
Dentist: Dr Vernon

FRIDAY: Gillian's birthday party, Royston Café (from 6 p.m.)

Meet Mia THURSDAY lunchtime, 1 p.m. + get present for Gillian

b Tell each other about John and Rachel's arrangements. How many times will John and Rachel see each other next week?

Example: *John's meeting Rachel at the Blue Note Café on Monday at 6.30 p.m.*

Speaking

5 a In groups of four, ask and answer the questions. Find out who:

1 walks the most.
2 cycles the most.
3 uses public transport the most.

b Report your findings to the class.

Reading

6 a Look at the picture of Joe Marshall. Why do you think he rides a unicycle to work?

1 He enjoys it.
2 It's quick and safe.
3 He likes people looking at him.
4 It's good exercise.
5 It's good in traffic jams.
6 It's cheap.

b Read the online article to check your ideas.

http://www.newgadgetsontheroad.co.uk

One-wheeled wonder

The electric unicycle is the real king of the road

Forget public transport. For computer programmer Joe Marshall, the daily journey to work across one of the most crowded cities in the world is fun. "It's like playing on the way to work," he says.

It takes Joe about 40 minutes to travel the nine-mile journey across London by electric unicycle. That's about the same as it takes on the bus or the underground, and ten minutes quicker than by car. "Electric unicycles are as fast as bikes," he says, "and they're the best thing in traffic jams because you can turn in a really small space. It's great, too, because you accelerate or stop by leaning forward or backward."

But aren't electric unicycles more dangerous than bikes? Marshall doesn't think so. "Electric unicycles are safer than they look and easier to ride," he says. "And drivers are more careful with me than with cyclists." Electric unicycling is more common than many people think. "More and more people are seen with electric unicycles on the streets. I think it's getting a trend because riding an electric unicycle feels like floating", Marshall says. "The longest trip I did on an electric unicycle was last year with a group of people riding across Ireland."

But what about all the looks you get? "You can't worry about what people think," he says. "Most of them are all right, but I get a lot of comments, like 'Where's the other wheel?' A few days ago, an old lady came up to me and said, 'That's really stupid. Buy a car!' "

Reading & Speaking

7 a Read the article in 6 again. Who thinks unicycles are fun / dangerous / stupid?

b What do you think of Joe's form of transport?

c What's the most unusual form of transport you know? Compare your answer with your partner's.

Getting around

Going on a journey

Vocabulary — Things for a trip

8 Match the things in the list with the things in the pictures.

Remember …			
suntan lotion		tissues	
sunglasses		passport	
money		toothbrush	
address book		comb	
mobile		pen	
map + guide book		rucksack	
		umbrella	

9 a Make a list of things you take with you when you:

- go out for an evening with friends.
- go to school.
- go away on a school trip.

b Compare with a partner.

Listening

10 Listen to Mary talking to her mum just before she leaves for a language course in Salzburg.

32 h4kd6z

1 Who is going to meet Mary at the airport?
2 How long is she going to stay in Salzburg?

11 Listen to Mary talking to her dad. Decide whether the statements are true (T) or false (F).

33 tk7933

T   F

1 Mary's flight was very comfortable.
2 The meeting point wasn't very easy to find.
3 The language school's directions weren't very good.
4 Mary enjoyed her first Austrian meal.

12 Now listen to Mary's conversation with her friend Ian in Edinburgh. Answer questions 1–4 again. Are they true (T) or false (F)?

34 in93kk

T   F

1 Mary's flight was very comfortable.
2 The meeting point wasn't very easy to find.
3 The language school's directions weren't very good.
4 Mary enjoyed her first Austrian meal.

Vocabulary — Prepositions of movement

13 a Read Jaynie's description of a journey she likes. How does she get to the centre of Lewisham?

One of my favourite journeys is walking from my home in Lower Sydenham to the centre of Lewisham. I go out of my front door and across Southend Lane and then, after a few minutes, I go down some steps and into a quiet riverside park. It's really beautiful, with lots of trees, flowers and green grass. I walk for about forty minutes near the river and then go through Ladywell Fields, a large park. Then I go up some steps and right at the top is Bardsley's, my favourite café.

89

Getting around

b Fill in the correct prepositions. Which ones do you remember from Jaynie's description on p. 89?

A _____ B _____ C _____ D _____

E _____ F _____ G _____ H _____

Writing & Speaking

14 a Write a short description of a journey you like. Jaynie's description on p. 89 will help you.

b Read your descriptions to each other. Which do you think is the most interesting?

Listening

15 Charlie wants to visit a friend at his new house in Basingstoke, England. Look at his coach ticket.

1 Where is he travelling from?
2 Where is he going?
3 Is it a single or a return ticket?
4 What is the departure date?
5 How much did the ticket cost?

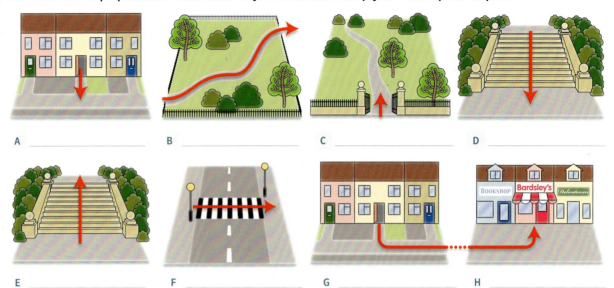

```
Express Coach
PASSENGER TICKET

From: London Victoria
To: Basingstoke
Type: OPEN RETURN
Service: 022
19 May
Adult: 01  Child: 00
Total fare: £18.00
```

16 Listen to Charlie buying his ticket. Circle the correct words.

1 He wants to go to Basingstoke   today / tomorrow .
2 With a day return ticket, he comes back   today / tomorrow .
3 With an open return, he can come back   any time / at the weekend .
4 The day return is   more expensive / cheaper .

Vocabulary

Buying a ticket

17 a Match the questions 1–6 with the answers A–F.

1 How much does an open return ticket cost?
2 What time does the next coach leave?
3 Is it direct?
4 How long does it take to Basingstoke?
5 Which coach do I get?
6 Where do I get it?

A The direct coach? About an hour and a half.
B Number 342.
C It leaves at 4.15, in fifteen minutes.
D To Basingstoke? It's £18.00.
E Just outside those doors. You'll see the sign.
F No. You need to change coaches once.

b Use these words to make five new questions using the highlighted expressions in 17a.

bus   a single   train   a day return   Birmingham

Speaking

18 a You want to buy a ticket. Work in A/B pairs.
- A, read your role cards on p. 145. B, read your role cards on p. 148.
- Think of questions to ask about prices, times and other travel details.

b Take turns to buy a ticket. Have conversation 1 first, then conversation 2. Change role cards and have two more conversations.

Getting around

At the airport

Vocabulary — Airports

19 a Do you ever travel by plane?

- Do you like flying? Why? / Why not?

b Match these places (1–6) with pictures A–F.

1 boarding gate
2 baggage collection
3 check-in
4 customs
5 security
6 passport control

A B C
D E F

c What parts of the airport do you have to go through before you fly? What about when you arrive? Put the places in order.

20 a Look at Belinda's boarding pass.

1 Where is she travelling to?
2 What airline is she using?
3 What time is her flight?

b Find Belinda's flight on the board.

1 Is her flight on time?
2 What time does it leave?
3 What gate is it leaving from?

RAMOS / BELINDA MISS (ADT) — British Airways

London LHR
GATE 20

BA 0059
to Tokyo NRT

27 AUG
12:35

GATE OPENS
11:55

SEAT
23 K

✈ DEPARTURE

Destination

Code	City	Flight	Scheduled	Actual	Gate	Status
DUB	Dublin	EI 153	11:50 AM	–	–	Cancelled
FCO	Rome	BA 548	12:20 PM	12:20 PM	4	Boarding
BOM	Mumbai	AI 119	12:20 PM	12:40 PM	11	Delayed
KUL	Kuala Lumpur	MH 329	12:25 PM	12:25 PM	21	On time
NRT	Tokyo	BA 0059	12:35 PM	12:45 PM	20	Delayed
YYC	Calgary	AC 851	12:45 PM	12:45 PM	18	On time

Getting around

Getting a flight

Listening **21** **a** Listen to Belinda checking in. What does she give to the person?

36   7f6gi3

b Listen again. Complete the sentences 1–5.

1 Can I see your _____, please?
2 Do you have any _____ luggage?
3 Did you pack your _____ yourself?
4 Are you carrying _____ for anyone else?
5 Boarding is at _____ from _____ 20.

c Match sentences 1–5 with Belinda's answers A–E.

A Here you are.   B Thanks.   C Just this bag.   D Yes, I did.   E No.

22 **a** Listen to Belinda. Where is she now?

37   ys56sy

b Listen again. Tick (✓) every time you hear these things.

bag   belt   keys   laptop   shoes   wallet   mobile

c Complete the conversation with words from 22b. Write them in the gaps on the right.

Officer 1: **1**?
Belinda: I've put them in my **2**.
Officer 1: OK. Is there a **3** in here?
Belinda: No.
Officer 1: And your **4**, please.
Belinda: Oh, OK.
Officer 2: Come forward, please. **5**? **6**?
Belinda: Uh, they're in my **7**.
Officer 2: **8**?
Belinda: That too.
Officer 2: Are you wearing a **9**?
Belinda: Oh yes, sorry.
Officer 2: That's fine, thank you.
Belinda: Thanks.
Officer 3: Could you open your **10**, please?
Belinda: OK.
Officer 3: That's fine. Enjoy your trip.
Belinda: Thanks.

1 _____
2 _____
3 _____
4 _____
5 _____   6 _____
7 _____
8 _____
9 _____
10 _____

Speaking **23** **a** Work in groups of three. You are at an airport. Look at your role cards and complete them.

- A, you work at check-in. Look at p. 145.
- B, you work for airport security. Look at p. 147.
- C, you are a passenger. Look at p. 148.

b Have two conversations: one at check-in, and the other at security. Change roles and have the conversations again.

Getting around

Telling a story

Vocabulary — Storytelling expressions

24 Which expressions in the box:

1 start a story?   2 link a story?   3 end a story?

Later, …	It was two in the morning.	It was really strange.
… and then …	I was with some friends.	In the end, …
I had a great time.	Well, this was a few weeks ago.	After that, …

Listening

25 a Listen to Patrick's story about Japan.

1 What was he frightened of?
2 What was the receptionist frightened of?

b Listen to the story again. Who:

1 took Japanese lessons?   4 looked frightened?
2 shouted 'Kuma'?   5 went into Patrick's room first?
3 made a phone call?   6 laughed?

Writing

26 Have you ever had a funny experience mixing up words in a foreign language, or can you imagine how it would happen? Write a short story about it and use the storytelling expressions from the box in 24.

Grammar — Articles

→ Grammar reference and practice, p. 159

27 Look at the examples from Patrick's story and (circle) the correct form in the grammar box.

Use a / the / no as an article when you talk about a person or thing for the first time:
The first thing I saw was a huge spider on the wall.

Use a / the / no as an article when the reader or listener knows which thing:
When the receptionist saw the spider on the wall, she started laughing too.

Use a / the / no article when you talk about things in general: I hate spiders!

28 You use the in a lot of fixed expressions and before some adjectives. Add expressions 1–3 from Patrick's story to the table.

I was (1) in the south of Japan (2) at the time.   (3) The first thing I saw was a huge spider on the wall.

Time expressions	Place expressions	Before some adjectives
in the morning	in the middle of …	the best, the worst, the most
at the weekend	in the corner of …	the same
at the moment	at the end of …	the last, the next

29 a Complete the sentences with a, an, the, or no article (–).

1 When was ___ last time you saw a spider?   3 Is there ___ art gallery near here?
2 Do you like ___ pasta?   4 Can you open ___ door, please?

b Write two or three more questions with expressions from the table in 28.

c Ask and answer all the questions in pairs.

93

Getting around

30 a Work in A/B pairs. A, look at these pictures and read Holly's story here. B, look at the pictures and read Jack's story on p. 148.

in my car in the Rocky Mountains in Canada → lots of mountains and trees → see a family of bears, mother and two cubs → stop car → get out and take photos → cubs look frightened, mother gets angry → walks towards me → can't open car door …

b Think of a good ending for Holly's story. Imagine you are Holly. Prepare to tell the story. Think about:
- the past simple of the verbs (see → saw).
- where to use storytelling expressions (Later, …).
- where to use the (stop the car; the mother bear).

c Work in A/B pairs. Tell your stories.

31 Now listen to both stories. Are the endings like yours?

Speaking

32 a Think of two or three of your own journeys. For example, a time when:
- you missed a flight or a train.
- something dangerous happened.
- you saw something interesting.
- you had a very long journey.

b Prepare to tell your stories. Think about these questions:
1 When was it?
2 What was the reason for your journey?
3 What happened?
4 How did you feel?

c Tell each other about your journeys. Which journeys were fun? Which were difficult?

Writing

33 Write one of your stories (120–150 words). Add pictures or drawings if you can.

Keyword: *get*

get = receive, obtain, buy

34 **Get** with a noun usually means **receive**, **obtain** or **buy**. Complete the sentences with these words.

seat   dollars   newspapers   comments   pocket money   calls

1 How many phone _____ do you usually get every day?
2 I get my _____ at the end of the month.
3 Did you get some US _____ for the trip?
4 I want to get a good _____ .
5 Can you get some _____ ?
6 I get a lot of _____ , like 'where's the other wheel?'

Getting around

35 Ask and answer the questions.
1 How many emails, texts and phone calls do you get every day?
2 What presents did you get for your last birthday?
3 Where's the best place to get good coffee?

get = travel, arrive

36 In which sentences does get mean arrive? In which sentences does it mean travel on?
1 You can get the number forty-three bus.
2 Can we talk when I get home?
3 If we have too much luggage, we get a taxi.
4 It's a bit difficult to get there by public transport.

37 Talk in pairs. How do you get to:
- your doctor?
- the cinema?
- the public swimming pool?
- your favourite relative?

38 What is the first thing you do when you get to school or get home after school?

Across cultures: Saying sorry

39 The word sorry has a lot of different uses in English. Match pictures A–E with situations 1–5.

Sorry, but there's a problem with my shower.

Sorry, is this the train to Bristol?

Oh, I'm sorry!

Sorry?

I'm very sorry, your card's not working.

You can use sorry when:
1 you want to apologise.
2 you don't understand or can't hear someone.
3 you ask for information from people you don't know.
4 you want to complain about something.
5 you give bad news.

40 Read what people from different countries say about saying sorry, and discuss the questions 1–3 in pairs.

In Spain, you use different words to say *sorry*. When you can't hear something, you say *perdón? Or qué?* When you want to complain, you say *lo lamento* or *discúlpame* or *lo siento*.
(Manuel)
A

In Britain, people apologise a lot. When you bump into someone, or when someone bumps into you, both people usually say *sorry*.
(Matthew)
B

In Sudan, if you are not happy about something, you just complain about it, you don't say *sorry*.
(Khalid)
C

In Switzerland, the word for *sorry* is *Entschuldigung*, but if we can't hear someone, we don't normally say *sorry*, we just say *was? Uh?*
(Nathalie)
D

1 Does your language have one word for saying sorry, or different words for different situations?
2 Do you think people apologise a lot in your country? What about other countries you know?
3 What do you say in situations A–D above?

Getting around

Explore writing: Giving directions

41 You are attending the computer game convention in Dublin and you have booked a room via a private booking site. Your host has sent you directions on how to get to her house. Circle the correct answers and write them in the gaps.

1	A out of	B from	C down	D across
2	A out of	B down	C up	D from
3	A to	B from	C across	D into
4	A down	B up	C from	D into
5	A through	B down	C up	D from
6	A out of	B up	C into	D across

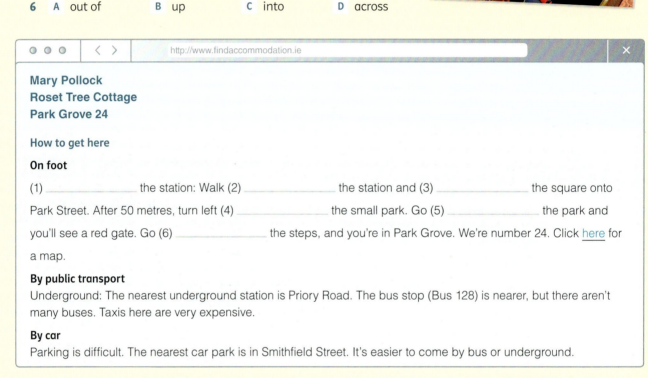

**Mary Pollock
Roset Tree Cottage
Park Grove 24**

How to get here

On foot

(1) _____ the station: Walk (2) _____ the station and (3) _____ the square onto Park Street. After 50 metres, turn left (4) _____ the small park. Go (5) _____ the park and you'll see a red gate. Go (6) _____ the steps, and you're in Park Grove. We're number 24. Click here for a map.

By public transport
Underground: The nearest underground station is Priory Road. The bus stop (Bus 128) is nearer, but there aren't many buses. Taxis here are very expensive.

By car
Parking is difficult. The nearest car park is in Smithfield Street. It's easier to come by bus or underground.

42 Read the directions again. Which map is correct?

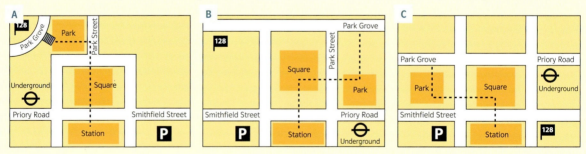

43 You are planning a party at your home. Write your invitation using:
- the present progressive to explain what you are doing (*We are having a party.*).
- directions to tell people how to get there from the station. Use the present simple to talk about the transport connections (*The last train into town leaves at 12:05 a.m.*).

Getting around

Explore listening: A trip to Cambodia

44 Before listening, match the words (1–7) with the definitions (A–G).

1	volunteer work	A	to think/believe
2	entire	B	very good, tasty
3	ancient	C	free work for other people
4	crickets	D	to not pay attention
5	to suppose	E	insects that live in hot climates
6	delicious	F	whole, complete
7	to ignore	G	very old

45 You are going to listen to Alexander talking about his trip to Cambodia. First you will have 45 seconds to study the task below, then you will hear the recording twice. While listening, match the beginnings of the sentences (1–6) with the sentence endings (A–I). There are two sentence endings that you should not use. Write your answers in the spaces provided. The first one (0) has been done for you.

After the second listening, you will have 45 seconds to check your answers.

TIP: Check your answers while listening for the second time.

0 About two summers ago, Alexander went to Cambodia, _____.   I
1 He ate spiders and crickets, _____.
2 Hardly anyone drives a car, _____.
3 The hotel owners said, "Just ignore the mice, _____."
4 After the capital of Phnom Penh, _____.
5 He also got to see Angkor Wat, _____.
6 Most people there are Buddhists, _____.

A and they were delicious
B which cost only 10 American dollars
C but call us if there are rats
D where you can get any kind of meat
E which is one of the seven wonders of the ancient world
F and they are very religious
G they went on a trip to the countryside
H ninety per cent of people use scooters
I where he did volunteer work

Self-assessment ✓✓ ✓ !!

- make arrangements, talk about timetables
- buy a travel ticket
- check in and board a flight
- tell a story
- talk about a journey
- write invitations and give directions

Goals
- find information in a cinema programme
- talk about films
- make and respond to suggestions
- make arrangements to meet
- talk about hopes and plans
- planning a weekend break
- write and reply to an invitation
- write a thank-you note

Vocabulary

Films

41 g9k43d

1 a Listen to eight short extracts from films. Match each extract with a kind of film.

a documentary ☐   a comedy ☐   an action film ☐   an animated film ☐
a drama ☐   a science fiction film ☐   a horror film ☐   a romantic film ☐

b Think of some examples of each kind of film.

Example: *Well, Shrek's an animated film …*

c What kinds of film do you like? What kinds do you not like? Why?

Reading

2 Read the cinema programme. What kind of film is on each day?

Example: *Monday: Fantastic Beasts and Where to Find Them, a fantasy film. Tuesday …*

🎬 THE PICTURE HOUSE 🎥

FANTASTIC BEASTS AND WHERE TO FIND THEM
(Britain, 133 min)
Mon 30 Oct, *7.00 p.m.*

A fantasy film straight from the incredible imagination of J.K. Rowling. This prequel to the Harry Potter series follows Newt Scamander, a young English wizard, across the pond with his extraordinary suitcase of magical creatures. The thrills come quicker even than the adventures at Hogwarts. Prepare to be amazed by this fantastic film.

JUNO (Canada/USA, 96 min)
Tue 31 Oct, *7.30 p.m.*

16-year-old Juno gets pregnant and faces a difficult decision: abortion or adoption? Mr and Mrs Loring, who have been waiting for a baby for years, seem to be the ideal parents. Gradually Juno realises that nothing is as it seems as her life becomes more and more complicated.

THE OTHERS (Spain, 100 min)
Wed 1 Nov, *2.30 p.m. & 7.30 p.m.*

It is 1945, and Grace Stewart (Nicole Kidman) and her children live alone in a huge house. One of the children sees people no one else can see, and things become stranger and stranger. Are Grace and her children really alone? *The Others* is considered to be one of the scariest films of its time.

2 DAYS IN PARIS (France, 96 min)
Thu 2 Nov, *7.30 p.m.*

This beautiful film was written, directed by and starred Julie Delpy. It's an intelligent romantic comedy about a French photographer and her American boyfriend on a two-day visit to her family in Paris, which they hope will be better than their previous visit to Venice. It also stars Delpy's real-life parents and her cat, Max.

YEELEN (Mali, 105 min)
Fri 3 Nov, *8.00 p.m.*

This classic drama was directed by Malian film-maker Souleymane Cissé and was the best film of the 1987 Cannes film festival. Yeelen is set in the 13th century and tells the story of Niankoro, a young man who uses magic to fight his father, a dangerous magician. Who will have the more powerful skills?

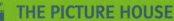

FAMILY FILM **DESPICABLE ME 3** (USA, 90 min)
Sat 4 Nov, *11.30 a.m., 3.00 p.m. & 6.30 p.m.*

Gru, Lucy and the Anti-Villain league are on the tail of new evil mastermind Balthazar Bratt, an 80's child star who has turned to crime. This hilarious comedy could be funnier even than the first two, and of course contains the wonderful minions, perhaps the funniest animated characters of all time, who are captured to perfection.

Box Office The Picture House, Hay Street, Perth / Ticket Prices Adults $13.50. Over 60s / students / under 15s $9.00

Getting together

Comparing

Grammar 3 Read the film reviews again.

Comparatives and superlatives

Which film:
1 is longer than the others?
2 is funnier: *Despicable Me 3* or *The Others*?
3 won an award for being the best film?

4 a Complete the table with comparative and superlative adjectives.

→ Grammar reference and practice, p. 159

	Comparative	Superlative
One syllable	**+er**	**+est**
quick	quicker	
safe		
long		the ____
Two syllables or more	**more ...**	**the most ...**
careful		the most careful
crowded	more crowded	the ____
dangerous		the most dangerous
Two syllables -y	**+ier**	**+iest**
easy		the easiest
Irregular		
good	better	the ____
bad	worse	the worst
far	further	the furthest
much/many	more	the most
little	less	the least

b What are the comparative and superlative forms of these adjectives? Use the table to help you.

cheap   busy   clean   expensive   interesting   nice   comfortable

c Read through the film reviews on p. 98 again and underline all the comparative and superlative adjectives.

Speaking 5 Practise conversations 1–4 in pairs. Then use the adjectives in brackets to change the conversations.

1 A: What's the best way to the cinema?
B: Well, you could get the bus, but it's easier to walk. (interesting, nice)

2 A: What's your favourite film?
B: I don't know if I have a favourite, but *Dumb and Dumber* is the funniest I've ever seen. (hilarious, silly)

3 A: What was the most expensive film of 2017? (bad, good)
B: Well, I think it was *Star Wars VIII*.

4 A: Do you think Odeon cinemas are busier than Empire cinemas? (clean, small)
B: They normally are, yeah.

Writing 6 What was the last film you saw? Write five sentences about it using comparative and superlative adjectives.

99

Getting together

Producing a film

Grammar 7
Passive

a Which sentence, 1 or 2, is used to describe the film *Yeelen* in the film reviews on p. 98?

1 This classic drama was directed by Malian film-maker Souleymane Cissé.
2 Malian film-maker Souleymane Cissé directed this classic drama.

b Why does the writer use the passive? Does the writer want to emphasise the classic drama or the director?

8 a Complete the sentences in the box with the correct form of *be*.

→ Grammar reference and practice, p. 161

Present simple passive:

am / is / are + past participle

The Others (1) _____ considered to be one of the scariest films of its time.

The minions (2) _____ captured to perfection.

Past simple passive:

was / were + past participle

This film (3) _____ written by Julie Delpy.

All the people in the cinema (4) _____ amazed by *Fantastic Beasts*.

b Read the film reviews on p. 98 again and underline all the passive verb forms.

9 We often use the passive when it is not important who does the action, or it is unnecessary to know. Therefore, it is often used to describe processes.

a Read the words and complete the process of producing a film. Use the correct form of the words provided. Add *by* where necessary.

The film production process

1 First / a writer / choose / the studio.
   First, a writer is chosen by the studio.

2 Then / draft script / write.
   _____

3 Next / a director / find.
   _____

4 Then / actors / invite / the director.
   _____

5 Once / actors / have been / chosen / a storyboard / produce.
   _____

6 Then / rehearsals / arrange.
   _____

7 After / enough rehearsals / the movie / film.
   _____

8 Then / the film / edit.
   _____

9 Finally / the film / show / in cinemas.
   _____

b Think of a process you know well. Write a description using the passive.

Choosing a film

Vocabulary — Suggestions

10 a John and Mia decide to go to the cinema. Complete their conversation.

Why don't we   Would you like to   OK   We could   I don't know

Mia: Some of these films look quite interesting.

John: Yeah, that's true. (1) _____ go and see one some time this week?

Mia: Yeah, (2) _____. (3) _____ see *Juno*? I heard it's really good.

John: Hmm. (4) _____. It sounds a bit boring. (5) _____ see *The Others*.

Mia: Well, I don't usually like horror films, but that one sounds good.

b Listen to check.

11 a Put the expressions from 10a in the correct groups.

Making suggestions	Saying yes	Saying no / not sure
Why don't we … ?		

b Add these expressions to the correct groups in 11a.

Good idea.   I don't really want to.   Shall we … ?   I'm not sure.   How about … ?
Fine with me.   Let's …   That sounds good.   No, thanks.

Speaking

12 Practise the conversation in 10a with different expressions. Take turns to be John and Mia.

13 a You are going to The Picture House with a group of friends. Choose two films from the programme (p. 98) you would like to see, and two films you do not want to see.

b In groups, decide which film to see together.

c In pairs, ask and answer the questions.

1 How often do you watch films at the cinema?

2 When was the last time you saw a film? What was it? Did you enjoy it?

3 Do you ever watch films more than once? Give examples.

4 Do you like watching films from other countries? Give examples.

Getting together

What are you doing tonight?

Reading

14 a Look at the picture on the right and read the first email. Can you guess how Rachel answers John's questions?

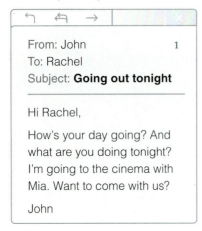

From: John 1
To: Rachel
Subject: **Going out tonight**

Hi Rachel,

How's your day going? And what are you doing tonight? I'm going to the cinema with Mia. Want to come with us?

John

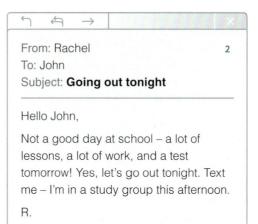

From: Rachel 2
To: John
Subject: **Going out tonight**

Hello John,

Not a good day at school – a lot of lessons, a lot of work, and a test tomorrow! Yes, let's go out tonight. Text me – I'm in a study group this afternoon.

R.

b Read Rachel's reply. Check your ideas.

15 a Read the messages John and Rachel send later. Put them in order from 1–6.

MESSAGES

Today 5:52 pm

☐ Sorry, bus stuck in traffic. Call me after film.

☐ Can't come. Stuck @ school til 6.30.

☐ What time's the film?

☐ Cool, cu then.

☐ Hi. Going to *The Others* at The Picture House. Having a snack 1st @ about 6.15. Can u come?

☐ 7.30. Meet @ 7.00 outside cinema?

☐ Where are you? We're waiting 4 you!

b Answer the following questions.

Who:
1 invited Rachel to the cinema?
2 had a snack together?
3 had a difficult day?
4 saw the film?
5 couldn't get to the cinema on time?

Listening

43   646s7w

16 a Listen to John and Rachel's phone call after the film. Can they meet this week?

b Listen again. Make notes.

1 Where are John and Mia going now? _____

2 Does Rachel want to go with them? Why? / Why not? _____

3 What are Rachel's plans for Friday? What are her plans for Monday? _____

Getting together

Arranging a film night

Listening 17 a How often do you watch films at home? When? Who with?

b Listen to Jane, Rita and Matthew arranging a film night at Rita's home.

1 When are they going to meet?
2 Tick (✓) the films they talk about.

    Pan's Labyrinth   *Casablanca*   *The Bourne Supremacy*   *Yeelen*

3 Which film do they decide to watch?

Vocabulary 18 a Match 1–4 with A–D.

Talking about films

1 What's it like?
2 Who's in it?
3 What's it about?
4 It's about this young man with magical powers.

A It's about a young girl and it's set in Spain … in the 1940s, I think.
B That sounds interesting.
C Matt Damon.
D Well, it's an action film, I guess.

b In pairs, test each other. Take turns to say 1–4 and remember A–D.

Speaking 19 a *Media task*. You want to watch a film at the cinema with some friends. Go to the website of your local cinema (English language if possible).

Think about:
- when you are free this week.
- two films you would like to see.
- how to describe the films – use the passive too.

Example: *The new Star Wars films were not directed by George Lucas anymore.*

b Talk in pairs.

Decide:
- when to meet.
- where to meet.
- which film to watch.

c Tell the rest of the class what you have decided.

103

Getting together

Hopes and plans

Reading 20 **a** What are your plans for the future? Exchange your ideas with your partner.

b Read the interview with the German actor Jo Weil on his future plans.

Interview: Jo Weil

In October 2016 popular German actor Jo Weil chatted with Digital Journal about his latest acting projects, his hosting gigs and plans.
"I'm very excited because at the moment I'm working on two new acting projects — and both are in the UK again," he said. "After the great experience with shooting the lead in the British Feature Film *Sodom* I really hoped to be able to do more English-speaking work. So, this is like a dream come true. This week I'll fly to London to film *Angel North* — it's a pilot for a science-fiction series. My part is totally different from other parts I've played so far, plus it's a genre I would like to work more in. So, I'm really looking forward to that. Later in the year, I'm going to play a not so nice guy in the horror feature *The Toymaker*. We are hoping to film by the seaside in South Wales. It's going to be a lot of fun. And good news for all my fans in the US, *The Toymaker* already has a distributor for the States. So, in late spring you'll be able to watch my work 'for real', too."
On his future plans, Weil said, "I'm definitely going to spend more time and do more work in London. Also it would still be a dream come true if I'd get to work on a film or TV show in the US. But of course, I'll also keep my focus on working in Germany, too. I have a wonderful manager and two fantastic talent agents (in London and Munich). I can't thank them enough for the amazing job they do so I'm very optimistic that many good projects will come up …"
Regarding his hosting, he said, "At the moment I'm the host of *Lifestyle with Jo Weil* on *Wirtschaft TV*. It's an online network for which I'm going to do celebrity interviews on red carpets and at big events. We filmed the first interviews in Mallorca in Spain and it was so much fun. I did not have enough time to prepare, but it went really well. I'm really looking forward to filming the next episodes. There is also another hosting project in the pipeline. It's a cool new format that will combine some things I personally like very much. So please keep your fingers crossed that I'll have enough time to start filming sometime soon."
Weil continued, "My main focus was to push my English-speaking acting work and to live some time in London. Both were successful — but cost me too much energy. My 'normal' projects in Germany took up too much time for me to pursue my singing career. If I do something, I want to be able to give it a hundred percent of my energy. So, I am going to give my music some rest and focus on acting and hosting. But I am hoping that in the future I will have the chance to record new songs."
For his fans, Weil concluded, "Thank you so much for all your support. Working in this business can be very challenging and hard at some points. It's always great to know that I have all these wonderful people who are there for me. This means a lot to me."

21 Look at the interview again and make a list of Jo's current and past projects. Is there anything he'd like to do but can't do at the moment?

Current projects	Past projects	Can't do at the moment

Getting together

Grammar 22

will, be going to, be hoping to, would like to

a Complete the sentences in the table with these words.

I'm   are   He's   I'd   Would   Are   Is   Will   I

→ Grammar reference and practice, p. 161

⊕		
1	_____	will/'ll …
2	_____	going to keep his focus on working in Germany.
3	_____	hoping to …
4	_____	like to …

❓			
5	_____ he ever work on a film in the US?	✅ Yes, he will. / ❌ No, he won't.
6	_____ he going to stay in London next year?	✅ Yes, he is. / ❌ No, he isn't.
7	_____ they hoping to film the interviews in Mallorca?	✅ Yes, they are. / ❌ No, they aren't.
8	_____ you like to move back to Germany one day?	✅ Yes, I would. / ❌ No, I wouldn't.
9	What _____ you going to do this weekend?	

b Look at the *grammar reference* on p. 161. Then put the phrases highlighted in Jo Weil's interview (p. 104) into the correct categories.

will = assumptions / predictions	be going to = intentions / plans	be hoping to = hopes for the future	would like to = wishes for the future

c Look at the hopes and future plans of young people. Complete the statements.

1 I _____ going _____ study in the States for six months.

   I hope I _____ meet some nice people.

2 I _____ hoping _____ go to university next year.

3 I _____ like _____ have children in the future.

4 I _____ going _____ start a new job next month.

Writing 23

Your career counsellor would like to know what your plans are for the future and why. Write a short text (80–100 words) about your future plans.

- Begin with *When I leave school, I'd like to …*

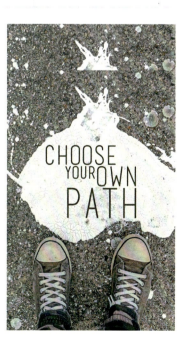

105

Getting together

Planning a weekend break

Reading 24 Look at the tourist information about La Mauricie, a national park in Canada. Match pictures A–D with a place or activity on the website.

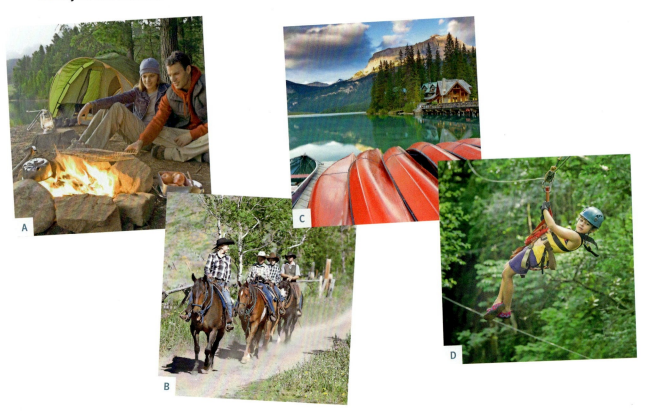

http://www.nps.gc.ca/mauricie

LA MAURICIE Canada

Accommodation

Camping du Parc ***

We welcome you to Camping du Parc, a friendly campsite close to … more

Au Joyeux Druide, Hotel and Art Gallery ***

Our house is on a hill by the Shawinigan River. Here you'll find comfortable rooms … more

Le Baluchon ****

Our inn is in a beautiful location near islands, waterfalls, hills and a forest. … more

Chalet Joel Migneault **

Rent this warm, quiet chalet in the heart of nature on Lake Chrétien. … more

Outdoor activities

From tree to tree

An extraordinary family activity. Come and experience this new treetop adventure … more

Riding Centre, Saint-Georges

Come and enjoy our horses with a qualified instructor. … more

Black bear observation

Watch for bears safely with our experienced guides. … more

National Park of Canada, Mauricie

A paradise for outdoor lovers with 536 km^2 of lakes and forests. Canoeing and hiking … more

Getting together

Listening 25

🎧 45 🌐 3fx4rb

a Listen to Dennis and Millie planning a weekend in La Mauricie. Tick (✓) the things they talk about on the website on p. 106.

b Listen again and take notes. Where are they going to:

1 stay? _____
2 go on Saturday? _____
3 go on Sunday? _____

Vocabulary 26

Planning

Can you remember Dennis and Millie's conversation? Complete the sentences with these words.

expensive   Saturday   nice   accommodation   uncomfortable

Introducing / Changing topics

1 What are we going to do about _____ ?
2 What are we going to do on _____ ?

Opinions

3 I think it's too _____ .
4 This campsite looks _____ to me.

Agreeing / Disagreeing

5 Yeah, OK. • Fine.
6 But camping is really _____ .

Speaking 27

a Work alone. You are going to La Mauricie for a weekend with some friends. Read the information about La Mauricie on p. 149 and take notes:

- where to stay.
- what to do on Saturday.
- what to do on Sunday.

b Talk in groups and plan what to do. Then explain your ideas to other groups. Did you choose the same or different things?

Writing 28

a *Media task*. Go on the internet and find information about different kinds of holidays and take notes.

b Choose one destination and make a website. On your website give information about:
- accommodation.
- outdoor activities.

107

| Language skills | Extras | Explore |

Getting together

Keyword: *about*

29 Which sentences use about with a topic? Which use it with a number? Underline the topics and numbers.

1 *Juno* is about a difficult decision in a teenager's life.
2 I've got an idea. I read about this film called *Yeelen*.
3 We're having a snack first at about 6.15.
4 So what do you think about action films?

about with topics

30 a Match 1–7 with A–G to make conversations.

1 "You look stressed. Is there a problem?"
2 "Can I see the room this evening?"
3 "Do you know that my brother's getting married?"
4 "Don't forget the party on Friday."
5 "Hello, can I help you?"
6 "How was your day?"
7 "So, do you want to buy these jeans?"

A "Hmm. I don't know. I'll think about it."
B "Yes, there is! Do you know anything about computers?"
C "Sure. How about six thirty?"
D "It was terrible! I don't want to talk about it."
E "What party? No one told me about that."
F "Yes, please. I have a question about my ticket."
G "Yes, I heard about it."

b Test each other in pairs. Use the above phrases with about for an answer. Be careful, you might have to change them slightly.

1 "Can I come and play with your new game console this evening?"
2 "Don't forget our film evening on Saturday!"
3 "Did you know that Sue's passed her driving test?"
4 "Hello, can I help you?"
5 "Are you sure you want to order sushi for tonight?"
6 "How was your weekend?"

about with numbers

31 a Talk in teams. Guess the answers. Use about.

1 When did Yuri Gagarin go into space?
2 How many teeth does an adult elephant have?
3 When were the first modern Olympics?
4 How high is Mount Everest?
5 How many people are there in a cricket team?
6 How long is the Great Wall of China?
7 How long does it take for light to travel from the sun to the earth?
8 When did people start writing?

Example: A: *Gagarin went into space in about 1960, I think. Or was it in 1962?*
B: *It was definitely before 1969 because thats's when Armstrong walked on the moon.*

b Listen to check. Which team has the best guesses?

Getting together

Explore writing 1: Invitations and replies

32 In pairs, ask and answer the questions.

1 When and where do you usually get together with your friends?
2 How do you usually invite people or get invited to parties? By email, phone, text, or face-to-face?

33 a Put emails A–C in order.

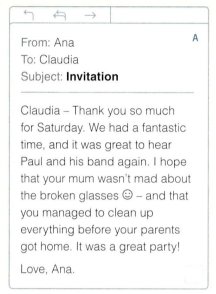

b Put text messages D–H in order.

☐ D Hi – Are you free next weekend? Can you come hiking with my brother and parents? Ana ☺

☐ E Sounds great but volleyball match with my team on Sat. Free on Sunday. OK? Claudia

☐ F Sure, no problem. See you then. C.

☐ G Dear Ms Duncan, thanks for taking me yesterday. Lovely day, Claudia

☐ H Sorry, Dad's busy Sunday. Let's get together next weekend then? Ana

c Read all the emails and text messages again. Which are invitations / replies / thank-you notes?

34 a Match the beginnings (1–6) and endings of the invitations (A–F) below.

1 This is to invite you to
2 Please let me know
3 I hope you
4 Are you free
5 Would be great
6 Can you come

A hiking with my brother and parents?
B to see you there.
C next weekend?
D my 16th birthday party.
E can come.
F if you can come.

b Look at the invitations to check. Can you think of more ways to complete 1–6?

Example: *This is to invite you to our flat for lunch.*

35 Complete these expressions from the replies and thank-you notes in 33.

1 We had a _____ .
2 It was great _____ .
3 Sounds _____ .
4 Sorry, _____ .
5 Lovely _____ .
6 Let's get together _____ .

109

Getting together

36 *Ellipsis.* In emails and text messages, we often don't use words like *I*, *we*, *be*, *do*, *that*, *the*, etc. to make them shorter.

Example: ~~I had a~~ Lovely day! ~~I'm~~ Free on Sunday.

Make these sentences shorter for an email or text message. Cross out the words you don't need.
1 That sounds absolutely fantastic.
2 I'm very busy this weekend. I can't come to the picnic. I hope you have a good time.
3 It was lovely to see you. Do you want to meet again next weekend?
4 We're going to see *The Others* at The Picture House. We're having ice cream first.

37 a Choose an event and write an email invitation.
- a birthday party
- a picnic
- an end-of-term party
- a graduation party

b Read another student's invitation. Write a reply.

c It is after the event. Write a short note to say thank you.

Explore writing 2: A review of your favourite film

38 a Daniel, your friend from England, emails you a review of his favourite film. Read the review. Does the film sound good to you?

From: Daniel
To: Ana
Subject: **Film review_Volver**

Dear Ana,

... I watched *Volver* last night – it's amazing! You should watch it. It's a drama written and directed by Pedro Almodóvar. I think it was produced in 2006. The story is set in a village in Spain, and it's about a family – two sisters, their aunt and the teenage daughter of one of the sisters. Another character is the sisters' dead mother, who comes back to help them in a difficult time. You know, 'volver' means 'to return' in Spanish. It stars Penélope Cruz, but I think the cast really work as a team. Apparently, six actresses shared the Best Actress Award at the Cannes Film Festival.

I think *Volver* is a warm, funny film about the relationship between women. But it isn't just for girls! I can only recommend it.

All the best,

Daniel

b Reply to Daniel's email with a review of your favourite film. Write an email (80–100 words) using some of the highlighted expressions above.

Explore speaking: Presenting your favourite film

39 *Media task.* Prepare a presentation (3 min) about your favourite film. Include the following points:
- **what?** film title, kind of film
- **when?** production date
- **where?** country of production; where it is set
- **who?** director, actors
- **what is it about?** storyline
- **why?** reasons why you like it so much
- (Comment on the music too.)

Language skills | Extras | **Explore**

Getting together

Explore reading: A festival programme

40 Look at the *Summer in the City* programme in 32. Tick (✓) the kinds of events that are featured.

Theatre ☐   Children's events ☐   Dance ☐   Film ☐   Jazz ☐
Folk music ☐   Classical music ☐   Walks ☐   Talk ☐   Rock music ☐

41 Read the festival programme. First decide whether the statements (1–5) are true (T) or false (F) and put a cross (☒) in the correct box. Then identify the sentence in the text which supports your decision. Write <u>the first four words</u> of the sentence in the space provided. There may be more than one correct answer; write down <u>only one</u>. The first one (0) has been done for you.

Summer in the city
Saturday 12 July

CINEMA UNDER THE STARS

Piazza Grande 22.00
The Man Without a Past
by Aki Kaurismäki (Finland, 2003)
Free

KIDS' SUMMER

Guasto Gardens 20.00
Clowns a fun show for the under-12s, inspired by Fellini's clowns. After the show, kids and their families are invited to sleep under the stars in the park. Free, but book in advance 339 3450228

SPECIAL EVENT

Arena Sport 21.30
Fura dels Baus
Spectacular performance by the celebrated Catalan theatre company in their new all-women production, *Imperium*. €30
Information and tickets from Tourist Information Office, Piazza Grande, Mon–Sat 14.00–19.00

CITY WALKS

Starting from Piazza Piccola 21.00
Secrets of the Middle Ages: the city in the 13th and 14th century. The walk lasts approximately two hours.
€8 Book in advance 348 4499321

OPEN-AIR JAZZ

Via del Porto 21.30
Music from the Max Aurora trio
Entrance and first drink
€5

SCANDELLARA FESTIVAL

Scandellara Park 21.00–02.00
Jurassic Rock in concert 22.00
Plus DJ. Free

CLASSICAL COURTYARD

De Pisis Gallery main courtyard 21.30
Music by Schubert, Beethoven and Dvorak. Donatella Virzi, piano.
Free

	Statements	T	F	First four words
0	The city walks end at midnight.		✗	*The walk lasts approximately*
1	The Catalan theatre company has no men in its show.			
2	Tickets for the show *Imperium* can be bought every day of the week.			
3	Adults can't sleep in the park after *Clowns*.			
4	The open-air jazz concert is free.			
5	The band playing at the open-air jazz concert has three members.			

Self-assessment   ✓✓ | ✓ | ‼

- find information in a cinema programme
- talk about films
- make and respond to suggestions
- make arrangements to meet
- talk about hopes and plans
- planning a weekend break
- write and reply to an invitation
- write a thank-you note

First of all, think about what you have learned up to now. Are you close to "I can do this well" or closer to "I need to work on this"?

Put a mark where you think you are at the moment. Then do the tasks and check your answers with the key on p. 187. Put another mark in a different colour where you see yourself now you've done the task.

Reading
- I can understand an article about a film.
- I can understand a story about a journey.

Reading 1 Read about the film *The Darjeeling Limited*. First decide whether the statements (1–6) are true (T) or false (F) and put a cross (☒) in the correct box. Then identify the sentence in the text which supports your decision. Write <u>the first four words</u> of this sentence in the space provided. There may be more than one correct answer; write down <u>only one</u>. The first one (0) has been done for you.

The Darjeeling Limited

Although I find Wes Anderson's films interesting, I have never liked the false charm of the characters and their families. I was surprised that I liked his new movie, *The Darjeeling Limited*. It is the name of the train that three American brothers take to travel across India. It was written by Anderson himself with Roman Coppola and Jason Schwartzman, who is often found in Anderson's movies.

A writer, Jack Whitman (Schwartzman), meets a former girlfriend in a Parisian hotel. Shortly after, he boards a train in India to meet his two older brothers, all in their thirties. Suddenly we see an old American businessman (another Anderson regular, Bill Murray), racing by taxi through an Indian street to catch the same train. He just misses it, but Jack's brother, Peter (Adrien Brody), passes him on the platform, catches up with the train, and walks through the crowded third-class carriages to his first-class carriage. This is a beautiful comic scene about age, frustration and class.

Jack and Peter have an older brother, Francis (Owen Wilson), who has arranged and is paying for this journey from Mumbai to the Himalayas. Francis is a rich businessman, who uses his money to pay for his adventures and romantic dreams. His head is wrapped in bandages, a tooth is missing and he walks with a stick – he was injured in a motorcycle accident. The trip was planned as 'a spiritual journey', to celebrate the year that has passed. The brothers last met at the funeral of their father in New York.

Peter is married with a pregnant wife back in the US, while Jack writes autobiographical stories that he pretends come from his imagination.

The Darjeeling Limited is dramatic and funny – an amazing story is put into 90 minutes. After the brothers argue about who should have their father's razor and sunglasses, Jack and Peter are bossed around by Francis, who orders food for them and holds their passports. Later, Peter buys a deadly snake, which escapes in the compartment[2]. Because of this, they are thrown off the train by the conductor[3], along with their luggage.

Finally, a journey that began as a tribute to their dead father ends in a visit to the Himalayan monastery where their strong, independent mother (Anjelica Huston) has just been named the leader.

---

[1] **carriage:** a train waggon
[2] **compartment:** a separate section of the train where people can sit
[3] **conductor:** a person who checks / sells the tickets on a train

The brothers argue, fight, and remember the old days but a new kind of friendship develops as they make their comic journey. *The Darjeeling Limited* is a wonderful creation, a combination of Indian colour and faded imperial grandeur[4] – and one of the great train movies.

Source: adapted and abridged from Philip French, "The Darjeeling Limited", 25 November 2007, https://www.theguardian.com/film/2007/nov/25/comedy.drama1

	Statements	True	False	First four words
0	The author loves the characters in Wes Anderson films.		✗	*Although I find Wes*
1	The script was only written by Wes Anderson.			
2	Francis can be adventurous.			
3	Jack and Peter try to control Francis.			
4	The brothers choose to leave the train.			
5	The brothers' mother is an anxious person.			
6	The brothers' relationship improves over the journey.			

Writing   ✓✓   ✓   ‼

- I can respond to an invitation.
- I can describe a journey.

Writing 2 — Read the email from your friend, Nehir, from primary school. Write a reply to Nehir's email. In your reply, you should:
- react to your friend's invitation.
- describe your most recent holiday.
- point out how you liked your last holiday.

Write about 150 words.

From: Nehir
Sent: 20 April
To:
Subject: **Birthday party**

Hey mate, how's it going? Seems like ages since we've seen each other.

Well, I'm going to be 16 next month – I can't believe it. I'm going to have a party at my parents' house in London and I've invited everybody from our old class – I'd absolutely love it if you could come … Please say yes!

I can't remember if I told you last time we spoke, but I'd just come back from Spain. I was there with my parents. It was great, we did a tour of Andalusia in the south. It's very, very beautiful but also incredibly hot – too hot if I'm honest. You told me that you were going away with your parents but you hadn't booked it yet – where did you go and how was it?

Can't wait for your reply.

Love,

Nehir

---

[4] **grandeur:** greatness or glory

Listening
- I can understand a conversation about films.
- I can understand descriptions of people.

Listening 3 You are going to listen to Katie giving an interview on the radio. First you will have 45 seconds to study the task below, then you will hear the recording twice. While listening, choose the correct answer (A, B, C or D) for each question (1–5). Put a cross (☒) in the correct box. The first one (0) has been done for you.

After the second listening, you will have 45 seconds to check your answers.

0 Katie
- A doesn't like Wes Anderson films.
- B has never seen a Wes Anderson film.
- **C really likes Wes Anderson films.** ☒
- D has never heard of Wes Anderson.

1 Katie
- A likes *Grand Budapest Hotel* best.
- B thinks *Grand Budapest Hotel* is his best looking film.
- C thinks *Moonrise Kingdom* is his best looking film.
- D thinks that *Grand Budapest Hotel* was nominated for an Oscar.

2 She
- A saw her first film in 1998.
- B saw *The Royal Tenenbaums* which was her first Wes Anderson film.
- C cried after watching *Rushmore*.
- D cried after watching *The Royal Tenenbaums*.

3 Royal
- A has always had a good relationship with his children.
- B is a happy and likeable character.
- C easily gets annoyed.
- D is very much like the actor who plays him.

4 Steve Zissou
- A is not very optimistic.
- B is not very strange.
- C was played by Bill Murray in all Wes Anderson's films.
- D makes films.

5 Katie
- A thinks Wes Anderson films are comedies.
- B thinks Wes Anderson films are dramas.
- C thinks Wes Anderson films are tragedies.
- D knows that *Isle of Dogs* is animated.

Language

- I can correctly form the comparative and superlative.
- I can use the passive voice.
- I can correctly use the present simple or progressive for future events.

✓✓   ✓   ❗❗

Language 4 Complete this text with the correct form of the verb in brackets. The first one (0) has been done for you.

0 *Juno* is the _____ film I've ever seen. (good)
1 What film is _____ – *Yeelen* or *The Others*? (expensive)
2 What kind of transport is _____ – the Maglev train or a Habal-Habal? (safe)
3 What's the _____ job? (dangerous)
4 Do you think a coco taxi is _____ than a sled? (quick)
5 Last week, I watched the _____ film ever. (silly)

0	best	3	
1		4	
2		5	

5 Complete this text with the correct form of the verb in brackets. The first one (0) has been done for you.

0 In 2013, *Moonrise Kingdom* _____ for an Oscar. (nominate)
1 The film _____ in 2012. (release)
2 The lead adult role _____ by Edward Norton, and he got really good reviews. (play)
3 In this new film, three brothers _____ across India and it is lots of fun. (follow)
4 When a dangerous snake is released into the carriage, all three of them _____ off the train by the conductor. (throw)

0	was nominated	3	
1		4	
2			

6 (Circle) the correct form of the verb.

1 Hurry up, Jon! The film starts / is starting at 8 o'clock.
2 This Saturday I meet / am meeting my father for a coffee.
3 Express trains to London leave / are leaving at 15:30, 17:00 and 18:00.
4 Where do you go / are you going this weekend?
5 Wednesday? I can't make it I'm afraid, I go / am going to Paris next week.

115

Goals
- talk about health
- buy things in a pharmacy
- understand instructions on medicines
- give advice
- write an email apologising

Vocabulary

The body and health

1 a Do the quiz. the correct answers.

BODY sense: Test your knowledge

1 Your head weighs about 3.5 / 5.5 / 8.5 kilos.
2 The stomach can hold four / six / eight litres of food.
3 You use 5 / 12 / 20 muscles to smile. You use about 50 / 70 / 80 muscles to speak.
4 Our eyes never grow / stop growing . Our nose and ears never grow / stop growing .
5 The body loses half a kilo / more than half a kilo / a kilo of skin every year.
6 Over 20% / 40% / 50% of the bones in your body are in your hands and feet.
7 The smallest bone is in your ear / nose / little toe . It's the size of a grain of rice.
8 Your thumb is the same length as your nose / big toe / ear .
9 Children have 18 / 20 / 22 first teeth. Adults have 28 / 30 / 32 teeth.
10 Your heart beats about 50,000 / 100,000 / 200,000 times every day.

48   zw9x2t

b Listen to check.

2 Look at the highlighted words in the quiz. What other body words do you know? Check in the picture dictionary, *The body*, p. 168.

3 Match problems 1–8 with pictures A–H.

I've got a	(1) headache. (2) cold. (3) sore throat. (4) temperature.
	(5) pain in my back. (6) problem with my knee.
I feel (really / a bit)	(7) sick. (8) tired.

A ☐   B ☐   C ☐   D ☐   E ☐   F ☐   G ☐   H ☐

4 Make conversations. Talk about different problems from 3.

Are you OK? / Are you all right? ⟶ Yes, I'm OK, thanks.
Yes, I'm fine.

Not really. / No, not too good. ⟶ Oh, I'm sorry about that.
I've got a … / I feel …   I'm sorry to hear that.

Are you OK?

What are your symptoms?

Listening & Reading

5 Marc, from Lyons in France, is in the UK on a language trip. He goes to a pharmacy. Listen to the first part of Marc's conversation with the pharmacist. What problems does Marc have?

49 ec2q8s

6 Match the pharmacist's questions (1–3) with Marc's answers (A–C).

1 What are your symptoms?
2 Are you allergic to anything?
3 Are you taking any other medicine?

A Just dairy products.
B No, not at the moment.
C I've got a pain in my back.

7 a Read the medicine packages below. Which medicine is best for Marc? Why?

Hotlem

For cold symptoms, including headache, sore throat and high temperature.
How to take: Put one sachet of powder into a cup and fill with hot water (not boiling). You can add sugar or honey.
How much to take: Adults and children over 12 years: 1 sachet every 4 to 6 hours. Do not take more than 4 sachets in 24 hours. Do not give to children under 12.
WARNING: CONTAINS PARACETAMOL.
DO NOT TAKE IF YOU ARE ALLERGIC TO PARACETAMOL.

Paracetamol

500 mg tablets

For the relief of aches and pains, including headache and toothache.
KEEP AWAY FROM CHILDREN
DO NOT TAKE WITH ALCOHOL
If symptoms continue, go to your doctor.
DOSE:
- Adults and children over 12 years: 1 to 2 tablets every 4 to 6 hours. Do not take more than 8 tablets in 24 hours.
- Children 6 to 12 years: half to one tablet every 4 to 6 hours. Do not take more than 4 tablets in 24 hours.

Not for children under 6.

50 a4i3d8

b Listen to the second part of Marc's conversation. Does he buy Hotlem or Paracetamol? Is this medicine a painkiller? What if it doesn't work?

c Read the packages again. Are these sentences true (T) or false (F)?

1 You shouldn't give Hotlem to a ten-year-old.
2 Hotlem has paracetamol in it.
3 An adult can take six sachets of Hotlem in 24 hours.
4 You can drink wine with paracetamol.
5 An adult shouldn't have more than eight tablets in 24 hours.
6 You can give paracetamol to a five-year-old.

Speaking

8 Work in A/B pairs.
- A, you are the pharmacist.
- B, you feel ill. Have a conversation and buy some medicine. Change roles and have another conversation.

Example: A: *Hello. Can I help you?* B: *Yes. I'd like something for …*

Are you OK?

Home remedies

Speaking 9 What do you do in situations 1–4?

1 You've got toothache.
2 You've got a really bad pain in your back and you don't know why.
3 You've got a temperature.
4 You feel tired and you have no energy.

Do you:
- take a day off school?
- see a doctor or dentist?
- take some medicine?
- ask someone for advice?
- go to a pharmacy?
- do nothing / something else?

10 a Pictures A–D show different remedies. Can you match them with these problems?

Example: *Maybe onions can help stomach ache.*

1 headache ☐   2 toothache ☐   3 a high temperature ☐   4 stomach ache ☐

A black toast with honey   B an onion   C a wet teabag   D salt water

b Read the blog entries to check your ideas.

---

http://knowledge.com/homeremedies

KNOWLEDGE.COM The world's best advice site ... written by you.

Monica, Canada
monica_a@kmail.com

Black toast with honey

A friend of mine stayed in a hotel in India and the manager gave this to her for stomach ache. It really works. Just take a piece of bread and toast it until it's black. Then put honey on the toast and eat it. You don't really need the honey, but it makes it taste better. It doesn't look good, but it can really help. So if you get stomach ache, try this remedy.

Norma, USA
norma_u@kmail.com

An onion

If you get a high temperature, use an onion. It sounds strange, but it helps. Cut one large onion in half and tie half an onion to the bottom of each of your feet. You shouldn't wear socks of course, just bare feet! I use this on my kids and it works every time. The remedy came from a relative from down south.

Heli, Finland
heli_f@kmail.com

A wet teabag

Here are my tips for toothache. You should put a wet teabag on the sore tooth. I always have a wet teabag in the fridge so it's there when I need it. Another idea: take a garlic clove and put it on the tooth. Both these ideas help me nine times out of ten. But if they don't work for you, you should go to a dentist.

Lameed, Egypt
lameed_e@kmail.com

Salt water

When I was a child, I got a lot of headaches and my grandmother always did this for me. Put a few drops of warm salt water in your ears. Don't use really hot water. Do this three or four times for both ears. Then lie down and close your eyes for about ten minutes.

Are you OK?

Writing **11** What do you think of the home remedies on p. 118? Would you like to try them? Why? / Why not? Describe one or two of the remedies and say what you think about them. Write about 75–90 words.

Vocabulary **12** You can use the *imperative* or *should* to give advice. Complete the sentences with the following words.

Giving advice

socks   teabag   water   feet   garlic

✓			✗		
(You should)	Take a _____ clove and put it on the tooth.		Don't You shouldn't	use really hot _____ wear _____	, of course,
	Put a wet _____ on the sore tooth.			just bare _____	.

13 a Think of advice for each of these problems. Write five sentences.

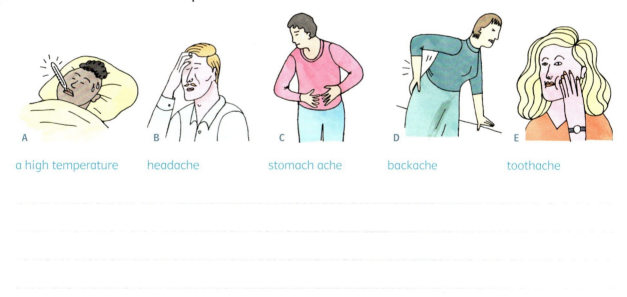

A a high temperature   B headache   C stomach ache   D backache   E toothache

b Talk in groups. Listen to each other's advice and guess the problem.

Example: A: *You should take a paracetamol and lie down for half an hour.*   B: *Is that for a headache?*

Are you OK?

If you get stomach ache ...

Grammar 14 — Giving advice with *if*

Look at the *if* sentences in the table. Then put the words of this sentence in order and add it to the examples below.

If / an onion / get / a temperature, / you / use .

→ Grammar reference and practice, p. 162

***If* + present simple, imperative**
If you get stomach ache, try this remedy.
If you try the salt water remedy, don't use really hot water.

***If* + present simple, *should / shouldn't* + infinitive**
If they don't work for you, you should go to a dentist.

You can change the order of *if* sentences:
If you get stomach ache, try this remedy. or Try this remedy if you get stomach ache.

15 a Match problems 1–6 with advice A–F. There is more than one correct answer.

1 you've got a very bad cold
2 you're allergic to paracetamol
3 your feet hurt
4 you've got stomach ache
5 you feel very tired
6 you've got a problem with your knee

A you shouldn't eat a large meal
B be careful what medicine you take
C don't go to school
D don't go for a run
E put them in hot water with mustard
F you should go to bed early

b Now say the six sentences with *if*.

Example: *If you've got a very bad cold, don't go to school.*

Listening 16

51 w7ij8g

Listen to Amina from Lebanon, Angharad and Nathalie from Switzerland, and Ruth from England talking about their own remedies for a cold. Tick (✓) the remedies they talk about.

1 eat oranges
2 drink black tea with honey
3 take paracetamol
4 eat chicken soup
5 drink hot honey and lemon juice
6 get on with work
7 inhale steam from hot water
8 go to the doctor

Speaking 17 Talk about these questions in groups.

1 What do you think of their remedies?
2 What do you do when you've got a cold? What about people you know?
3 What's the most popular remedy? What's the most unusual remedy?

Example: *If I have a cold, I put my head over a bowl of hot water and inhale the steam.*

Are you OK?

Giving advice

Reading 18 a Read the magazine article. What is the main topic?

1 better relationships with classmates
2 a better school environment
3 exercising at school

TIPS OF THE WEEK
Stay healthy at school

Classrooms are not always healthy environments. Here are some tips for improving them and your health.

- Try to sit near a window. Natural light makes you feel happier.
- Fresh air is good for you, so you should open the window if possible.
- If you want to improve the appearance of your classroom, get some plants.
- Sit properly and make sure the top of your computer screen is at eye level.
- A bad sitting position can give you headaches and back pain.
- Don't sit near an air-conditioner. It dries out your eyes and skin.
- Nice wall colours can improve your mood, so change the colour of your classroom walls. The right colour can even help you to be more creative. White, blue or green are better than dark or bright colours.
- Don't use the lift. You should always use the stairs. This keeps you fit.

b Find:
- seven things you should do.
- two things you shouldn't do.

c Do you do any of the things in the article? Why? / Why not?

Vocabulary 19 Cover the article. Complete the sentences with these words.

Giving reasons for advice

Fresh air   The right colour   Using the stairs   Plants   Natural light

1 _____ makes you feel happier.
2 _____ is good for you.
3 _____ improve the appearance of your classroom.
4 _____ helps you to be more creative.
5 _____ keeps you fit.

20 a You want some advice. Choose one of these topics or use your own ideas. How to:

- improve your room cheaply.
- give a short presentation in class.
- study effectively at home.
- organise a picnic for your friends.
- entertain a group of children.
- organise a party for 20 people.

b Work in pairs. Ask each other for advice and give advice using the examples below.

- **ask for advice:** *I want to improve my room, but I'm not sure what to do.*
- **give advice:** *You should / shouldn't … Don't … If you …*
- **give reasons:** *Fresh air's good for you.*

Writing 21 Two of the most common problems for teenagers are school stress and money problems. Write a blog entry giving advice on these issues (8–10 sentences on each topic). Use the texts in 10b and 18a to help you.

121

Are you OK?   Language skills   Extras   Explore

Keyword: *of*

Containers and quantities

22 Complete the sentences with the words from the boxes.

a lot   bit   bottle   couple   lots   pair

1. I'm looking for a _____ of blue shoes.
2. I always have a _____ of water on my desk.
3. I can speak English and a _____ of French.
4. There are _____ / _____ of interesting shops near here.
5. I had a _____ of lessons yesterday.

23 What other words can you use instead of the underlined words?

Example: *a pair of socks, …*

Places and times

24 Which sentences are about places? Which are about times?

1. There's a beautiful park in the centre of town.
2. Cairns is a town in the north of Queensland, Australia.
3. People always phone me when I'm in the middle of dinner.
4. There's a table in the corner of my bedroom.
5. I get my pocket money at the beginning of the month.
6. I usually have one or two tests at the start of the week.

25 Ask and answer the questions. Make notes.

1. What are your favourite places in the centre of your home town / in the north of your country / in the south of your country?
2. What do you always / usually do at the start of the week / at the end of the month / at the end of the year?

Info point: Measuring

You can measure things like length, width, height, distance, weight/mass and volume. You can also measure time and temperature.
Measurements can be in SI units (SI = the International System of Units – a metric system) or in Imperial units. Imperial units are used in the USA; both SI and Imperial units are used in the UK.

Measuring answers questions like:
How long is the line?   How tall is your classmate?
How wide is the street?   How long does it take to travel to Salzburg by train?
How deep is the swimming pool?   How cold is the water in the lake?
How far away is the next bus stop?   How much milk is there in the plastic cup?

26 Study the table on p. 123 and complete it with the words from the boxes.

distance   liquids   feet   mass   pints   vernier callipers   periods of   Fahrenheit   scales   height

Are you OK?

Measuring instrument	You can measure...	SI units	Imperial units
(1) _scales_ : digital or analogue, with more or less precision	weight / (2) _____ .	g (grams) kg (kilograms) t (tonnes)	oz (ounces) lb (pounds) short tons
tape measure	length, width, depth, (3) _____ .	mm (millimetres) cm (centimetres) m (metres) km (kilometres)	in (inch – inches) ft (foot – (4) _____) yd (yard – yards) mi (mile – miles)
(5) _____	the (6) _____ between two sides of an object.	mm tenths and hundredths of a mm	inches thousandths of an inch
calibrated / measuring jug / measuring vessel, beaker	volumes, especially volumes of (7) _____ .	ml (millilitres) l (litres) cm³ (cubic centimetres) m³ (cubic metres)	pt ((8) _____) for beverages (1 pt ≈ 0.568 l) gal (gallons) for fuel (1 UK gal ≈ 4.5 l) bbl (oil barrels) (1 barrel of oil ≈ 160 l of oil)
thermometer: digital or analogue	temperature.	0 °C (Celsius) 100 °C	32 °F ((9) _____) 212 °F
stopwatch: digital or analogue	(10) _____ . time, e.g. cycles, laps, runs.	There is just one system of units: years, months, weeks, days, hours, minutes and seconds.	

27 How do you convert SI units to Imperial units and Imperial units to SI units? Go on the internet and find a comprehensive conversion table to complete the following tasks.

28 a *Media task.* Now research the following information (at home, at the supermarket or online):
- the length dimensions of two technical appliances (e.g. of a TV / a washing machine) the weight of two food items from the supermarket
- the volume of two liquid products like drinks, perfumes, motor oil or detergents

b Write down their measurements in both SI and Imperial units and report your findings to the class.

Example: *A netbook has a size of 10". The 10 inches refer to the diagonal dimension of the netbook. One inch is equal to about 2.5 centimetres, so the diagonal size is approximately 25 centimetres.*

29 Complete the table with the words from the boxes. Decide what the temperature ranges feel like.

°Fahrenheit	°Celsius	This feels...
40 s	5–10	
50 s	10–15	
60 s	15–21	
70 s	21–26	
80 s	26–32	
90 s	32–37	

hot   comfortable   warm

boiling   hot   chilly   cool

30 Read the description of the barometer and complete it with the words in the boxes.

accurately   pressure   mercury   expands   amplified   calibrated   compresses

Barometers are used to measure atmospheric (1) _____, and have been in use since the 17th century. Early barometers used (2) _____, but were soon replaced with the mechanical barometers seen here. They have a sealed, partially evacuated metal box inside. As the air pressure rises or falls, the box either (3) _____ or flexes outward. The box is attached to a metal spring and, as the box responds to the changes in air pressure, the spring (4) _____ or contracts. This movement is (5) _____ with a system of levers, which are then attached to a chain. The chain moves the pointer on the dial, which is (6) _____ (marked with numbers) so you can read the air pressure (7) _____ .

b Look at the diagram and label the parts with the words in the boxes.

pointer   evacuated box   levers   chain   metal spring

1 _____
2 _____
3 _____
4 _____
5 _____

31 a *Media task.* Choose one measuring instrument from the list.

- tape measure
- milometer (AE: odometer)
- altimeter
- laser range finder
- vernier callipers
- barometer
- tyre-pressure gauge
- measuring cup
- analogue scales
- drawing compass
- digital fever thermometer
- stopwatch

b Go on the internet and research the answers to the following questions.

- What is it used for?
- What parts does it consist of?
- How much does it cost?

c Present your findings to the class in the next lesson (2–3 minutes). Make sure that you know how to pronounce the name of the instrument.

Use phrases like:

With a … you can …
It is used to measure …
Before … , you must …
It consists of …

The display shows …
It is very precise / shockproof / water-resistant …
It is made of plastic / metal …
It costs …

Explore writing: An email apologising

32 What are the names of the people in photos 1–3? Read A–C to find out.

From: Olivia Johnson
To: John
Subject: **Today's interview**

A

Dear John,

I'm afraid I have a terrible cold and will have to cancel today's interview. I appreciate that you have prepared for today, but unfortunately I just can't make it. I'm so sorry to disrupt your plans, but could we reschedule for next week sometime? I'm really looking forward to meeting you and hearing about your vision for the company.

Kind regards,

Olivia Johannsen

CEO, Alphabetic Plastics

From: Claude Dubois
To: Ms Partridge
Subject: **Apartment booking**

B

Dear Ms Partridge,

I'm very sorry, but unfortunately we've had a problem with the computerised booking system and the apartment you reserved is unavailable at the time you require. We would instead like to offer you a larger apartment in the same street, at no extra cost. We would be grateful if you could confirm if that is acceptable.

Apologies for the inconvenience,

Claude Dubois

General Manager, Parisian Apartments

From: Virat
To: Armando
Subject: **Meeting this morning**

C

Hi Armando,

I'm really sorry, my train has been cancelled so I won't be able to make the meeting this morning. I know how important the project is – sorry to let you down at such short notice. Thanks for all your hard work so far and I hope it all goes according to plan … Looking forward to catching up this afternoon, as long as the trains get their act together …

Virat

33 a Read the emails again and say which things went wrong / were not possible.

b How did Olivia, Virat and Claude say sorry? Cover the emails and match 1–5 with A–E. Then read again to check.

1 Apologies
2 I'm afraid
3 Sorry to
4 I'm very sorry, but
5 I'm really sorry,

A I have a terrible cold.
B let you down at such short notice.
C for the inconvenience.
D unfortunately there has been a problem.
E my train has been cancelled.

34 When we say sorry, we usually say why. Look at the emails above and find out:

1 why Olivia didn't interview John.
2 why Virat couldn't go to the meeting.
3 why Claude couldn't reserve the apartment.

Are you OK?

35 Complete the sentences with these words.

hope   could (x2)   looking   would   unfortunately (x2)

1 _____ we reschedule for next week?

2 _____ there has been a problem.

3 _____ I just can't make it.

4 I _____ it goes according to plan.

5 I'm _____ forward to meeting you.

6 We _____ like to offer you a larger apartment.

7 _____ you confirm if that is acceptable?

36 a Together with a partner, choose one situation (A–C) for an email.

It's Sunday afternoon. You have a very bad cold. Tomorrow you have to give a presentation to your department, but you think you should stay in bed. Write an email to explain the problem to your boss.

A

You and your business partner are supposed to go to Stockholm to meet a potential client. Your flight has been cancelled and you will be delayed until tomorrow. Email them to explain the situation.

B

You work in a clothes shop and this morning you reserved a jacket for a valued customer. Your colleague didn't see the 'reserved' sign and sold it to another customer in the afternoon. A replacement will be available next week. Write an email to the first customer to explain the situation.

C

Discuss the following questions.

1 Who are you writing to?
2 How can you say sorry?
3 What reasons can you give?
4 Can you use any expressions from 27b and 29?

b Work alone and write your email.

c Look at your partner's email. Can you improve your emails together?

37 Read other students' emails. What do you think of their reasons?

Explore listening: Staying healthy

38 Look at the photos. Which do you think is most important for a healthy lifestyle?

exercise

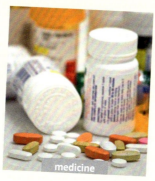
medicine

diet

sleep

39 You are going to listen to Lona talking about how she tries to stay healthy. First you will have 45 seconds to study the task below, then you will hear the recording twice. While listening, choose the correct answer (A, B, C or D) for each question (1–5). Put a cross (☒) in the correct box. The first one (0) has been done for you.

After the second listening, you will have 45 seconds to check your answers.

0 Lona thinks it is important to
- A feel good.
- B go to sleep around 8 p.m.
- C have a sleeping pattern. ☒
- D sleep 8 hours a day.

1 In her opinion, going to the gym is
- A as enjoyable as dancing.
- B good exercise.
- C fun with friends.
- D not very exciting.

2 She goes to dance classes
- A with a couple she knows.
- B before she goes out with friends.
- C a couple of times a week.
- D to enjoy the music.

3 When she can afford it, Lona
- A goes to a restaurant.
- B buys organic food.
- C bakes her own bread.
- D buys brown sugar.

4 She drinks ginger in warm milk
- A when she has a cold.
- B when she is in India.
- C when she has no tea at home.
- D when she wants to lose weight.

5 She takes honey
- A when there is nothing else.
- B to improve the taste of ginger.
- C when her mum tells her to.
- D because it tastes good and gives energy.

Self-assessment   ✓✓ | ✓ | ! !
- talk about health
- buy things in a pharmacy
- understand instructions on medicines
- give advice
- write an email apologising

Goals
- talk about experiences
- say what you've never done and always wanted to do
- talk about places you've been to
- find out information about things
- start and finish conversations

Reading 1 a **Talk in groups of four.**

Find out who:
- has met a famous person.
- has played an instrument at a concert.
- has raised money for charity.
- has ordered something online.
- has eaten something exotic.
- has used an online booking service.
- has played a musical instrument.
- has been at a sports camp.

Example: A: *Have you ever touched* a wild animal? B: *No, I haven't,* but *I have always wanted* to stroke a lion.
- Yes, *I have*. <u>Two years ago</u> I touched a big brown bear at a zoo.

b **Read the text and <u>underline</u> all verbs in the present perfect tense.**

Grandpa Frank's story

I'm 82 now and I have been retired for 18 years. My life has been very interesting; I have seen many countries and met lots of people. I have always been active and interested in different cultures. In the last few years I have spent most of the time here in my small house and garden in the suburbs of Washington DC.

Travelling for me started when I joined the army in 1953. I thought I would fight in the Korean war but when I joined up it had already finished. I moved to Berlin as soon as I had completed my basic training, so Europe, and not Asia, was the first continent for me to discover. Well, I've been to so many countries since then that I can hardly remember them all. I've been to Poland, Russia, Latvia and Romania, but have also travelled to Spain, Italy, Switzerland and France more than three times. Actually, I have explored all of the countries around the Mediterranean Sea, except Morocco. I had the chance to go there in 1987, but then there was a bad storm and the cruiser I was on had to stop in Tunis. It wasn't the first time the weather had spoiled my travel plans but it was pretty annoying. It was towards the end of my holiday, so I could not wait for better weather and had to return to the States.

I've never been to Australia or to the Scandinavian countries, but I would love to go there. Maybe I will manage to book a trip to Stockholm next Christmas.

As I have travelled a lot, I've seen a lot of wonderful places and have eaten and drunk some strange things. I had light blue Ryuhyo Beer in Japan and ate grilled grasshoppers in Indonesia – I hadn't eaten insects before and they tasted really funny. I have always wanted to brew my own beer, but I haven't managed to do so yet. I once worked in a bar for a week in Paris – before that I had always wanted to own a pub, but it was such hard work I changed my mind.

Yeah, I know, I've been around for a few years that doesn't mean I have stopped planning. It doesn't matter how old you are, it matters how active you stay in your mind.

Experiences

Grammar — Present perfect verbs

2 In the article, Frank says *I've never been* to Australia.
Is he talking about:

1 the past?
2 the present?
3 his whole life up to now?

3 Complete the sentences with *'ve* (have) or *'s* (has).

→ Irregular verbs, p. 165

Present perfect (*have / has + past participle*)

1 I _____ never played football.
2 You _____ never been to a gym.
3 He _____ never eaten clam chowder.
4 We _____ never had a garden.
5 They _____ never worked in an office.

clam chowder: a soup with seafood, traditionally served in a small loaf of bread

4 What are the past participles of these verbs? Look at irregular verbs on p. 165 to check.

Regular (*-ed*)		Irregular			
1 play	played	5 go	been / gone	9 see	
2 like		6 do		10 eat	
3 smoke		7 have		11 understand	
4 want		8 read		12 take	

5 Make sentences with the present perfect.

1 I / never / do / any extreme sports.
2 I / never / understand / maths.
3 We / never / have / a TV at home.
4 My brother / never / smoke.
5 My parents / never / fly / to the USA.
6 I / never / be / interested in football.
7 My mother / never / like / cooking.
8 Jo / never / work / in an office before.

Writing

6 a Write six sentences with *never* about yourself or people you know, three true and three false.

b Listen to each other's sentences. Which do you think are true? Which are false?

Experiences

Have you ever … ?

Grammar **7** You can use the present perfect to talk about your life up to now. Complete the sentences with been, seen and heard.

Present perfect

→ Grammar reference and practice, p. 163

Present perfect *has / have + past participle*

❓ 1 Have you been to Berlin? ✅ Yes, I have.
   2 Have you ever seen the Great Wall of China? ❌ No, I haven't.

➕ 3 I've _____ to most of the Mediterranean countries.
   4 I've _____ it on television.

➖ 5 I haven't _____ there.
   6 I've never _____ of it.

ever = at any time (in your life)

8 Look back at Grandpa Frank's story, form questions with the words below and find the answer in the text.

1 be / in the army?
2 go / to Switzerland?
3 have / an interesting live?
4 live / in Germany?

5 travel / to Stockholm?
6 drink / green lemonade?
7 stop / planning trips?

Example: A: *Has Frank ever been to Australia?* B: *No, he hasn't.*

Speaking **9 a** Make a list of:

1 five famous cities around the world: London, Chicago, …
2 five cities / towns in the country where you are now: Bregenz, Villach, …
3 five places in the town or city where you are now: the castle, the theatre, …

b In groups, find out who has been to the places on the list. Then use follow-up questions to find out more.

Example: *Have you been to … ?* ▪ *Have you seen … ?* ▪ *Have you heard of … ?*
        What's it like? ▪ *Does it have … ?* ▪ *Is it … ?* ▪ *Would you like to … ?*

Writing **10** *Media task.* You would like to submit an article about one of the sights or attractions in Austria to an online travel magazine. Research a place on the internet and write about it.

In your text you should:

- include some facts and figures.
- give important background information.
- mention possible tourist activities.

Begin, for example, with *The Neusiedler See is located* … and write 120–140 words.

Your article should be informative and interesting for English-speaking people your age.
You can use the article on p. 132 to help you.

Experiences

I've always wanted to ...

Listening **11 a** Listen to Andrei and Anne talking about things they have always wanted to do. Match the speakers to the pictures.

53 x9at83

I've always wanted to swim with dolphins.

I've always wanted to go to Egypt.

b Listen again. Why do they want to do these things?

Speaking **12 a** Think of some things you have always wanted to do.

b Tell each other about the things. Ask questions to find out more.

Example: A: *I've always wanted to ride an elephant.* B: *Really? Why?*

Vocabulary **13 a** Which of these things can you see in the place where you live?

Sights

a castle   a cemetery   a church steeple   a fountain   a market   a museum   a palace   a park
a sculpture   a skyscraper   a statue   a tomb   a town hall   a waterfall   caves   city walls   gardens ruins

→ Picture dictionary, *Sights*, p. 168

b Talk in groups.

1 Can you think of famous examples of the sights in 13a?
Example: *The Empire State Building in New York is a famous skyscraper.*

2 What kind of sights do you like / would you like to see?

Reading **14** Look at pictures 1–3. What do you know about these places? Have you been to any of them?

Great Barrier Reef, Australia

Taj Mahal, India

Ellis Island, New York, USA

Experiences

15 a Work in groups of three.

- A, read about Ellis Island below.
- B, read about the Great Barrier Reef.
- C, read about the Taj Mahal.

Find out what these numbers mean.

1 **Ellis Island:** 1892–1954, 12 million, 2 %
2 **Great Barrier Reef:** 900, 2,600, 1 billion, 1981
3 **Taj Mahal:** 1631, 20,000, 25 million

b Tell each other about the places.

Ellis Island is a short boat ride from Manhattan. It was the historical door to the USA for millions of immigrants. The Ellis Island Immigration Station opened in 1892 and closed in 1954. During this time, the US Bureau of Immigration dealt with twelve million immigrants. The immigrants that were allowed to enter generally spent about two to five hours at Ellis Island. Officials asked them 29 questions including name, occupation, and the amount of money they carried. Those with health problems or a criminal background were sent back to their home countries or put in the island's hospital. About two per cent were not allowed to enter the USA. This is why Ellis Island was sometimes called 'Heartbreak Island' or 'The Island of Tears'. Now a museum, millions of people have visited Ellis Island.

The Great Barrier Reef is located in the Pacific Ocean, off the north-eastern coast of Australia. The world's largest reef is made of billions of corals. It has over 2,900 individual reefs and 900 islands. It is over 2,600 kilometres long and can be seen from outer space. The reef is also a paradise for snorkelling and scuba diving. It is a popular tourist destination, especially the area around the town of Cairns. Tourism is important for the region, earning $1 billion per year. A large part of the reef is protected by the Great Barrier Reef Marine Park, which helps to limit the negative consequences of fishing and tourism. In 1981, the Great Barrier Reef became a World Heritage Site[1].

The Taj Mahal is the tomb of Mumtaz Mahal. She was the third and favourite wife of Shah Jehan, the Moghul emperor of India. When Mumtaz died in childbirth in 1631, the emperor decided to create a beautiful building in memory of his beloved wife. It took 20,000 workers more than 20 years to complete it. The Taj, in the city of Agra on the Yamuna river, is now one of the most famous places in the world. Since 2000, it has had more than 25 million visitors. Today Mumtaz and her husband lie in the Taj together, but some people say that Shah Jehan wanted his own tomb to be in a second, black Taj, on the other side of the river.

c Which of the places sounds the most interesting? Why?

Writing 16 *Media task.* Research a place on the internet that you have always wanted to see or have already seen and find fascinating. Write an article about this place. Collect your articles in class and turn them into an online magazine on "The best places to see." Maybe you would like to place the articles on your school website?

Your article should:

- state why you have always wanted to see it or why it has impressed you so much.
- include some facts and figures.
- give important background information.
- mention possible tourist activities.

Write about 140 words. You can use the descriptions in 15 to help you.

---

[1] **World Heritage Site:** a place (such as a forest, mountain, lake, desert, monument, building or city) that is listed by the UNESCO as being of special cultural importance. World Heritage Sites in Austria are, for example, the historic centres of Graz, Salzburg and Vienna als well as the Wachau.

... but it had already finished.

Grammar — Past perfect

17 Go to Frank's story on p. 128. In the article, he says *I moved to Berlin as soon as I had completed my basic training*. Which happened first? Tick (✓) the correct answer.

1 I moved to Berlin ☐   2 I had completed my basic training ☐

When we are talking about a past event (e.g. *I moved to Berlin*) we often use the past perfect to show that something else had happened before that (e.g. *as soon as I had completed my basic training*).

18 Complete the sentences with finished, eaten and left.

→ Grammar reference and practice, p. 164

Past perfect: *had + past participle*

❓ 1 Had she already gone when you arrived?   ✓ Yes, she had.
2 Had you ever eaten sushi before you went to Japan?   ✗ No, I hadn't.

➕ 3 The war had already _____ when I joined the army.
4 Romesh arrived really late for the party and I had already _____ .

➖ 5 I hadn't _____ insects before and they tasted really funny.

19 Read through Frank's story on p. 128 again and find other examples of the past perfect tense.

20 Think of two events in your life and put them in order using the past simple and past perfect tenses.

Example: *When I arrived at the station today, the train had already left.*

Getting information and recommendations

Listening
54 je2q64

21 a Your class is planning an end-of-year trip. You want to go to a nice place. How do you choose it?

Do you:
- ask your teachers?
- discuss it with your parents?
- look for places on the internet?
- ask friends about places they know?
- go to a travel agency?
- do something else?

b Listen to Alexander from Vienna asking his friends at boarding school about day trips.

1 Why does he want to go on a day trip?   2 Does he choose Hampton Court, Windsor or Cambridge?

Vocabulary — Getting information

22 a Can you remember what they said? Match 1–8 with A–H.

1 Have you been to Hampton Court?   A OK, I'll think about it. Thanks.
2 You could ask Sue.   B Neither.
3 What was it like?   C Good, I'll take them there.
4 Have you visited Windsor?   D Good idea, I'll ask her.
5 It's really nice.   E Windsor? The castle you mean?
6 Which one should we go to?   F Yes, I went there last year.
7 Take them to Cambridge. They'll love it. Really. G Well, you can take the train.
8 Do you know how to get there?   H It was all right, but quite expensive.

b In pairs, take turns to say sentences 1–8 and remember the answers.

Experiences

23 Choose one situation and think of things to ask about. Then work in pairs and ask each other for information and recommendations.

1. You're taking a visitor out. Think of some places to ask other students about.

2. You want to do a new sport or activity. Think of some sports and activities you've never tried.

3. You'd like to take some interesting books on holiday with you. Think of some books you've heard of, but haven't read.

4. You'd like to buy some really cool clothes. Think of some shops you'd like to ask other students about.

5. You're thinking about going on holiday somewhere different. Think of some places you've never been to.

Example: A: *Have you been to that new club in town?* B: *No, but have you tried … ?*

Safety signs in holiday accommodations

Vocabulary
Safety signs

24 Safety signs are usually split into three categories – mandatory action signs, caution signs and prohibition signs. Match the categories (1–3) with the correct meaning (A–C)

1. mandatory action signs
2. caution signs
3. prohibition signs

A. warn you about a hazard
B. order you to do something
C. tell you that you must not do something

25 a Look at the signs below. Which colour is used for each category of sign?

A
B
C
D
E
F
G
H
I

b Look at the signs again. Write the number of the correct sign next to its definition.

1. No Smoking D
2. Wear A Life Jacket
3. Caution – Wet Floor
4. Caution – Hot Surface
5. No Mobile Phones
6. No Diving
7. Danger – Electricity
8. Wear Protective Gloves
9. Wash Your Hands

Experiences

Reading

26 Look at the *Fire Action Information* found in a hotel room, and match the signs to the correct text.

- A Operate the fire alarm using the nearest available call point.
- B Fire action: If you discover or suspect a fire
- C Proceed to the assembly point at: 6, Station Road
- D Leave the room shutting the door behind you.
- E IMPORTANT
  Before you go to bed make sure you know the means of escape in case of fire and know how and where to operate the fire alarm and how to call the Fire Brigade.
- F ON HEARING THE ALARM
  Leave the building IMMEDIATELY.
- G Do not stop to collect personal belongings. Do not re-enter the building.

1 2 3 4 5 6 7

Keyword: *at*

27 Add the highlighted expressions to the table.

1 I was at boarding school in England at the time.
2 Middle children are good at meeting new people.
3 I met Ed when he was 16. I was at his father's house.
4 I usually go to bed at midnight.
5 My sister works as a nurse at the hospital.
6 She wasn't at the party.

Times	Places	Group events	Good at …
at 7.00	at home, at work	at a lecture	good at English
at the moment	at my parents' flat	at a match	not very good at swimming

28 a Add *at* to sentences 1–6. Find someone who:

      at
1 was ∨ a party last night.
2 met their girlfriend or boyfriend school.
3 is reading a good book the moment.
4 often works the weekend.
5 was a music festival recently.
6 is good sport.

b Use the sentences in 28a to ask questions to other students. Try to find out more information.

Example: A: *Were you at a party last night?* B: *Yes, I was.* A: *Where was it?*

Keyword: *take*

take with nouns

29 a Complete the sentences with these words.

    boat trip   message   medicine   tablets

1 OK, and do you prefer taking _____ in a drink or tablets?
2 Do not take more than four _____ in 24 hours.
3 Sorry, he isn't here at the moment … Can I take a _____ ?
4 And would you like to take a _____ around Sydney harbour?

b You can use *take* to talk about travel and medicine. Find examples above. Can you think of more examples?

Experiences

30 a Can you remember the last time you:
- took a train?
- took a shower?
- took a message?
- took a really good photo?
- took a trip to somewhere new?
- took a tablet for a headache?

b Talk together giving some details (when, where, why, …).

take with time

31 a Underline an activity and (circle) a time in these sentences.
1 Travelling home takes (a whole day).
2 It takes about twenty minutes to walk to the centre of Edinburgh.
3 It takes 40 minutes to travel the nine-mile journey across London by unicycle.

b Complete these sentences so that they are true for you. Then compare with a partner.

Example: *It takes 25 minutes to answer my emails. How long does it take to answer yours?*

1 It takes _____ to answer my emails.

2 It usually takes about _____ to get home from school.

3 Starting up my computer takes _____.

4 It usually takes _____ to make breakfast.

5 Cleaning my room takes _____.

6 It takes _____ to read the newspaper.

Across cultures: Your experiences

32 a Listen to Jessica, David and Lynne talking about their experiences of other cultures. Match each person with a country and a topic.

Australia   Brazil   the USA   food   people   music

b Talk together. What did they say about each topic? Listen again to check.

33 Match 1–6 with A–F.

1 I was surprised that
2 It's something people do
3 I remember standing
4 I couldn't believe how
5 I got interested in Brazil
6 I've never been there, but

A I've read a lot about it.
B friendly people were.
C because of the music.
D on special occasions.
E on a street corner.
F I really enjoyed the food.

34 a Think of your experiences of other cultures. For example:
- listening to music or eating food from other countries.
- meeting people from other countries.
- reading books or watching films from other countries.
- seeing art or cultural exhibitions from other countries.
- travelling to another country.

b Talk about your experiences with other students and make notes. Choose the most interesting experiences and share them in class.

Explore listening: World travellers

35 Work together with a partner and talk about your travel experiences so far.

Tell each other about:
- the countries you have been to.
- the places you liked / didn't like, and why.
- the most interesting food you have ever eaten.
- your best and worst travel experience.

36 You are going to listen to a recording about world travellers. First you will have 45 seconds to study the task below, then you will hear the recording twice. While listening, match the beginnings of the sentences (1–6) with the sentence endings (A–I). There are two extra sentence endings that you should not use. Write your answers in the spaces provided. The first one (0) has been done for you.

After the second listening, you will have 45 seconds to check your answers.

| 0 | Tim interviewed Michelle _____ . | B |

1. It is difficult for her to name the most beautiful country _____ .
2. The little guesthouse in Marrakesh felt exotic _____ .
3. Michelle says the fried crickets in Bangkok _____ .
4. One of her worst experiences was _____ .
5. Michelle wants to visit Indonesia _____ .
6. Australia is a great country to travel in _____ .

A	didn't taste bad
B	in a kitchen during lunchtime
C	forgetting her bag on a train
D	because every place is special in its own way
E	because of its size and diversity
F	because of its great diving sites
G	tasted like potato chips
H	getting very ill in Pakistan
I	because of the colourful tiles everywhere

Explore speaking 1: Presenting a famous place

37 a *Media task.* The class is divided into three groups. At home, group A researches Hampton Court on the internet, group B Windsor Castle, group C Cambridge. Find out:
- what they are.
- where they are.
- what you can do / see there.
- anything else you think is interesting.

b In class, each group:
- compares and combines their findings.
- makes a poster with the most important information to display in class.
- prepares and gives a presentation together (2–3 mins).

Use phrases like:
… is a famous palace. / … is known for its …
… is located in …
It features … / One of the main attractions …
Visitors can …

Experiences

Explore speaking 2: Starting and finishing conversations

38 a Listen to three conversations (1–3). Match them with pictures A–C.

A

B

C

b Read conversations 1–3 to check.

1
Sue: Hello.
Max: Hello, Sue. This is Max.
Sue: Oh, hi, Max. How are things?
Max: Fine, thanks. Listen, can you talk now?
Sue: Well, actually, I'm going out in ten minutes. Is it important?
Max: Erm, no, not really. Can I call you back later?
Sue: Yeah, any time after eight is fine. I'll talk to you later, OK?
Max: OK, thanks. Bye.

2
Julia: Chris … Excuse me, have you got a moment?
Chris: Yes, of course.
Julia: Thanks. I wanted to ask you about the school play …

Julia: … well, the break's almost over, Chris. Thanks for your help.
Chris: Any time.
Julia: Thanks. See you at school tomorrow.
Chris: Yes, see you.

3
Simon: Peter! How are you? I haven't seen you for a long time.
Peter: I'm great, thanks.
Simon: Hey, are you doing anything now?
Peter: No, not really.
Simon: Have you got time for a coffee and a chat?
Peter: Sure, great idea …
Simon: … well, it was good talking to you, Peter.
Peter: Yeah, really nice.
Simon: Anyway … I'll text you some time.
Peter: Yeah, that would be nice. Take care.
Simon: You too. Bye.

39 Put the highlighted expressions from the conversations in 36 into the right groups.

Starting a conversation	Finishing a conversation
How are things?	I'll talk to you later.

138

Experiences

40 a How can you reply to the expressions in 37? In groups, think of ideas.

Example: A: *How are things?*   B: *Fine, thanks. / I'm great, thanks …*

b Compare your ideas with the responses in the conversations.

41 a Don't look at the conversations. Make sentences with these words.

1 Can / talk?
2 Are / doing / anything now?
3 Excuse / got / moment?
4 haven't / seen / long time
5 Have / got / time / a cup of coffee?
6 I'll talk / later
7 See / party
8 It / nice talking / you
9 I'll call / time
10 Thanks / help

b In pairs, take turns to say sentences 1–10 and reply.

42 Read the two situations.

Conversation 1

It's Saturday afternoon. You meet a former teacher of yours in a shopping centre.
1 Say hello and check your teacher remembers you.
2 Ask about your old school and talk about your new one.
3 Finish your conversation.

Conversation 2

It's Monday. You phone a friend to talk about your weekend.
1 Say hello and check your friend has time to talk.
2 Ask about your friend's weekend. Talk about your weekend.
3 Finish your conversation.

43 Have two conversations in A/B pairs.

- A, start conversation 1. Then, B, start conversation 2.

Example: *Hi, Masha, how are you? Have you got time for a chat?*

Self-assessment   ✓✓   ✓   ❕❕

- talk about experiences
- say what you've never done and always wanted to do
- talk about places you've been to
- find out information about things
- start and finish conversations

First of all, think about what you have learned up to now. Are you close to "I can do this well" or closer to "I need to work on this"?
Put a mark where you think you are at the moment. Then do the tasks and check your answers with the key on p. 188. Put another mark in a different colour where you see yourself now you've done the task.

Reading
- I can understand a blog post about experiences.
- I can understand vocabulary about health.
- I can understand sentences in the present perfect.

Reading 1 Read the following blog post by Mirabelle, a pharmacist who works for Médecins Sans Frontières in South Sudan. Some parts of the blog post are missing. Choose the correct part (A–K) for each gap (1–8). There are two extra parts that you should not use. Write your answers in the boxes provided. The first one (0) has been done for you.

Mirabelle and two of her colleagues at Yida

Fast-Paced Education in the Field

It only seems like yesterday that I arrived in Yida, (0) _____ been here three months and I'm ready for a break. I've learned so much in those three months – I've done a full inventory of the pharmacy's stock, I've placed an international order, and I've assisted in general vaccinations[1] and a measles[2] vaccination. Over the past three months (1) _____ lot about tropical diseases and treatment[3]. As a pharmacist, I care about drug quality and people getting these drugs. In Yida, our pharmacy is the only one that provides HIV treatment and so patients travel a long way to get here. But I've also dealt with three other diseases, which (2) _____:

Leprosy[4]: This is not a disease we study at school, so (3) _____ about it. I quickly read the Médecins Sans Frontières documentation to find out about the disease and see which drugs are recommended. There was not enough information, so I decided to search online for published literature. However, it was hard to find recent articles, so I used the World Health Organisation (WHO) website.

First, I needed to understand what causes the (4) _____. The good news is that it can be treated, if caught early, there'll be no damage to skin, muscles, or eyes. WHO has provided treatment free to any patient in the world with leprosy since 1995. The treatment for leprosy is given in (5) _____. Patients must be given lots of advice because the disease is very infectious. We also need to find out if they (6) _____. I'm glad all our patients can receive the treatment they need to cure this horrible disease.

Malaria: I can tell you all about the symptoms of malaria. But my knowledge of the treatment is not great. Again, this is not a disease (7) _____ before.

Measles: We are currently doing a mass measles vaccination campaign in the Yida Camp. The kids hate the injections, but it is for the best. I make sure that the vaccines are cold. This is my first vaccination campaign and I want to learn all the tricks it takes to vaccinate hundreds of kids in 45 °C heat.

Once (8) _____ you never forget it, so I'm thankful for this opportunity to learn about these diseases, not only in books, but in real life too …

---
[1] **vaccination:** an injection to prevent people from getting illnesses [2] **measles:** highly infectious virus, can be dangerous, patients show red spots all over their bodies. [3] **treatment:** the medicine you give a patient to cure him / her from a disease
[4] **leprosy:** chronic infectious disease caused by a bacteria

A	I have also learned a	0	H
B	you give them paracetamol	1	
C	three different tablets	2	
D	I had never seen before	3	
E	I had no idea	4	
F	have any allergies	5	
G	I've ever studied	6	
H	but I've already	7	
I	you've learned something	8	
J	disease and its symptoms		
K	a high temperature		

Writing ✓✓   ✓   !!

- I can write an email apologising.

Writing 2 You are a pharmacist and you should fly to Yida camp tomorrow to join the team at *Médecins Sans Frontières*. Due to a snowstorm, your flight has been cancelled. Write an email to Stephanie Miller, the Human Resources Coordinator.

In your email, you should:

- explain the situation.
- point out how you feel about it.
- state that you will be on the next available flight to South Sudan next Monday.

Write about 150 words.

Listening

- I can understand a conversation about hopes for the future.
- I can understand advice and recommendations.

Listening 3

You are going to listen to a conversation between Carmela and her school's career adviser, Mr Patel, about her plans for the future. First you will have 45 seconds to study the task below, then you will hear the recording twice. While listening, choose the correct answer (A, B, C or D) for each question (1–6). Put a cross (☒) in the correct box. The first one (0) has been done for you.

After the second listening, you will have 45 seconds to check your answers.

0 Carmela
- A knows what she wants to study.
- B doesn't want to go to university.
- C hasn't had any thoughts about her future.
- D wants to study at university. ☒

1 Carmela
- A doesn't like working with people.
- B wants to work in an office.
- C has already worked in a shop.
- D got the advice to work in an office by Mr Patel.

2 Carmela
- A thinks a degree is not necessary for getting a good job.
- B thinks a medical degree takes too long.
- C would like to be a doctor.
- D should be a doctor according to Mr Patel.

3 Carmela
- A likes science.
- B wants to study for quite some time.
- C likes blood and gore.
- D doesn't like sciences.

4 Carmela
- A already knows what to do to become a pharmacist.
- B should study certain subjects.
- C was told that choosing subjects is not important.
- D has already chosen which subjects to study.

5 Mr Patel
- A says it is easy to become a pharmacist.
- B thinks that all you need to become a pharmacist is a degree.
- C claims that anyone can join the Royal Pharmacists Association.
- D says that Carmela needs a degree to become a pharmacist.

6 Mr Patel
- A thinks that Carmela doesn't want her own pharmacy.
- B doesn't know if Carmela could have her own pharmacy.
- C doesn't think Carmela could open her own pharmacy.
- D hopes that Carmela wants to open her own pharmacy.

Language
- I can give health advice.
- I can describe hopes for the future.
- I can describe a great place (cathedral, statue, etc.).

Language 4

Health advice. Circle the correct word. The first one (0) has been done for you.

0 What are my (symptoms) / medicines ? Well, I've got a pain in my back.
1 Add this sachet[5] / tablet of powder to hot water and drink it.
2 I'm allergic / aching to cat hair.
3 He can't speak at the minute, he has a terribly ache / sore throat.
4 If you have a headache, you should take a painkiller / symptom .
5 I've got terrible toothache, I'm going to the dentist / doctor tomorrow morning.

5

Hopes for the future. Complete the sentences with the phrases from the boxes. The first one (0) has been done for you.

would like   am hoping to   ~~will~~   I'd like to   are going to   is hoping to

0 Liam has worked so hard this year, he _will_ pass his exams easily.
1 I have never been to China, but I _____ go in the next few years.
2 Karen and Steve _____ have a joint 16th birthday party.
3 Anil is studying really hard because he _____ get a place at an American university.
4 Where do I want to work? Ideally, _____ work for a big company, like Siemens.
5 I'm very happy here in Austria, but one day I _____ to move back to England.

6

Getting information and recommendations. Match the sentences 1–5 with the answers A–G. There are two extra answers that you should not use.

1 Have you ever been to Australia?
2 What was it like?
3 Did you see the Opera House?
4 If I could choose between Australia and New Zealand, which one should I go to?
5 Do you know how to get a visa?

A Well, they are both incredible. Go to both!
B You can fly there easily.
C Yes, I went to the Olympics in 2012.
D Oh, it was amazing. It's the most beautiful country I've ever seen.
E Well, you just have to go to the embassy[6].
F Good idea, I'll do that.
G The one in Sydney? Yeah, you can't miss it!

---

[5] **sachet:** small packet
[6] **embassy:** official representation of a country in a foreign country

Activities

Unit 1, exercise 9b

Manuel: Wow, Mona, it's really crowded here. Do you know many people here?

Mona: Well, yeah, let's see. Look over there, the woman with the long, dark hair – that's Dora Newfield, the head of the parents' association. She is a very nice lady. She was a kindergarten nurse before she moved here, so she handles all the pupils', teachers' and parents' requests very well.

Manuel: Oh, wow. So, I can contact her if I have a question, that's really good to know … and isn't she talking to Mr Larkins? Wasn't he your French teacher? He was always so strict, right? Your marks weren't so good, and you weren't happy about it.

Mona: Huh, no, he is from Scotland and teaches English. He is so much fun! Sometimes he speaks in a really strong accent to make us laugh!

Manuel: Hey, over there I can see Rob and Sally, the twins, behind Ms Newfield. Rob is drinking some juice. The twins were a year ahead of me and they were always together at our old school and here they are next to each other again; funny …

Mona: Where? … Oh, yes, I can see them now. I think they also organised the charity cinema evening last May. They were the ones who chose that interesting film about the teenagers who wanted to break out of their boring life, right?

Manuel: Yeah, I remember. That was great, wasn't it? Who are they talking to?

Mona: Alina, the new student representative. She is in the third form, just like me. She was elected four months ago. She is so stylish and always knows where to get the latest fashions!

Manuel: Well, yeah, I can see that!

Mona: Ah, and, look, to their left, isn't this Jakob from your class?

Manuel: Oh, yes, you're right. He is from Slovenia. He's a great baseball player. Last year his team won the local baseball championship. He frequently plays after school and also offers training lessons to younger pupils.

Mona: Great! I haven't met him yet, but I know who he is talking to: George, you know, the second form student who's also a tennis instructor.

Manuel: Wow. Behind George is Alexandra, Jakob's next-door neighbour.

Mona: Yeah, I know Alexandra. She is really nice. Wasn't she in the fitness centre last Saturday when we went swimming there?

Manuel: Hmm … you're right, that was her! Who is Alexandra talking to?

Mona: That's Ms Robson.

Manuel: Ah, yeah. Ms Robson was your maths teacher last year, right?

Mona: Ms Robson, yeah, she teaches maths. She's got this cool habit of looking at our faces after explaining something new. She always knows when we are confused, so she asks a lot of questions to figure out what exactly we didn't understand. I really like her!

Manuel: Oh and look! Behind Ms Robson is Erkan and Michelle.

Mona: Where? Oh, there. Is Erkan Michelle's boyfriend?

Manuel: Yes, they are together. They fell in love at our old school farewell party. Remember? Michelle told us about her great holidays in France and that her grandma is actually French.

Mona: Hmm, I can't remember… Anyway, Erkan looks handsome with his black hair. Isn't he Spanish?

Manuel: No, his parents are from Turkey. They were refugees when they came here. I think Erkan was only two years old then …

Mona: Oh. Well, what do you think about the open day event?

Manuel: It's cool … Hey, there's someone from my class. I'll go join him. See you later.

Mona: Yeah.

Unit 4, exercise 22b

Melinda: Hi everybody, we're going to draw a few lines and shapes. So get ready – and here we go!

Chester: Right! So everybody has a sheet of paper in front of them and a sharpened pencil or pen.
Now, draw a line in the middle from top to bottom. Then, on the right side of the line, draw a triangle towards the bottom of the page.

Melinda: Just above the triangle draw a circle of about the same size. Next, draw another line from left to right that cuts the line in the middle. But it should be above the circle, towards the top of the page.

Chester: Now two more instructions and you're done. Draw a circle as large as possible on the left-hand side of the line in the middle. The circle should be below the line that runs from left to right. And finally, write your name inside the larger circle.

Melinda: So … Do you think you got it right?

Unit 3, exercise 37

Student B

Conversation 1
Student A wants to book a holiday bungalow in Cornwall. You are the cook there and don't have all the information. The manager will be back tomorrow. Take a message.

Student B

Conversation 2
Your name: Martin (or Martine) Duplessis
Nationality: French
Your phone number: 0033 299 9867 9106
Email: DuplessisM@smail.fr You want to book the tree house hotel advertised on www.natureretreat.uk

Unit 4, exercise 6

Tell your partner:

1 name of invention
2 function of invention
3 name of inventor
4 date / place of invention

Student B
Spencer Silver, a chemist for 3M in Kentucky, US, accidentally found a glue which was just strong enough to hold paper to a surface. This was in 1968, but post-it notes weren't sold until 1974.

Unit 7, exercise 23

Student A

You work at the airline check-in desk.
Your name is _____.
Remember that you need to:
- check the passenger's passport.
- give the passenger a boarding pass.
- tell the passenger which gate to go to, and what time they are boarding.

Use the information on the 'Departures' board on p. 91.
Remember that boarding time is normally 40 minutes before departure time.

Unit 7, exercise 18

Student A

Conversation 1
You are at the train ticket window in Central Station in Colville. You want to go to Riverton, a nearby town. Ask questions to find out travel details. Buy a ticket.

Conversation 2
You work at the ticket window in a coach station in Albany City. Answer the customer's questions.
Coach ticket: price one way $25.60, day return $45.00, open return $52.75. Next one leaves in 15 minutes and takes 3 hours 45 minutes; change coaches once. Another one leaves in 30 minutes and takes 3 hours; it is direct. Coach number 613. It is outside, look for sign.

A
Activities

Unit 5, exercise 3c

Interviewer: So I'm joined by Katie Smith, manager of the new Whitewater shopping mall in North London. Welcome Katie!
Katie: Hi, thanks for having me.
Interviewer: Congratulations on the opening today, erm, what was the guiding philosophy behind the mall?
Katie: Well, the main idea was to have everything under one roof. And it's a very beautiful roof, by the way, which lets in lots of light.
Interviewer: If the sun is shining …
Katie: Right, that's not guaranteed here in North London! But we have lots of different shops here, for instance in our clothes shops, we have all the latest brands in menswear and womenswear, and we have shops that sell everything from sportswear to evening dresses.
Interviewer: So from sports shops to shops for prom dresses!
Katie: Absolutely, and we also have a lot of shoe shops, so you can find the right pair to match your clothes.
Interviewer: Can you buy accessories here too?
Katie: Of course, we have many retailers of jewellery and bags as well. These shops also sell many different kinds of suitcases, so you will be OK no matter how much luggage you take on holiday.
Interviewer: Do you have any entertainment outlets? What if I want to buy some video games?
Katie: Yes, we have many shops covering media, including music, video games and films. Most of them are on the first floor, so you can get there using the escalators.

Interviewer: How much demand is there for physical media in the internet age? I don't like DVDs. I think streaming is so much easier.
Katie: Well, of course, many people these days choose to stream their films, games and music, but we feel that there is still a demand for expertise. Our sales assistants have so much knowledge they can use to help our customers. Some information can only be found out by asking a person. For example, we also have a car show room where our experts can explain to you the differences between a Ferrari and a Lada.
Interviewer: Oh really, that's great. Well, I know I'd rather have a Ferrari than a Lada. How many customers do you expect each week?
Katie: Our estimates vary, but I can say that we expect that much of our business will be at weekends.
Interviewer: What about restaurants? Can I get some food here?
Katie: Yes of course, we have lots of restaurants catering to different tastes, such as Indian, Thai and Italian.
Interviewer: What about Vietnamese? I prefer Vietnamese to Thai.
Katie: Actually no, we don't have any Vietnamese restaurants, but we have almost everything else. There's not much we don't have. We also have an organic candy store that sells everything from vegan chocolate to sugar free lollipops. I like them because they are not so sweet.

Unit 5, exercise 24

book¹ [bʊk] noun
1 a set of pages with writing on them fastened together in a cover: *I've just read a really good book.*
2 a set of pages fastened together in a cover and used for writing on: *an address book*
book² [bʊk] verb
to arrange to use or do something at a time in the future: *I've booked a hotel room.* ▪ *We've booked a trip to Spain for next month.*

match¹ [mætʃ] noun (pl. matches)
1 a sports competition in which two people or teams compete against each other:
a football match
2 a thin, wooden stick which makes fire when you rub one end of it against a rough surface: *a box of matches*
match² [mætʃ] verb
If two things match, they are the same colour or type: *I can't find anything to match my green shirt.* ▪ *Your socks don't match.*

Unit 5, exercise 31

Student B

You need to get to the bookstore to pick up the audiobook they have reserved for you. Then you'd like to look at some elegant clothing for the school ball next month. Shoes for that occasion would be nice too. You're also looking for a present for your friend who is really into rock climbing.
For lunch you'd like Chinese food.

A Activities

Unit 3, exercise 31c

Student A

Hazelwood, Dublin 9, North Dublin City

- share with four other students (but own bathroom)
- television, phone, internet
- central heating not included
- washing machine
- dishwasher
- near bus stop to city centre
- parking
- no smoking
- visits 9 a.m. – 1 p.m., weekends only

Unit 6, exercise 4

Unit 7, exercise 4a

Monday
12.30: meeting school Mag. Editor
5 p.m.: school choir
6.30 p.m.: meet John Blue Note Café

WEDNESDAY
4.30 p.m.: dentist (ouch!)

THURSDAY
4 p.m.: shopping with Mia
– b-day present for Gillian

FRIDAY
04.15 sharp: see Dane Court people off in front of main hall
7 p.m.: Gillian's party

TUESDAY
3rd lesson: maths test!!!!
5.30 p.m.: meet Dane Court people, show them town

Unit 7, exercise 23

Student B

You work for airport security.
Your name is _____.

Remember that you have to:
- check the passenger's passport.
- X-ray all hand luggage.
- X-ray shoes.
- check for laptops.
- look in the passenger's bags.

A
Activities

Unit 7, exercise 18

Student B

Conversation 1
You work at the train ticket window in Central Station in Colville. Answer the customer's questions.
Train ticket: price one way $11.00, day return $19.00, open return $25.00. Next one leaves in 15 minutes and takes 1 hour 10 minutes; change trains once. Another one leaves in one hour and takes 45 minutes; it is direct. Go to platform 5.

Conversation 2
You are in Albany City at the coach station. You want to go to another city, Kenover, by coach. Ask questions to find out travel details. Buy a ticket.

Unit 7, exercise 23

Student C

You are the passenger.
Your name is _____.
- Where are you going? Choose a destination from the 'Departures' board on p. 91.
- How many pieces of hand luggage do you have?
- Do you have a laptop in your hand luggage?

You need to go to check-in first, then go through security.

Unit 7, exercise 30

on holiday to France with some friends → get bus and ferry to France → have something to eat in ferry restaurant → fall asleep → wake up in ferry restaurant → my friends not there → ferry empty → at Calais in France → run to bus → too late → see bus driving off ferry … ?

Think of a good ending for Jack's story. Imagine you are Jack. Prepare to tell the story. Think about:
- the past simple of the verbs (go → went).
- where to use the (get the bus; the ferry to France).
- where to use storytelling expressions (Later, …).

Unit 6, exercise 22

Student B

1 $\dfrac{(5 + 3) \times 2}{(5 - 3) \times 2} =$

2 $\dfrac{1}{2} + \dfrac{1}{8} =$

3 $\sqrt{(114 + 7)} =$

4 $[(6 - 2) \times 8] \div 4 =$

5 $\dfrac{25}{5} + 2^3 =$

6 $10 - 2 \times 4 + 2 \times 5 =$

Activities   A

Unit 8, exercise 27

http://www.nps.gc.ca/mauricie

LA MAURICIE Canada

Accommodation

Camping du Parc ***

We welcome you to Camping Du Parc, a friendly campsite close to La Mauricie National Park in Québec, Canada. We offer a quiet site under the trees, a sky full of stars and a good campfire.

On site: a nice little beach, playgrounds, a safe cycling path.

Nearby: some golf clubs, many fishing spots, in the heart of La Mauricie.

Au Joyeux Druide, Hotel and Art Gallery ***

Our house is on a hill by the Shawinigan River. Here you'll find comfortable rooms, a games room, and good home-grown food. We're also a gallery of modern art.

3573, Rue Bellevue, Shawinigan (Québec)

Le Baluchon ****

Our inn is in a beautiful location near islands, waterfalls, hills and a forest. We offer you comfort, a healthy break and excellent food.

3550, Chemin des Trembles, Saint-Paulin (Québec)

Chalet Joel Migneault **

Rent this warm quiet chalet in the heart of nature on Lake Chrétien.

On site: hiking, mountain biking, volleyball, swimming, canoeing, kayaking and much more.

496, rue des Peupliers, Saint-Gerard-des-Laurentides (Québec)

Outdoor activities

From tree to tree

An extraordinary family activity! Come and experience this new treetop adventure, unique in Mauricie. Climb trees and cross rope bridges on our specially designed course.

Open: May to October, reservations preferable.

Admission: children: from $16; adults: $25.95; special rates for families and groups.

Riding Centre, Saint-Georges

Come and enjoy our horses with a qualified instructor. Ride alone, in a group or as a family. Ponies available for children. Riding lessons for children and adults.

Open: all year

Rates: adults: $10 / hour; children: $5 / hour; special family and group rates

Black bear observation

Watch for bears safely with our experienced guides. Learn what to do if you see a bear in the forest! Over 95% of people see bears.

Open: June to September, at sunset.

Rates: adults: $20; students: $10; special family and group rates.

National Park of Canada, Mauricie

A paradise for outdoor lovers with 536 km^2 of lakes and forests. Canoeing and hiking in summer and cross-country skiing in winter are the main activities.

Open: May 12 to October 15, 7 a.m. to 10 p.m.

Admission: $3.50 to $7 per person.

Unit 3, exercise 31b

Student B

Oxmantown Road, Dublin 7, North Dublin City

- one person, no sharing
- television
- no phone or internet
- central heating included
- washing machine
- no dishwasher
- no smoking
- no parking
- visits after 8 p.m.

Grammar reference and practice

Intro

Subject pronouns and possessive adjectives

Bedeutung

Besitzanzeigende Pronomen (*possessive adjectives*) drücken aus, dass jemandem etwas gehört. Sie werden auch in Verbindung mit Namen, Adressen und Telefonnummern verwendet.

Form

Subjektpronomen	Besitzanzeigende Pronomen
I'm Anna.	My name's Anna.
Are you Maria? Are you Maria and Stefan?	What's your name? What are your names?
He's a student.	This is his phone number.
She's from Korea.	What's her address?
It's a beautiful cat.	What's its name?
We're from Italy.	Our home town is Milan.
They're from Norway.	What are their names?

Practice

Complete the sentences with the words in the box above.

1 "What's _your_ name?" – "I'm Anna. Nice to meet you."
2 They're from Japan but _____ children were born in Europe.
3 What languages do _____ speak, and what's your first language?
4 Her name's Astrid and _____ 's from Mexico.
5 _____ name's Sameh and he's from Egypt.
6 We only speak English but _____ children speak three languages.
7 "What's your phone number?" – "Well, _____ mobile number is 07786-330074."
8 _____ name is Fay and she's from Australia.

Unit 1

Possessive 's and s'

Bedeutung

Ein Nomen mit besitzanzeigendem 's hat dieselbe Bedeutung wie ein besitzanzeigendes Pronomen (*her*, *his*, *their* …):
James is Isobel's husband. Alasdair is her son.
Isobel is Alasdair's mother. Rob is his brother.
James is Alasdair and Rob's father. Isobel is their mother.

Form

Singular

Isobel + 's = Isobel's husband
my friend + 's = my friend's name
Alasdair and Rob + 's = Alasdair and Rob's family

Plural

In diesem Fall wird kein zusätzliches *s* hinzugefügt:
parents + *'* = *my parents' house*

Practice

1 Singular. Add 's to the correct word in each sentence.

1 Are you Rob brother? — _Rob's_
2 This is Sally, my brother girlfriend. _____
3 Are you Lucia English teacher? _____
4 My friend boss is really nice. _____
5 Maria Teresa family is from Madrid. _____
6 What's that man name? _____
7 Is that your sister bag? _____
8 My cat name is Alfie. _____

2 Plural. Circle the correct word.
1 This is my   parents / parents'   new car.
2 His   parent's / parents   live in Kyoto.
3 Hi. Are you   Charles / Charles's   father?
4 Natasha and Anna are my   sisters / sisters' .
5 Her   grandparents / grandparents'   flat isn't very big.
6 What are your   colleagues / colleagues'   names?

Checking information

Bedeutung

Zum Überprüfen von Annahmen können negative Frageformen mit dem besitzanzeigenden 's verwendet werden.

Form

Isn't Carl your neighbour's gardener? Yes, he is my neighbour's gardener.

Practice

Form the question to check the information.

1 Greg and Sue / from Brighton?

  Aren't Greg and Sue from Brighton?

2 Erkan / Michelle's boyfriend?
3 Susan and Mary / best friends?
4 The English teacher / from Newcastle?
5 The bicycles / in the cellar?
6 Grandma / at the hairdresser's?
7 Robert and Mona / on holiday in Greece right now?

be past: was, were

Bedeutung

Die Vergangenheitsform von *be* (*was*, *were*) wird verwendet, um über Dinge zu sprechen, die in der Vergangenheit geschahen, d. h. abgeschlossen sind.
When I *was* 19, I *was* a student.
In 2018, Leslie and I *were* classmates. Beth *was* in Dallas yesterday.

Form

Kurzformen:

⊖ was**n't** = was not / were**n't** = were not

Practice

Add *was*, *wasn't*, *were* and *weren't* to the correct places in the sentences.
1 After school he ∨ an accountant for ten years.   *was*
2 Excuse me, you at Wennington College in 2011?
3 "How do you know Carl?" "We classmates at the same school for a couple of years."
4 "Mario and Lucia at the party last night?" "No, they're on holiday."
5 I in Athens last Friday. It's a really interesting city.
6 "Where Mr Gomez at ten o'clock this morning?" "I don't know."
7 "How your exam?" "OK. It very difficult."
8 Alex and Paul at the same school, but they in the same class.

Adjectives and adverbs

Bedeutung

Adjektive geben Informationen über ein Nomen: der GEGENSTAND / die PERSON ist wichtig:

A *difficult* exercise

A *new* type of school

In Verbindung mit *to be* (= am / is / are / was / were etc.) werden immer Adjektive benutzt, auch wenn sie nach dem Nomen stehen. Sie beschreiben, wie etwas ist:

Our teacher was a *young* woman.

The German lessons were *difficult*.

Adverbien werden mit *-ly* gebildet und können drei verschiedene Wortarten beschreiben: a) ein Verb, b) ein Adjektiv, c) ein anderes Adverb.

Grammar reference and practice

a Adverbien beschreiben ein Verb: Die HANDLUNG ist wichtig

I could easily get there in ten minutes.

He wrote slowly in the German lessons.

b Adverbien beschreiben Adjektive:

The train is terribly slow.

She went to a really modern school.

c Adverbien können andere Adverbien beschreiben:

I wrote extremely slowly at school.

They scream at each other really loudly sometimes.

Practice

Circle the correct word.

1. Their new offices in the city look very impressive / impressively .
2. Airline food is never as good / well as it looks.
3. He reacted calm / calmly when I told him the bad news.
4. What we need is a total / totally motivated team.
5. Did you have a well / good flight?
6. They had to walk very careful / carefully over the old bridge.
7. I think it is an interesting / interestingly idea to live in a tree house.
8. We saw a hilarious / hilariously funny movie yesterday.
9. My grandma is extreme / extremely slow in the kitchen, but her food is excellent.

Unit 2

Present simple

Bedeutung

Die *Present Simple Tense* wird verwendet, um über Fakten zu sprechen (sind generell gültig), eine allgemeine Aussage zu machen oder über Gewohnheiten zu reden.
James is in his office. It's 8.30. Pierre lives in France. Rob and Adam work in the same office.

Verwenden Sie die Gegenwartsform von be (am, is, are), um Aussagen zu machen über:

- **who (wer):** *I'm Rob. / He's a student. / They're my friends.*
- **what (was):** *It's my bag. / They're my books.*
- **where (wo):** *My bag's in my car. / The books are here.*
- **how old (wie alt):** *I'm fifteen.*
- **times and dates (Uhrzeiten und Daten):** *It's 8.30. / It's 1 October 2012.*
- **the weather (das Wetter):** *It's hot. / It's sunny.*

Form

to be im *Present Simple*

➕	➖
I'm Rob.	I'm not Rob.
You're late.	You aren't late.
He's a teacher.	He isn't a student.
She's a doctor.	She isn't a journalist.
It's my bag.	It isn't my bag.
We're friends.	We aren't brothers.
They're Spanish.	They aren't Brazilian.

❓	✅ / ❌
Am I late?	Yes, I am. / No, I'm not.
Are you from Spain?	Yes, you are. / No, you aren't.
Is he a teacher?	Yes, he is. / No, he isn't.
Is she a doctor?	Yes, she is. / No, she isn't.
Is it your bag?	Yes, it is. / No, it isn't.
Are we late? / Are you her brother?	Yes, we are. / No, we aren't.
Are they here?	Yes, they are. / No, they aren't.

Andere Verben im *Present Simple*
NOTE: he, she, it + s

➕	➖
I know Rob.	I don't know Rob.
You sing in the same band as Rob.	You don't sing in the same band as Rob.
He works in Denver.	He doesn't work in Denver.
She has a green car.	She doesn't have a green car.
It feels like summer today.	It doesn't feel like summer today.
We get up at 7 o'clock every day.	We don't get up at 7 o'clock every day.
You live in the new skyscraper downtown.	You don't live in the new skyscraper downtown.
They usually go on holiday in August.	They don't usually go on holiday in August.

❓	✅ / ❌
Do I know Rob?	Yes, I do. / No, I don't.
Do you sing in the same band as Rob?	Yes, you do. / No, you don't.
Does he work in Denver?	Yes, he does. / No, he doesn't.
Does she have a green car?	Yes, she does. / No, she doesn't.
Does it feel like summer today?	Yes, it does. / No, it doesn't.
Do we get up at 7 o'clock every day?	Yes, we do. / No, we don't.
Do you live in the new skyscraper downtown?	Yes, you do. / No, you don't.
Do they usually go on holiday in August?	Yes, they do. / No, they don't.

Present simple questions: Fügen Sie *do* oder *does* hinzu, um eine Frage im *Present Simple* zu stellen.

Present simple negative sentences: (Verneinungen): Fügen Sie *not* hinzu, um die Verneinung im *Present Simple* zu bilden.

Kurzformen:

⊖ do**n't** = do not / does**n't** = does not

Die meisten Verben	Verben, die mit einem Konsonanten + -y enden
I work in an office. You work here. He / She work**s** there. We work at home. They work for a big company.	I study French. You study a lot. He / She stud**ies** every day. We study on Fridays. They study medicine.
Verben, die mit *-s, -z, -ch, -sh*, oder *-x* enden	**Unregelmäßige Verben**
I miss you. You miss me. He miss**es** his girlfriend. We miss you. They miss us.	I have a cat. You have three sisters. She ha**s** a new car. We have a big family. They have a brother.
catch → catch**es** watch → watch**es**	go → go**es** do → do**es**

Practice

1 Complete the conversations with the correct form of *be* in the present simple.

1 "Where _are_ you from?" – "I _____ from Australia."
2 "Vigo _____ in Portugal."
3 "No, it _____ . It _____ in Spain."
4 "_____ you Rob's classmate?"
5 "No, I _____ . I _____ his brother."
6 "Sorry, _____ I late?" – "Yes, you _____ . Forty-five minutes!"
7 "How old _____ your children?"
8 "_____ you interested in yoga?" – "Yes, we _____ ."
9 "_____ this your coffee?" – "No. Maybe it _____ Jo's."
10 "Excuse me, where _____ the cinema?" – "Sorry, we _____ from around here."

2 Complete the sentences with the correct form of the verb in brackets.

1 When we're away from home, I _miss_ (miss) my parents. My friend _____ (miss) his bed.
2 My mum and dad _____ (speak) three languages. I only _____ (speak) one.
3 I _____ (have) two rabbits and my sister _____ (have) five.
4 In the summer we usually _____ (stay) with our friends in Portugal. They sometimes _____ (stay) with us too.
5 My friends _____ (live) in the same town as me, but my sister and her husband _____ (live) abroad.
6 I _____ (study) Japanese, but my friend Simon _____ (study) French.
7 My brother _____ (want) to travel in Europe. My friends _____ (want) to travel in South America.
8 My mum _____ (cook) dinner at the weekend. We all _____ (cook) during the week.

3 Put the words in the correct order to make questions.

1 you / in / this neighbourhood / Do / work ?
Do you work in this neighbourhood?
2 you / Do / near here / live ?
3 does / Where / live / your brother ?
4 What / do / play / sports / you ?
5 you / in the evening / watch TV / Do / always ?
6 she / go on holiday / Where / does / usually ?

4 Complete the sentences with *don't* or *doesn't*.

1 They _don't_ work here. They're here for the meeting.
2 "Where's the café?" – "Sorry, I _____ know. I'm new too."
3 Roberto _____ live in Venice. He lives in Rome.
4 I'm sorry, I _____ eat seafood. It makes me ill.
5 Can you help us? We _____ know where to go.
6 My sister's at home a lot. She _____ have a job.

153

G Grammar reference and practice

5 Mixed exercise: Present simple

a Fill in the gaps below using the words in the boxes. Make sure you add –s for the 3rd person singular.

enjoy   travel   go (2 x)   sell   open
work   meet   play   have

1 I _____ the window, before I go to sleep.
2 Most people _____ an eight-hour day.
3 I _____ to the cinema twice a week.
4 Christa sometimes _____ shopping in the evening.
5 We nearly always _____ golf at the weekends.
6 Jürgen and Leo _____ cars for Ford.
7 Carl _____ in an office.
8 I _____ to school by underground.
9 I usually _____ my friends at the weekend.
10 Alfred _____ holidays.

b Use the words from 5a to complete the questions.
1 _____ Alfred _____ holidays?
2 _____ Mark usually _____ swimming at the weekend?
3 _____ Mark _____ the window before he goes to sleep?
4 _____ most people _____ an eight-hour day?
5 _____ he _____ in an office?
6 _____ they usually _____ golf at the weekend?
7 _____ they _____ cars for Ford?
8 _____ Michelle always _____ by underground?
9 _____ Henry _____ his friends at the weekend?
10 _____ Susan _____ to the cinema twice a week?

a, an, some

Bedeutung

a / *an* (= ein/e) wird mit Nomen im Singular verwendet um ein Element aus einer Menge zu bezeichnen.
Can I have a cup of coffee, please? Would you like an orange? I will be home in an hour. (das "h" von hour wird nicht ausgesprochen, daher ist der erste Buchstabe ein Vokal)

Das Wort *some* (= einige, etwas) wird häufig in Verbindung mit zählbaren Nomen im Plural verwendet, wenn eine genaue Mengenangabe unwichtig ist. *Some* verwendet man auch bei unzählbaren Nomen im Singular.

Can I have some oranges, please? Can I have some books, please? Can I have some orange juice?

Form

Verwenden Sie *a* vor Wörtern, die mit einem Konsonanten (b, c, d, …) beginnen: *Can I have a newspaper, please?* Wenn das darauffolgende Wort mit einem Vokal (a, e, i, o, u) am Beginn ausgesprochen wird, verwendet man *an*: *Can I have an apple, please? I will be home in an hour.*

Practice

Add *a*, *an* or *some* to the sentences.
1 I live in Toronto. It's ∨ great city.   *a*
2 I really want new boots.
3 Would you like cup of coffee after your dinner?
4 I want to get good job.
5 My flat has spare room.
6 My home town has good clubs.
7 I want to go to café for lunch.
8 I'm architect.
9 Could you bring biscuits?
10 It's old computer, but I like it.

_____

Unit 3

Subject and object pronouns

Bedeutung

Pronomen können verwendet werden, um über Personen, Dinge und Aktivitäten zu sprechen.
My grandparents are great. I love them so much.
Where's Susan? Is she here?
I like watching TV. It's fun.

Grammar reference and practice

Form

Subjektpronomen	Objektpronomen
I	me
you	you
he	him
she	her
it	it
we	us
they	them

Subjektpronomen stehen in einem Satz meistens **vor** dem **Verb**.
I like watching TV.

Objektpronomen folgen **nach** den **Verben** und **Präpositionen**.
I love them.
I like talking to my boyfriend and watching TV with him.

Practice

Circle the correct word.

1. He / him   likes fishing in the sea with his friends.
2. Is   she / her   busy now?
3. Bob can meet   we / us   at 5.00 tomorrow evening.
4. She / her   is a really nice person.
5. I like talking to   he / her .
6. We / us   play football at the weekend.
7. My cat doesn't like my boyfriend, but she loves   I / me .
8. Are   they / them   friends or just classmates?
9. Money doesn't make   you / we   happy.
10. I don't read newspapers. I don't like   they / them .

Adverbs of frequency

Bedeutung

Adverbs of frequency geben an, wie oft man etwas tut oder wie oft etwas geschieht. Die Bandbreite geht von nie (*never*) bis immer (*always*).

100%	always
90%	usually
80%	frequently
70%	often
50%	sometimes
30%	occasionally
10%	seldom
5%	rarely
0%	never

Form

Adverbs of frequency stehen zwischen Subjekt und Prädikat (Verbphrase): *I often go swimming.*
Wenn die Verbphrase nur aus *am, is, are, was, were* besteht, sind die *adverbs of frequency* NACH dem Verb:
Anna is usually outdoors with her dog Benny.

Besteht die Verbphrase aus mehreren Verben, sind die *adverbs of frequency* NACH dem ersten Verb:
Bob can often meet his friends because they all live in the same area.
Damien will never be a couch potato.
Chin-Mae doesn't often read books. She is too busy working.

Adverbs of frequency können auch am Beginn des Satzes stehen und werden dadurch besonders betont:
Occasionally I go to school by bike.

Sentence structure

Die Struktur in englischen Sätzen ist weniger flexibel als im Deutschen, d.h. es gibt eine fixe Abfolge von Adverbphrasen im Satz.
Zusätzlich zu *adverbs of frequency* gibt es auch *adverbs of manner* (Art und Weise), *place* (Ortsangabe) and *time* (Zeitangabe).

1. *Adverbs of manner* beantworten die Frage: Wie? – HOW?
2. *Adverbs of place* beantworten die Frage: Wo? – WHERE?
3. *Adverbs of time* beantworten die Frage: Wann? – WHEN?
4. *Adverbs of frequency* beantworten die Frage: Wie oft? – HOW OFTEN?

Nachdem es fixe Stellen im Satz gibt, an denen Adverbphrasen stehen können, ergibt sich dieses **Grundmuster**:

A (time)   S   A   V   O   A (manner, place, time)

On Sundays Damien often does parkour in his neighbourhood. (Where?)
Damien worked out hard last Sunday. (How? When?)

Steht mehr als eine Adverbphrase am Satzende, sind sie in dieser Reihenfolge: *1 manner, 2 place, 3 time*.
Zum Betonen einer bestimmten Information – und auch für besseren Stil – kann man das letzte Adverb an den Satzanfang stellen:

Damien often does parkour in his neighbourhood on Sundays. or
On Sundays Damien often does parkour in his neighbourhood. (WANN? – *on Sundays* – wird besonders betont.)

Practice

Change the order of the words to make a correct sentence.
1. not / things / usually / forget / do / I .
2. in the / out / often / evening / we / go .
3. factory / a / 24 hours / day / works / this .
4. never / I / name / can / his / remember .
5. always / the weekend / flat / cleans / at /the / my mother .
6. and / seldom / out / during / Greg / the / week / Harry / go .

Unit 4

Past simple

Bedeutung

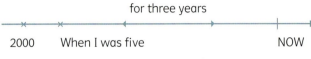

Verwenden Sie das *Past Simple*, um über Ereignisse zu sprechen, die in der Vergangenheit geschahen und abgeschlossen sind.
Pavel made the Stereobelt in 1972.
My family moved from Nigeria to Scotland when I was five.
I lived in France for three years.
He travelled to Iceland 14 years ago.

Typische Phrasen, die mit der *Past Simple* verwendet werden sind: *last week …, in 2018, six months ago, when I was …, by the end of 2016 …,* diese Phrasen können am Satzanfang oder am Satzende stehen.
Last week I got a new puppy.
I got a new puppy last week.

Form

Die Form des *Past Simple* ist für alle Personen dieselbe.
I went to the cinema last night. / We moved to Scotland.

Negative Sätze werden mit dem Hilfsverb *didn't* gebildet, da *didn't* bereits in der **Past Tense** ist, ist das **Verb im Infinitiv**.
I didn't go to the cinema last night. NICHT: *didn't went* – 2 x Past Tense ist zu viel.
We didn't move to Scotland.

Wenn *was, were* alleine die Verbphrase bilden, wird die Verneinung nur mit *wasn't, weren't* gebildet. Es ist KEIN "*didn't*" notwendig.
She was very tired yesterday. → *She wasn't very tired yesterday.*

Fragesätze werden mit dem Hilfszeitwort *did* gebildet. Das Subjekt ist zwischen *did* und dem **Verb im Infinitiv**.
Did you go to the cinema last night? Did you move to Scotland?
Yes, I did. / No, I didn't.

Wenn *was, were* alleine die Verbphrase bilden, wird der Fragesatz nur mit *was, were* vor dem Subjekt gebildet. Es ist KEIN "*did*" notwendig.
She was very tired yesterday. → *Was she very tired yesterday?*
He was lazy on Sunday. → *When was he lazy?*

Manche Verben sind im *Past Simple* regelmäßig und enden mit -ed.

move / moved   listen / listened   like / liked

Einige Verben sind im *Past Simple* unregelmäßig.

go / went   make / made   buy / bought   have / had

→ Siehe *Irregular verbs* auf S. 178.

Practice

1 Complete the conversations with *did* or *didn't*.

1 "_____ you have a nice weekend?"
"Well, no, I _____. It was terrible."

2 "When _____ you buy that mobile phone?"
"I _____ buy it. My sister gave it to me."

3 "_____ you see your friends last weekend?"
"Yes, I _____. We had a great time."

4 "How much _____ your laptop cost?"
"I _____ pay a lot – about $150. I bought it from a friend."

5 "Who _____ you see at the party?"
"I _____ go. I stayed at home."

6 "_____ you like the film?" "Well, the story was OK, but I _____ like the actors."

2a Put these sentences into the past simple tense.

1 Tom holds her hand.
2 Martha buys oranges.
3 He thinks that she is stupid.
4 The telephone rings.
5 My sister rides the bus to work.
6 The manager wears a blue jacket.
7 I hear a noise in the dark room.
8 She gives him her bike.
9 She puts the bag on the table.

2b Turn the above sentences into negative sentences.
1 Tom **did not hold** her hand.

2c Turn the sentences in 2a into questions.
1 **Did** Tom **hold** her hand?

G

Grammar reference and practice

Unit 5

Countable and uncountable nouns

Bedeutung

Zählbare Nomen gibt es im Singular und Plural. Verwenden Sie **a** oder **an** für zählbare Nomen im Singular. Nicht zählbare Nomen haben keine Pluralform. Verwenden Sie weder **a** noch **an** in Verbindung mit nicht zählbaren Nomen.

a book   some books   some pasta
(some pastas / a pasta)

five potatoes   some potatoes   a chicken   some chicken

Form

Zählbar	Nicht zählbar
How many lettuces would you like? I'd like a lettuce / one lettuce. I'd like six carrots / some carrots. I don't eat a lot of carrots.	How much lettuce would you like? – Have some lettuce in your sandwich. I'd like a lot of lettuce.

Practice

1 Complete the sentences with *a*, *an*, *some*, *much* or *many*.

1 I eat _____ orange every day.
2 Would you like _____ pasta?
3 Can I have _____ apple?
4 I had _____ toast for breakfast this morning.
5 I'd like _____ biscuits.
6 How _____ meat do you eat?
7 How _____ eggs would you like?

2 (Circle) the correct word.

1 How much / many cheese do you usually buy every week?
2 How much / many onions would you like?
3 How much / many coffees did you drink yesterday?
4 How much / many fruit do you usually eat every day?
5 How much / many onions did you buy?
6 How much / many chocolate do you eat?

Singular and plural nouns

Bedeutung

Verwenden Sie die Pluralform, um über mehrere Personen oder Dinge zu sprechen.
I have a car. My friend has two cars.

Form

	Singular (ein/e)	Plural (zwei und mehr)
an die meisten Nomen wird **-s** angehängt.	thing, shop	things, shops
an Nomen, die mit -sh, -ch, -ss, -x, -z oder -s enden, wird **-es** angehängt.	dish, boss	dishes, bosses
Für Nomen, die mit einem Konsonanten + y enden, gilt: y → -ies.	company, city	companies, cities
unregelmäßige Pluralformen	person, man, woman, child	people, men, women, children

Practice

Complete the sentences with the plurals of these words.

~~country~~   city   school   newspaper   sister
email   woman   party   friend

1 How many *countries* are there in South America?
2 I send _____ to my boyfriend every day.
3 I have three _____ and one brother.
4 I don't like big _____ . I prefer small towns.
5 When do you usually meet your _____ ?
6 I don't read _____ . I don't like bad news.
7 Ask the _____ over there. They work in this shop.
8 All the _____ in my town have good teachers.
9 I like dancing, but I hate going to _____ .

Grammar reference and practice

Unit 6

Present progressive

Bedeutung

Das *Present Progressive* (die Verlaufsform der Gegenwart) wird verwendet, um über gegenwärtige Aktivitäten zu sprechen: Dinge, die jetzt gerade geschehen oder unmittelbar bevorstehen.
I *can't talk* now. *I'm planning* my presentation for tomorrow. (jetzt) *They're working* quite hard these days. (zurzeit)

Das *Present Progressive* wird manchmal auch *Present Continuous* genannt.

Form

be + verb + -ing
I'm going to a party now. She's / He's planning a holiday abroad. You're / We're / They're working quite hard these days.
I'm not feeling well. She / He isn't working at the moment. He's not working … You / We / They aren't writing a report. You're not writing …
Am I working late tonight? Where are we / they / you going? Are you studying English? Is he working hard? Are they designing a website?

Kurzformen:
Sie können *are not* und *is not* wie folgt zusammenziehen:
He's *not* working at the moment. They're *not* having a sale this week. No, he's *not*. / No, they're *not*.

Practice

Complete the sentences with present progressive verbs.

1 "I'm a student." – „Really? What / you / study?"

   What are you studying?

2 "I / go / out now. Bye." – "Bye. Have a nice time."
3 "Kevin, what / you / do ?"
4 "I / talk / to someone on the phone."
5 "Is this a good time, Mary?" – "Sorry, no. I / make / dinner."
6 "Can I use the computer?" – "Sorry, but I / use / it at the moment."
7 "He / not / work / at the moment. He / do / a course in marketing."

Unit 7

Present tense: arrangements and timetables

Bedeutung

Das *Present Progressive* wird auch verwendet, um über zukünftige Vereinbarungen zu sprechen – oft in Verbindung mit einer Zeitangabe. Es sind dies meist fixe Arrangements in der nahen Zukunft.
I'm meeting Jon for coffee this evening. We're *flying* to San Francisco tomorrow.

Form

→ Siehe *Present Progressive* S. 170.

Present simple for information in a timetable
Für Informationen in offiziellen (Fahr-) Plänen wird das *Present Simple* verwendet und drückt eine Handlung in der Zukunft aus.
My bus *leaves* at 3.00 p.m. tomorrow.

Practice

1 Complete each sentence with the correct verb in the *Present Progressive*.

see	go (2x)	have (2x)	arrive	give	get (2x)
	meet	work	leave (2x)		

1 We _____ to Ireland for a language week.
2 Dad's train _____ from platform 6.
3 Sorry, I can't come. I _____ late tonight.
4 I think he _____ a taxi to the airport tomorrow.
5 I _____ a film with some friends tonight.
6 Professor Hunt _____ a lecture on Matisse this afternoon.
7 We _____ Vienna to travel to Hamburg tomorrow.
8 We _____ a meeting on Thursday afternoon, so don't forget to come.
9 I _____ to the hairdresser's this Saturday.
10 They _____ the 10.30 coach to Seattle.
11 I _____ a party on Friday. Can you come?

2 a Put the words in order to make questions.

1 after / are / class / going / Where / you ?
   Where are you going after class?
2 are / getting up / tomorrow / What time / you ?
3 Are / friends / seeing / tonight / you ?
4 are / birthday / How / next / spending / you / your ?
5 are / at / doing / the weekend / What / you ?
6 Are / having / a holiday / in / six months / the next / you ?
7 you / next week / doing / are / What ?
8 soon / you / for food / Are / going / shopping ?

2 b Ask and answer the questions in 2a.

Articles

Bedeutung

Verwenden Sie *a / an* (unbestimmter Artikel), wenn Sie zum ersten Mal über eine Person oder eine Sache sprechen.
Is there a post office on this street?

Verwenden Sie *the* (bestimmter Artikel), wenn der/die Zuhörer/in weiß, über welche Person oder Sache Sie sprechen.
Zum Beispiel:
Der/Die Zuhörer/in kennt die Person oder Sache, weil bereits zuvor darüber gesprochen wurde.
We've got two cars, a Fiat and a Honda. We use the Fiat to get around the city.

Der/Die Zuhörer/in weiß aus der Situation heraus Bescheid.
Can you close the door, please?

Der/Die Zuhörer/in kennt die Person oder Sache, weil diese einzigartig ist (auf der Welt oder in der betreffenden Situation).
The sun is really bright today.

Aus diesem Grund wird *the* oft in Verbindung mit Ordinalzahlen und Superlativen verwendet, da es nur eine/n „Erste/n" oder eine/n „Beste/n" gibt.
The first floor … The best café … The last time …

Verwenden Sie **keinen Artikel**, wenn Sie allgemein über Dinge sprechen. Man spricht in diesem Fall auch von einem *Nullartikel* (zero article).
I don't like coffee. the coffee
Bananas are my favourite fruit. The bananas …

Form

Sie können *a / an* vor zählbaren Nomen im Singular verwenden.
She's got a boy and a girl.

Verwenden Sie *the* vor
- zählbaren Nomen im Singular: *She's got a boy and girl. The boy's thirteen and the girl's ten.*
- zählbaren Nomen im Plural: *The shops are closed today.*
- nicht zählbaren Nomen: *Have you got the luggage?*

Verwenden Sie *the* nicht in Verbindung mit Possessivpronomen.
This is my uncle. The my uncle

Ein *Nullartikel* kann verwendet werden vor
- zählbaren Nomen im Plural: *I don't like snakes.*
- nicht zählbaren Nomen: *I love chocolate.*

Practice

Add *the*, *a* or (–) to these sentences.

1 Look at ∨ moon. It's beautiful. *(the)*
2 Would you like drink?
3 I've got sister and brother. My brother lives in Bregenz and my sister lives in Linz. (2×)
4 I love animals.
5 Excuse me, when's next train to Istanbul?
6 This is announcement for all passengers flying to Kuala Lumpur.
7 My brother has got fantastic flat near sea. (2×)
8 Cars are more expensive than motorbikes.
9 Do you prefer tea or coffee?
10 Is there bank near here?
11 At moment I'm simply resting on my bed.
12 Mary bought fantastic new dress.
13 This is best meal I have ever had.

Unit 8

Comparatives and superlatives

Bedeutung

Comparative
The train is more expensive than the coach. The train is cheaper than the plane.

Superlative
The coach is the cheapest way to get to Edinburgh. The plane is the most expensive.

Verwenden Sie bei Superlativen *the*, da es nur eine/n „Teuerste/n" oder „Billigste/n" geben kann.

159

G Grammar reference and practice

Form

Komparative	Rechtschreibregel	Beispiel
einsilbige Adjektive	+ *-er* + *-r*, wenn das Adjektiv mit *-e* endet	long**er**, saf**er**
eine Silbe, die mit einem kurzen Vokal und einem Konsonanten endet	der letzte Konsonant wird verdoppelt + *-er*	big**ger**
zweisilbige Adjektive	*more* + Adjektiv	**more** careful
zwei Silben, die mit *-y* enden	y → + *-ier*	eas**ier**
drei Silben und mehr	*more* + Adjektiv	**more** dangerous, **more** interesting
unregelmäßige Adjektive	good, bad, far, much / many, little	**better**, **worse**, **further**, **more**, **less**

Superlative	Rechtschreibregel	Beispiel
einsilbige Adjektive	+ *-est* + *-st*, wenn das Adjektiv mit *-e* endet	the long**est**, the saf**est**
eine Silbe, die mit einem kurzen Vokal und einem Konsonanten endet	der letzte Konsonant wird verdoppelt + *-est*	the big**gest**
zweisilbige Adjektive	*most* + Adjektiv	the **most** careful
zwei Silben, die mit *-y* enden	y → + *-iest*	the eas**iest**
drei Silben und mehr	*most* + Adjektiv	the **most** dangerous, the **most** interesting
unregelmäßige Adjektive	good, bad, far, much / many, little	the **best**, the **worst**, the **furthest**, the **most**, the **least**

Practice

1 Complete the sentences with the comparative form of the adjectives in brackets.

1 Buses in this city are a lot _____ than the underground. (slow)
2 New York is _____ away than London. (far)
3 I think that cycling is _____ than driving. (dangerous)
4 Central Market's interesting, but it's _____ than Riverside Market. (crowded)
5 Walking's _____ for your health than driving. (good)
6 You can get the bus or a taxi to the station, but it's a lot _____ to get a taxi. (expensive)
7 We could go to the cinema, but I think the concert looks _____. (interesting)
8 I like walking into town, but it's _____ to go by public transport. (quick)
9 The small shops near me are nice, but the supermarket's _____. (cheap)
10 I get _____ pocket money than my sister. (little)

2 Comparative or superlative? (Circle) the correct answer in each sentence.

1 I think Rio de Janeiro's   the most beautiful / more beautiful   city in the world.
2 An open return is   the most expensive / more expensive   than a day return.
3 I love Italian, Chinese and Japanese food, but I think Japanese food is   the healthiest / healthier .
4 I think driving's   the safest / safer than   riding a motorbike.
5 This is   the biggest / bigger   park in my town.
6 I'm   the tallest / taller than   my brother.
7 In fact, I'm   the tallest / taller   person in my family.
8 I bought a new computer, but it's   the worst / worse than   my old one.

G
Grammar reference and practice

Passive

Bedeutung

Das *Passive* wird verwendet, wenn wir nicht erwähnen wollen, wer etwas getan hat. Die Betonung liegt auf der Handlung selbst. Dies ist oft der Fall beim Beschreiben von Prozessen und Abläufen.
The school was built in 1978.
First, the water is heated, then the dumplings are put in.

Wenn angeführt werden soll, wer etwas getan hat, fügt man diese Information am Satzende mit **by** an.
The school was built in 1978 by Hardy & Sons.

Form

Form von *be* in der entsprechenden Zeitform	3. Form des Verbs (*past participle*)
The film was	written by Mark Mitchell.
The book will be	published next month.
The cinema is	equipped with a big screen.
Will the house be	painted dark green?
A new park is being	built next to the supermarket.

Um einen aktiven Satz passiv zu machen, wird das Objekt zum Subjekt des passiven Satzes.
The teacher explained the school trip in detail.
The school trip was explained in detail by the teacher.

Practice

1 Make passive sentences.
1 My bicycle / steal / yesterday.
2 Three years ago a lot of mobile phones / sell / in Austria.
3 Harry Potter / write / by J. K. Rowling.
4 The chemicals / heat / to 300 degrees, so that they melt.
5 Tiramisu / make / from eggs, mascarpone cheese and sugar.

2 Make these sentences passive.
1 Someone stole the headmaster's briefcase.
2 We write all reports by hand.
3 A company repaired the old roof.
4 We keep last year's files in a safe.
5 They sent a letter to the American embassy in Rome.

Future: *will, be going to, be hoping to, would like to*

Bedeutung

Verwenden Sie *will*, um Vermutungen (*assumptions*) über die Zukunft oder Vorhersagen (*predictions*) auszudrücken.
Maybe I'll move back to Liverpool when I'm an old man.
Peter will arrive in Dublin at 3.30 this afternoon.
The exams will be at the end of May.
2050 will be a leap year.

Sie können *be going to* verwenden, um über Absichten (*intentions*) und Pläne (*plans*) für die Zukunft zu sprechen.
Barry's going to stay in China for another few years.
I'm going to start a new course soon. I paid for the first month yesterday.

Sie können *be hoping to* verwenden, um über Hoffnungen (*hopes*) für die Zukunft zu sprechen.
I'm hoping to go to university next year.

Mit *would like to* können Sie über Wünsche (*wishes*) für die Zukunft sprechen.
I'd like to go to Japan one day.

Form

will + Infinitiv

- ✚ I'll be rich one day.
- ➖ I won't make a lot of money.
- ❓ Where do you think you'll be in twenty years?
  Will you spend the rest of your life in Austria?
- ✅ / ❌ Yes, I will. / No, I won't.

be going to, be hoping to + Infinitiv

- ✚ I'm going to start university after school.
  I'm hoping to move abroad one day.
- ➖ I'm not going to start university after school.
- ❓ Are you going to start university after school?
- ✅ / ❌ Yes, I am. / No, I'm not.
- ❓ What are you going to do next weekend?
  Is he hoping to start his new job next week?
- ✅ / ❌ Yes, he is. / No, he isn't.

would like to + Infinitiv

- ✚ I'd like to start university after school.
- ➖ I wouldn't like to work abroad.
- ❓ What would you like to do with your life?
  Would you like to go to university one day?
- ✅ / ❌ Yes, I would. / No, I wouldn't.

161

G Grammar reference and practice

Practice

1 Complete the sentences with *will* or *won't*.

1 Lisa's going to boarding school in England. I guess she _____ feel homesick.
2 No need to take raincoats. I'm sure the weather _____ be fine.
3 My parents are on holiday for two weeks, so they _____ be here tomorrow.
4 She _____ become a famous film star one day.
5 Do you think they _____ really move to Australia?
6 Let's start preparing for the exam. We _____ pass it otherwise.

2 Complete the sentences with *be going to* and the correct verb.

~~do~~   finish   go   stay   change   ask   visit   make

1 "Did they clean the car?" – "No, but they **'re going to do** it this afternoon."
2 "Have you ever been to India?" –
"No, but I _____ next year."
3 "How's your new job?" – "I don't like it.
I _____ jobs again soon."
4 "Did she finish the report?" – "No, she _____ it tomorrow."
5 "Is dinner ready?" – "No. I _____ it now."
6 "Can Sam come to the park later?" – "No.
He _____ at home and study."
7 "Did you ask Jessie to come to the party?" – "No.
I _____ her tonight."
8 "What are your plans for the summer?" –
"Oh, we _____ relatives in New Zealand."

3 a Put the words in the right order to make questions.

1 which / you / in / countries / think / will / you /visit / do / the next few years ?
Which countries do you think you will visit in the next few years?
2 most like to / which / person / would / you / meet ?
3 do / what / are / you / next summer / going to ?
4 learn / you / hoping to / are / one day / another language ?
5 like to / would / another country / you / live or work /in / one day ?
6 be / will / 25 / married / you / at the age of ?
7 are / you / what / do / at work or school /in the near future / going to ?
8 would / what / buy / like to / soon / you ?

3 b Ask and answer the questions in 3a.

Unit 9

Giving advice with *if*

Bedeutung

Sie können *if*-Sätze verwenden, um Ratschläge zu erteilen.
If you get stomach ache, try some black toast.

Form

If + Present simple	Imperativ
If you **get** stomach ache,	**try** some black toast.
If you **have** a temperature,	**don't go** to school.

If + Present simple	should (+ Infinitiv)
If this **doesn't work**,	you **should go** to a dentist.
If you **have** a cold,	you **shouldn't go** to school.

Die Reihenfolge der Satzteile ist variabel. Kommt zuerst der Teil mit *If*, dann wird zwischen die beiden Satzteile ein Komma (,) eingefügt.
If you get stomach ache, try some black toast. Try some black toast if you get stomach ache.
If you have a cold, you shouldn't go to school. You shouldn't go to school if you have a cold.

Practice

1 Match sentence beginnings 1–8 with the endings A–H.

1 If your TV doesn't work,
2 You should exercise more
3 Don't forget to take an umbrella
4 If you want a holiday job,
5 Check a dictionary
6 If you feel stressed,
7 If you want to see him,
8 You shouldn't go to the gym

A check the adverts in the newspaper.
B give him a call.
C if you have backache.
D call the repairman.
E you should go for a walk and try to relax.
F if you want to be fitter.
G if it rains.
H if you want to know the meaning of a word.

162

2 Add the words in brackets to the sentences. Add capital letters and punctuation.

1 Go and see the dentist ^if you have toothache. (if)
2 you want some fruit go to the shop (if, you should)
3 don't eat food with lots of salt you want to be healthy (if)
4 eat a lot late at night you want to sleep well (if, you shouldn't)
5 you go out forget your keys (if, don't)
6 go to bed early you feel tired (if, you should)
7 take these tablets you have a headache (if)
8 check the internet you want travel information (if, you should)

Unit 10

Present perfect

Bedeutung

Verwenden Sie das *Present Perfect*, um über Erfahrungen zu sprechen, die von der Vergangenheit bis in die Gegenwart andauern.

I went to France in 2004. I went to China in 2007. I went to India in 2009.

I've been to France, China and India.   NOW

Das *Present Perfect* wird nicht für Ereignisse verwendet, die in der Vergangenheit abgeschlossen wurden. Benutzen Sie dafür das *Past Simple*.
~~I've been to France in 1990~~. I **went** to France in 1990.
~~I've seen Frank yesterday~~. I saw Frank yesterday.

In Fragen können Sie *ever* (= jemals in Ihrem Leben) verwenden.
Have you ever been to France?

Form

Das *Present Perfect* wird mit *have / has* + *Past participle* (Partizip Perfekt, 3. Form des Verbs) gebildet.

I, you, we, they	he, she, it
⊕	⊕
I've seen all the James Bond films.	She's visited more than twenty countries.
⊖	⊖
We haven't met Frank. We've never met Frank.	He hasn't been to Japan. He's never been to Japan.
?	?
Have they been to Spain?	Has she met Frank?
✓	✓
Yes, they have.	Yes, she has.
✗	✗
No, they haven't.	No, she hasn't.

Kurzformen
⊕ I've = I have you've = you have
we've = we have they've = they have
he's = he has she's = she has it's = it has

⊖ haven't = have not   hasn't = has not

Die meisten *Past participles* sind regelmäßig und enden mit **-ed**. In diesen Fällen ist das *Past participle* mit der Verbform im *Past Simple* identisch.

like / liked   smoke / smoked   visit / visited

Einige *Past participles* sind unregelmäßig, haben aber die gleiche Form wie das *Past Simple*.

buy / bought   have / had   meet / met

Manche *Past participles* sind unregelmäßig und haben eine andere Form als das *Past Simple*. Diese Verben enden oftmals mit **-n**.

eat / ate / eaten   do / did / done   see / saw / seen

Das Verb **go** besitzt zwei Past participles: been und gone.
He's been to India. (= He went to India and he came back.)
He's gone to India. (= He went to India and he's in India now.)

→ Zu den *Past participles*, siehe *Irregular Verbs* auf S. 178.

Practice

1 a Make questions with the present perfect.

1 you / go to India?
   Have you been to India?
2 you / meet someone famous?
3 you / have a holiday abroad?
4 you / swim in the sea?
5 you / read a book more than once?
6 you / learn a foreign language apart from English?
7 your country / win the football world cup?
8 you / ride a motorbike?
9 you / do karate or judo?
10 you / be on a ship?

1 b Ask and answer the questions above in pairs.

2 (Circle) the correct verb in the present perfect or the past simple.

1 Have you seen / Did you see Stefan at the party last night?
2 She 's been / She went to Paris six times, and now she wants to go again.
3 I 've left / I left primary school about five years ago.
4 Where have you been / were you last night?
5 The first modern Olympics have been / were in Greece in 1896.

Grammar reference and practice

6 The modern Olympics   have been / were   in Greece twice.
7 My brother's a journalist. He   's visited   / He   visited   a lot of countries.
8 My great-grandfather was a journalist. He   's visited   / He   visited   a lot of countries in the 1890s.
9 I never   had / have   never   smoked   .
10 I   started / have started   school when I was five.

Past perfect

Bedeutung

Wenn wir über vergangene Handlungen sprechen und ausdrücken wollen, dass eine Handlung vor einer anderen stattfand, wird die erste Handlung in der *Past Perfect* (Plusquamperfekt, Vorvergangenheit) ausgedrückt. Solche chronologischen Abläufe werden oft mit **before** oder **after** ausgedrückt.
She **had eaten** a big pizza **before** she ordered ice cream.
We travelled to India **after** we **had spent** four weeks in Australia.
When I **arrived** at the station, the train **had already left**.

Form

Das *Past Perfect* wird mit *had + past participle* (*Partizip Perfekt*, 3. Form des Verbs) gebildet.

had + past participle
⊕ She had read all the Harry Potter stories **before** she saw the first movie. ⊖ We hadn't met her sister **before** last week's party. ❓ Had they been to Spain **before** they visited you in Paris? Yes, they had. / No, they hadn't.

Kurzformen

⊕ I'd = I had   you'd = you had
   we'd = we had   they'd = they had

   he'd = he had   she'd = she had   it'd = it had
⊖ hadn't = had not

Practice

Fill in the correct tenses (past perfect or past simple).

1 After the bear _____ (return) to the cave, it _____ (feed) the cubs.

2 When Mitch _____ (come) round the corner, the bus _____ just _____ (leave).

3 Before my sister started to _____ (play) the piano, she _____ (have) dancing lessons for four years.

4 I _____ (be) extremely tired after I _____ (study) maths for three hours.

5 Dad _____ (turn on) the TV after he _____ (eat) dinner.

6 They _____ (go) hiking in the Alps before they _____ (visit) their mother in Dortmund.

7 Mark _____ (sell) his guitar before he _____ (buy) a new waveboard.

8 After I _____ (do) all my homework, I _____ (read) my favourite novel until 1.00 am.

Irregular verbs

Infinitiv	Past simple	Past participle	Infinitiv	Past simple	Past participle
be	was/were	been	lead	led	led
beat	beat	beaten	learn	learnt/learned	learnt/learned
become	became	become	leave	left	left
begin	began	begun	lend	lent	lent
bite	bit	bitten	let	let	let
blow	blew	blown	lie	lay	lain
break	broke	broken	light	lit/lighted	lit/lighted
bring	brought	brought	lose	lost	lost
build	built	built	make	made	made
burn	burnt/burned	burnt/burned	mean	meant	meant
buy	bought	bought	meet	met	met
can	could	been able to	pay	paid	paid
catch	caught	caught	put	put	put
choose	chose	chosen	read [ri:d]	read [red]	read [red]
come	came	come	ride	rode	ridden
cost	cost	cost	ring	rang	rung
cut	cut	cut	rise	rose	risen
deal	dealt	dealt	run	ran	run
do	did	done	say	said	said
draw	drew	drawn	see	saw	seen
dream	dreamt/dreamed	dreamt/dreamed	sell	sold	sold
drink	drank	drunk	send	sent	sent
drive	drove	driven	set	set	set
eat	ate	eaten	shake	shook	shaken
fall	fell	fallen	shoot	shot	shot
feed	fed	fed	show	showed	shown
feel	felt	felt	shut	shut	shut
fight	fought	fought	sing	sang	sung
find	found	found	sit	sat	sat
fly	flew	flown	sleep	slept	slept
forget	forgot	forgotten	speak	spoke	spoken
freeze	froze	frozen	spend	spent	spent
get	got	got	stand	stood	stood
give	gave	given	steal	stole	stolen
go	went	been/gone	stick	stuck	stuck
grow	grew	grown	swim	swam	swum
hang	hung/hanged	hung/hanged	take	took	taken
have	had	had	teach	taught	taught
hear	heard	heard	tell	told	told
hide	hid	hidden	think	thought	thought
hit	hit	hit	throw	threw	thrown
hold	held	held	understand	understood	understood
hurt	hurt	hurt	wake	woke	woken
keep	kept	kept	wear	wore	worn
know	knew	known	win	won	won
lay	laid	laid	write	wrote	written

Picture dictionary

Unit 3

Places

 an airport
 a bank
 a bridge
 a bus stop

 a castle
a hospital
a market
 a museum

a school
 a theatre
 a college / a university
a train station

a factory
a farm
a motorway
 a petrol station

 a canal
 a beach
 hills
 mountains

 a field
 a forest
 an island
 a river

 a lake
 a park
 the sea
 a desert

Homes

a flat / an apartment
the fifth floor
the first floor
the ground floor

a block of flats / an apartment block

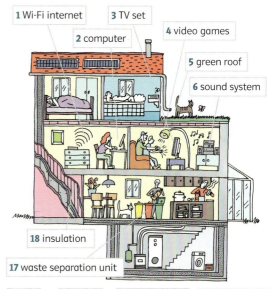

1 Wi-Fi internet
2 computer
3 TV set
4 video games
5 green roof
6 sound system
18 insulation
17 waste separation unit

8 tree
9 blinds
10 solar panels
11 triple glazed window
12 energy efficient windows
7 balcony
13 sliding door
14 conservatory
16 pond
15 bushes

166

P

Picture dictionary

Unit 5 **Food**

Meat

 chicken
 lamb
beef
sausages

Seafood

fish
salmon
prawns
shellfish

Carbohydrates

pasta
noodles
couscous
pastries

Vegetables

peas
lentils
olives
lettuce

mixed salad
beans
corn
courgettes

Fruit

peppers
an aubergine
squashes
mushrooms

watermelon
a melon
a banana
an apple

an orange
a lemon
a pineapple
a plum

cherries
a kiwi fruit
berries
a mango

Other

nuts
chips
herbs
spices

Unit 6 **Jobs**

an accountant
an architect
a builder
a cook / chef

a lawyer
a marketing assistant
a musician
a nurse

an office manager
a plumber
a shop assistant
a teacher

a doctor
an engineer
an IT technician
a journalist

a waiter
a police officer
a driver
a sales rep

167

Picture dictionary

Intro + Unit 6 — Study subjects

Arts, humanities, social sciences

architecture   art   drama   history

Professional

accounting   education   journalism   law

languages   economics   music   literature

marketing   medicine   engineering   management

Sciences

biology   chemistry   geography   mathematics*

* mathematics: in British English, people often say maths, and in American English math

Unit 10 — The body

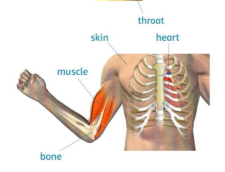

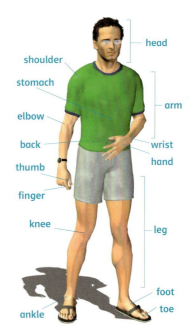

Labels: hair, eye, ear, nose, mouth, face, teeth, neck, throat, skin, heart, muscle, bone, head, shoulder, stomach, elbow, back, thumb, finger, knee, ankle, arm, wrist, hand, leg, foot, toe

Unit 11 — Sights

a castle   city walls   a fountain   a palace   ruins   a sculpture

a statue   a tomb   a waterfall   caves   gardens   a skyscraper

Vocabulary

AE	American English	
BE	British English	
coll.	colloquial (umgangssprachlich)	
etw.	etwas	
jmdm.	jemandem	
jmdn.	jemanden	
jmds.	jemandes	
pl.	plural	
sb.	somebody	
sth.	something	

Unit 0

to **fill in** sth. — etw. ausfüllen
Please fill in the contact form.

form — Formular

to **give** — geben
He did not give a reason for his decision.

information [ˌɪnfəˈmeɪʃən] — Information, Auskunft
He can give us some information about Spain.

to **introduce** sb. to sb. [ˌɪntrəˈdjuːs] — jmdn. jmdm. vorstellen

typical [ˈtɪpɪkəl] — typisch

1
Chinese [tʃaɪˈniːz] — Chinesisch; chinesisch
French [frenʃ] — Französisch; französisch
hometown — Heimatstadt
Hungarian [hʌŋˈɡeərɪən] — Ungarisch
introduction [ˌɪntrəˈdʌkʃən] — Bekanntmachung; Einleitung, Vorwort
Japanese [ˌdʒæpənˈiːz] — Japaner/in; japanisch
language [ˈlæŋɡwɪdʒ] — Sprache
to **number** sth. — etw. nummerieren
order — Bestellung; Reihenfolge
Russian [ˈrʌʃən] — Russisch; russisch
Slovak [ˈsləʊvæk] — Slowakisch
Slovakia [sləˈvækɪə] — Slowakei
Spanish [ˈspænɪʃ] — Spanisch; Spanier/in
to **speak** — sprechen
Turkey [ˈtɜːki] — Türkei
Turkish — Türkisch; türkisch
Wales [ˈweɪlz] — Wales
to **practise** sth. — etw. üben
the latest — das Neueste
cousin — Cousin/Cousine
aunt — Tante
mother tongue — Muttersprache
Arabic [ˈærəbɪk] — Arabisch
instructor — Trainer/in, Kursleiter/in
to **greet** sb. — jmnd. grüßen
Canada [ˈkænədə] — Kanada

3
enrolment — Einschreibung
first name — Vorname
mobile (phone) [ˈməʊbaɪl] — Mobiltelefon, Handy
Mr — Herr
title for a married or unmarried man
Ms [mɪz] — Frau
title for married and unmarried women
nationality [ˌnæʃənˈæləti] — Nationalität
surname [ˈsɜːneɪm] — Nachname
title [ˈtaɪtəl] — Titel; Anrede

4
each other — einander
They don't see each other a lot.

5
to **guess** [ɡes] — raten, vermuten
postcode — Postleitzahl
number — Nummer; (An-)Zahl

6
to **write** sth. — etw. schreiben
to **spell** sth. — etw. buchstabieren
Can you spell your surname?
to **cover** sth. [ˈkʌvə] — etw. bedecken/ zudecken

7
practice [ˈpræktɪs] — Übung
Practice makes perfect.
pronoun [ˈprəʊnaʊn] — Fürwort, Pronomen
table — Tisch; Tabelle
subject — Gegenstand, (Schul-)Fach
reference [ˈrefərəns] — Verweis

8
student card — Schüler-/Studentenausweis
US(A): (short for) United States (of America) — US(A), die Vereinigten Staaten (von Amerika)

9
academic secondary school [ˈsekəndəri] — Allgemeinbildende höhere Schule (Gymnasium)
dictionary [ˈdɪkʃənəri] — Wörterbuch
expression [ɪkˈspreʃən] — Ausdruck
favourite [ˈfeɪvərɪt] — bevorzugt; Lieblings-...
She's my favourite writer.
to **go** — gehen; fahren
Where do you go shopping?
new secondary school — Neue Mittelschule
nursery school [ˈnɜːsəri] — Kindergarten
own — eigene/r/s
primary school [ˈpraɪməri] — Volksschule
profile [ˈprəʊfaɪl] — Profil; Kurzportrait
administration [ədˌmɪnɪˈstreɪʃən] — Verwaltung
age — Alter
He's tall for his age.

10
to **work** — arbeiten; funktionieren
Does it work?
kind [kaɪnd] — Art, Typ
What kind of food do you like?
to **tell** sb. sth. — jmnd. etw. erzählen, sagen
to **use** sth. — etw. verwenden
break — Pause, Urlaub
I need a break.
economics [ˌiːkəˈnɒmɪks] — Volkswirtschaftslehre
to **finish** [ˈfɪnɪʃ] — abschließen, beenden
He finished his lunch.
nutrition [njuːˈtrɪʃən] — Ernährung
practical — praktisch, praxisbezogen
These plants have practical uses.
timetable [ˈtaɪmˌteɪbəl] — Stundenplan
vocational [vəˈkeɪʃənəl] — berufsbildend; beruflich
vocational college — Berufsbildende höhere Schule
accounting [əˈkaʊntɪŋ] — Buchhaltung

Vocabulary

	to **describe** sth. [dɪˈskraɪb]	etw. beschreiben
11	to **imagine** sth. [ɪˈmædʒɪn]	sich etw. vorstellen
12	to **check** sth. *I went to check that my friends were OK.*	etw. (über)prüfen/kontrollieren
	each	jede/r/s
	progress [ˈprəʊɡres]	Fortschritt
	self-assessment [ˌselfəˈsesmənt]	Selbstbeurteilung
	similar [ˈsɪmɪlə]	ähnlich
	time *I had a lovely time.*	Zeit; Mal
	unit [ˈjuːnɪt]	Einheit; Lektion
	well *Get well soon!*	gut, gesund
	independent [ˌɪndɪˈpendənt]	selbständig
	to **prepare for** sth.	sich auf etw. vorbereiten

Unit 1

	experience [ɪkˈspɪəriəns] *She has a lot of experience with animals.*	Erfahrung
	life (pl. **lives**)	Leben
	present [ˈprezənt]	gegenwärtig, anwesend
	open day	Tag der offenen Tür
1	to **meet** *Nice to meet you.*	(sich) treffen; (sich) kennen lernen
	classmate	Mitschüler/in
	to **put**	setzen, legen, stellen
	to **join** sb./sth.	sich jmnd./etw. anschließen
	crowd [kraʊd]	(Menschen)Menge
	to **be elected**	(zu etwas) gewählt werden
	actually	eigentlich
	student representative	Schülervertreter/in
	accent	(Sprach)Akzent
	local [ˈləʊkəl]	ortsansässig
3	**relationship** [rɪˈleɪʃənʃɪp]	Beziehung
4	**gap**	Lücke, Kluft
	kindergarten nurse	Kindergärtner/in
	to **move somewhere**	umziehen (an einen Ort)
	request [rɪˈkwest]	Anliegen, Anfrage, Bitte
	twins	Zwillinge
	charity [ˈtʃærəti]	Wohltätigkeit
	to **break out**	ausbrechen
	to **be good at** sth.	etw. gut können
5	to **find** *I find exams stressful.*	finden
	to **decide** sth. [dɪˈsaɪd] *She's decided to take the job.*	etw. entscheiden
	event [ɪˈvent] *They often watch sports events together.*	Ereignis; Veranstaltung
	individually [ˌɪndɪˈvɪdʒuəli]	einzeln
	like	Vorliebe
	dislike [dɪˈslaɪk] *I hope no policeman ever takes a dislike to you.*	Abneigung
6	to **compare** sth. [kəmˈpeə] *He compares internet advertising with ads on TV.*	etw. vergleichen
	headteacher	Schulleiter/in

7	**German**	Deutsche/r; Deutsch
	to **underline** sth. [ˌʌndəˈlaɪn]	etw. unterstreichen
	difficult [ˈdɪfɪkəlt]	schwierig
	gym (short for) **gymnasium** [dʒɪm]	Sporthalle, Fitnessraum
	interesting [ˈɪntrəstɪŋ]	interessant
	interview	Interview; Vorstellungsgespräch
	journey	Reise
	marks	Schulnoten
	old-fashioned	altmodisch
	pupil [ˈpjuːpəl]	Schüler/in
	skill *You need good communication skills to be a teacher.*	Fähigkeit, Fertigkeit
	strict [strɪkt]	streng
	to **take** *How long does it take to get there?*	nehmen; in Anspruch nehmen
	to **train as** sth. *Steve trains as an electrician.*	eine Ausbildung machen zu etw.
	type [taɪp]	Typ; Art
	village [ˈvɪlɪdʒ]	Dorf
	youth magazine [juːθ mæɡəˈziːn]	Jugendmagazin
	goalkeeper	Torfrau/-mann
	ten times	zehnmal
	building	Gebäude
	to **go by train**	mit dem Zug fahren
	boring	langweilig
	to **get** sth. **right**	etw. richtig machen
	to **be allowed to**	etw. dürfen
	to **warm up**	sich aufwärmen
	quietly [ˈkwaɪətli]	ruhig
	to **concentrate on** sth.	sich auf etw. konzentrieren
	to **scream**	schreien
	former school	vorige Schule
	marks	Schulnoten
	magazine	Magazin, Zeitschrift
8	**opposite** [ˈɒpəzɪt]	Gegenteil; gegenüber
9	**impressive**	beeindruckend
	to **argue**	streiten
	crowded *This train is always crowded*	überfüllt
	scary	gruselig, unheimlich
11	**adventurous** [ədˈventʃərəs]	abenteuerlich; abenteuerlustig
	outgoing	kontaktfreudig, offen
	creative [kriˈeɪtɪv]	kreativ, einfallsreich
	hard-working	fleißig
	sign of the zodiac, star sign [ˈzəʊdɪæk]	Sternzeichen
	temperamental	temperamentvoll, launisch
	enthusiastic	enthusiastisch
	impatient	ungeduldig
	irritable	gereizt, reizbar
	reliable	verlässlich
	jealous	eifersüchtig
	caring	liebevoll, fürsorglich
	adaptable	anpassungsfähig
	anxious	ängstlich
	loyal	loyal

Vocabulary

	unforgiving	unversöhnlich, unerbittlich		to shake *The two leaders smiled and shook hands.*	schütteln
	independent	unabhängig	21	female ['fiːmeɪl]	weiblich
	ambitious [æm'bɪʃəs] *He is very ambitious.*	ehrgeizig		male	männlich
	hot-headed	hitzköpfig		usually ['juːʒuəli] *I usually get home at about six o'clock.*	gewöhnlich
	intelligent	intelligent			
	optimistic	optimistisch	22	business ['bɪznɪs]	Wirtschafts-..., Geschäfts-...; Geschäft
	stubborn	stur			
	kind	freundlich, gütig	23	country ['kʌntri]	Land; Gegend
	protective	beschützend, fürsorglich		Japan [ˌdʒə'pæn]	Japan
	possessive	vereinnahmend, besitzergreifend	24	message *Can I take a message?*	Nachricht
	dependable	verlässlich, zuverlässig, belastbar		several years	einige Jahre
	supportive	unterstützend		to state sth.	etw. anführen, angeben
	indecisive	unentschlossen		contact details ['kɒntækt]	Kontaktdaten
	analytical	analytisch		exclamation mark	Rufzeichen
	witty	witzig, geistreich		rude	unhöflich
	nervous	nervös		purpose	Zweck
	entertaining [ˌentə'teɪnɪŋ]	unterhaltsam		to introduce oneself to sb.	sich jmnd. vorstellen
	charming	charmant		in advance	im Voraus
	moody	launisch		description [dɪ'skrɪpʃən]	Beschreibung
	Aries ['eəriːz]	Widder		hometown	Heimatstadt, Heimatort
	Taurus ['tɔːrəs]	Stier		closing	Abschluss(satz)
	Gemini ['dʒemɪnaɪ]	Zwilling	25	both *I like them both.*	beide
	Cancer ['kænsər]	Krebs		capital	Hauptstadt
	Scorpio ['skɔːpiəʊ]	Skorpion		cinema	Kino
	Sagittarius [ˌsædʒɪ'teəriəs]	Schütze		current ['kʌrənt]	jetzig, aktuell
	Leo ['liːəʊ]	Löwe		exam (short for) examination [ɪg'zæm]	Prüfung
	Virgo ['vɜːgəʊ]	Jungfrau			
	Libra ['liːbrə]	Waage		to live [lɪv] *She lives with her father.*	leben
	Pisces ['paɪsiːz]	Fisch			
	Capricorn ['kæprɪkɔːn]	Steinbock		to pass an exam	eine Prüfung bestehen
	Aquarius [ə'kweəriəs]	Wassermann		Spain [speɪn]	Spanien
15	occupation [ˌɒkjə'peɪʃən]	Beruf, Beschäftigung		to tick sth.	etw. ankreuzen/abhaken
16	highlighted	markiert, hervorgehoben		back *When did you get back?*	zurück
	internship (AE)	(Berufs-)Praktikum			
	to make	machen, herstellen		reply [rɪ'plaɪ]	Antwort
	neighbour ['neɪbə]	Nachbar/in		abroad [ə'brɔːd] *Are you going abroad this summer?*	im/ins Ausland
	to replace sth. with sth. *We want to replace the carpet with tiles.*	etw. durch etw. ersetzen			
			26	to stay	bleiben; wohnen
	private tutor	Privatlehrer/in, Nachhilfelehrer/in		to attend sth. *Alex is attending a school for the blind.*	etw. besuchen; an etw. teilnehmen
	colleague	Kollege/Kollegin			
	language school	Sprachschule		to choose sth. [tʃuːz] *Choose a book from more than 500 available.*	etw. auswählen
17	to be famous ['feɪməs] *The city is famous for its leaning tower.*	berühmt sein			
				ever	jemals
	to be married	verheiratet sein		to spend	verbringen; ausgeben
18	to mean *What do you mean?*	bedeuten; meinen		to study ['stʌdi] *He studies hard.*	lernen, studieren
	to understand sth.	etw. verstehen		tip	Tipp; Trinkgeld
19	greetings *We exchanged greetings.*	Grüße	27	false [fɔːls]	falsch
				American	Amerikaner/in; amerikanisch
20	to bow [baʊ] *The actors bowed after the performance.*	sich verbeugen		to contain sth. [kən'teɪn] *The box contains sweets.*	etw. enthalten
	to exchange [ɪks'tʃeɪndʒ]	austauschen			
	hug	Umarmung		to enjoy sth. *She's enjoying a day off.*	etw. genießen
	to hug [hʌg]	(sich) umarmen			

Vocabulary

except	außer	
Italy	Italien	
to justify ['dʒʌstɪfaɪ]	etw. begründen	
walk [wɔ:k]	Spaziergang	
Let's go for a walk.		
to watch	anschauen, zuschauen	
Are you watching this?		

Unit 2

	offer	Angebot, Vorschlag
	to request sth.	um etw. bitten, etw. anfordern
	to respond to sth. [rɪ'spɒnd]	auf etw. antworten/ reagieren
1	Sudan [su:dɑ:n]	Sudan
	Sudanese [ˌsu:dən'i:z]	sudanesisch
	spare [speə]	Gäste-...; Reserve-...
	Always carry a spare battery for your camera.	
	Switzerland	Schweiz
	to miss sth.	etw. vermissen
	cuisine	Esskultur
	sesame seed	Sesamsamen
	hard to find	schwierig zu finden
	to text	SMS senden
	at least	zumindest
	to look after sb./ sth.	auf jmnd./etw. aufpassen
	I need to look after my baby sister.	
	to remind someone of sth. [rɪ'maɪnd]	jmnd. an etwas erinnern
	available [ə'veɪləbəl]	verfügbar
2	to travel	reisen
	I'm travelling on my own.	
	skiing	Schifahren
	statement	Aussage(satz)
	newspaper	Zeitung
	orange juice	Orangensaft
	cheese	Käse
3	museum [mju:'zi:əm]	Museum
	soon	bald
	brackets	Klammern
	tourist	Tourist/in
	musician	Musiker/in
	to enjoy doing sth.	etw. gerne tun
	I enjoy travelling.	
	visitor	Besucher/in
	spare room	Gästezimmer
	to stay with sb.	bei jmnd. bleiben
	Slovenia	Slowenien
	a few days	ein paar Tage
	during the week	wochentags, unter der Woche
	meat	Fleisch
4	to be interested in (doing) sth.	an etw. interessiert sein
	My sister is interested in reading crime novels.	
5	campsite	Campingplatz
	sofa ['səʊfə]	Sofa, Couch
	China ['tʃaɪnə]	China
	comfortable ['kʌmftəbəl]	bequem, angenehm
	common	gewöhnlich, üblich

	Cuba ['kju:bə]	Kuba
	flat	Wohnung
	in common	gemeinsam
	He and I have something in common.	
	place	Ort, Platz
	to plan sth.	etw. planen
	We're just planning our holidays.	
	spare room	Gästezimmer
	Sweden ['swi:dən]	Schweden
	to get sth.	etw. bekommen; etw. besorgen
	How many emails do you get a day?	
	on one's own	allein
	I was on my own, without friends or family.	
	adventure	Abenteuer
	difference ['dɪfərəns]	Unterschied
	living room	Wohnzimmer
	to work full-time	Vollzeit arbeiten
	dinner	Abendessen
	smoker	Raucher/in
6	to remember sth.	sich an etw. erinnern
8	rucksack ['rʌksæk]	Rucksack
	chocolate	Schokolade
	biscuits	Kekse
9	clothes [kləʊðz]	Kleider, Kleidung
	cup	Tasse; Pokal
	rule [ru:l]	Regel
	This is the exception that proves the rule.	
	consonant ['kɒnsənənt]	Mitlaut, Konsonant
	vowel [vaʊəl]	Selbstlaut, Vokal
	some	einige, ein wenig
	Can you bring some apples? I'd like some apple juice.	
	a, an	ein, eine, einer
10	to be afraid	(be)fürchten
	I'm afraid I have to go.	
	Would you like ...?	Möchtest du (möchten Sie) ...?
	No, I'm afraid not.	Nein, leider nicht.
	Can I ...?	Darf ich ...?
11	conversation	Unterhaltung
	to drop sb. somewhere	jmnd. wo absetzen
	A helicopter dropped the rockstar on the rooftop.	
	competition [ˌkɒmpə'tɪʃən]	Wettbewerb
	to spend money on sth.	Geld für etw. ausgeben
12	guest [gest]	Gast
	to hope	hoffen
	I hope you're well.	
	to take care of sb./sth.	sich um jmdn./etw. kümmern
	What about ...?	Was ist mit ...?
	I don't like action films. What about you?	
	to ask a favour	um einen Gefallen bitten
	favour	Gefallen
	guy	Typ, Kerl
	lovely	nett, großartig

Vocabulary

	to **appreciate** sth.	etw. schätzen
	almond	Mandel
13	**architecture** ['ɑːkɪtektʃə]	Architektur
	boat trip	Bootsfahrt
	Let's take a boat trip.	
	fine	gut; gesund
	We're fine.	
	trip	Ausflug; Reise
	What else …?	Was sonst …?
	sight	Sehenswürdigkeit
	Are you interested in seeing some sights?	
	boat	Boot, Schiff
14	to **offer** sb. sth.	jmdm. etw. (an)bieten
	He offers her a job.	
	to **take turns**	sich abwechseln
15	**marketing assistant** ['mɑːkɪtɪŋ]	Marketing Assistent/in
	Milan	Mailand
	to **suggest** sth.	etw. vorschlagen
17	**village**	Dorf
	Athens	Athen
	bad-tempered	schlecht aufgelegt
18	**dish**	Speise; Schale
	popular ['pɒpjələ]	beliebt
	breakfast	Frühstück
	throughout	überall in
	Throughout Austria people eat potatoes.	
	to **save** sth.	etw. sparen
	food	Lebensmittel, Nahrungsmittel
	to **serve** sth.	etw. servieren
	cereals	Müsli, Getreide
	stewed fruit [fruːt]	Obstkompott
	bacon	Speck
	accompanied by sth.	von etw. begleitet; hier: gemeinsam mit
	We eat eggs accompanied by sausages.	
	sausage	Würstel
	mushroom ['mʌʃrum]	Pilz
	marmelade	(Orangen-)Marmelade
	accompaniments	Begleitung, hier: Beilage
	beans	Bohnen
	origin	Ursprung
	to **originate**	stammen aus, ausgehen von
	Potatoes originated in Peru.	
	rural	ländlich
	rich meal	reichhaltiges Essen
	Egyptian ['iːdʒɪpʃən]	ägyptisch
	ancient	uralt, antik
	to **flavour with** sth.	mit etw. würzen
	cumin	Kümmel
	onion ['ʌnjən]	Zwiebel
	garlic	Knoblauch
	parsley	Petersilie
	hard-boiled eggs	hart gesottene Eier
	cucumber ['kjuːkʌmbə]	Gurke
	recipe	Kochrezept
	side dish	Beilage
	to **grind** sth.	etw. mahlen

	ground sesame seeds	gemahlene Sesamsamen
	ingredient [ɪnˈɡriːdiənt]	Zutat
	chickpea	Kichererbsen
	paste	Paste
	black tea	Schwarztee
	mint leaves [liːvz]	Pfefferminzblätter
19	**holiday**	Urlaub; Feiertag
	We're on holiday here.	
	leaflet	Broschüre, Flugblatt
20	**child** (*pl.* **children**)	Kind
	design [dɪˈzaɪn]	Gestaltung, Entwurf
	island [ˈaɪlənd]	Insel
	medicine [ˈmedsən]	Medizin; Medikament/e
	flexible [ˈfleksɪbəl]	flexibel
	homestay course	Kurs mit Gastfamilienaufenthalt
	knowledge [ˈnɒlɪdʒ]	Wissen
	all year round	das ganze Jahr über
	preparation [ˌprepəˈreɪʃən]	Vorbereitung
	South Africa	Südafrika
	general [ˈdʒenərəl]	allgemein
	major	bedeutend; Haupt-…
	Malta [ˈmɔːltə]	Malta
	accommodation	Unterkunft, Quartier
	beach	Strand
	choice [tʃɔɪs]	(Aus-)Wahl
	You have to make a choice.	
	close [kləʊs]	nahe; eng befreundet
	We're very close.	
	to **combine** [kəmˈbaɪn]	kombinieren
	local	örtlich, regional
	Mediterranean [ˌmedɪtəˈreɪniən]	Mittelmeer
	numerous [ˈnjuːmərəs]	zahlreich
	to **be situated**	gelegen, liegen
	The school is situated near our home.	
21	to **confirm** [kənˈfɜːm]	bestätigen
	Please confirm that that's OK with you.	
	confirmation [ˌkɒnfəˈmeɪʃən]	Bestätigung
	to **contact** sb.	jmdn. kontaktieren
	to **look forward to** sth.	sich auf etw. freuen
	She's really looking forward to going out.	
	to **refer to** sth. [rɪˈfɜː]	sich auf etw. beziehen
	He refers to a magazine article.	
22	**reason** [ˈriːsən]	Grund
24	**a couple**	ein paar, einige
	There are a couple of shops near here.	
	Australia	Australien
	Croatia [krəʊˈeɪʃə]	Kroatien
	kitchen	Küche
	wish	Wunsch
25	**space**	Platz, Raum; Weltraum
	Did someone steal your parking space?	
	to **allow** sth.	etw. erlauben
	fridge	Kühlschrank

Vocabulary

	binge watching	mehrere Folgen einer Serie nacheinander ansehen
	to return a favour	sich für einen Gefallen revanchieren; sich erkenntlich zeigen
	during	während
	unfortunately	leider
	at short notice ['nəʊtɪs]	kurzfristig
	apart from *Should I bring anything else apart from chocolate?*	außer
	additional	zusätzlich
	closing remark	Abschlussbemerkung
26	capital letter	Großbuchstabe
	sightseeing ['saɪtˌsiːɪŋ]	Besichtigungen, Sightseeing
27	important [ɪmˈpɔːtənt]	wichtig
	to avoid [əˈvɔɪd] *I tried to avoid him.*	jmdn./etw. (ver)meiden
	to cost	(Geld) kosten
	department store	Kaufhaus
	entrance *Let's meet at the main entrance.*	Eingang
	guide (book) [gaɪd]	(Reise-)Führer
	queue [kjuː]	Warteschlange
	recording [rɪˈkɔːdɪŋ] *Students can view a digital recording later.*	Ton-/Filmaufnahme
	speech *I'm not good at giving speeches.*	Rede
	square [skweə]	quadratisch; Quadrat; Platz
	task [tɑːsk]	Aufgabe
	ticket	Ticket, Fahr-/Eintrittskarte
	tour guide	Reiseführer/in
	twice [twaɪs]	zweimal
	to give a speech	eine Rede halten
	to queue	sich anstellen

Competence check: Units 1–2

1	mountaineering camp	Bergsteigercamp
	water sports	Wassersport
	to be afraid of	sich fürchten vor
	rope-climbing [rəʊp ˈklaɪmɪŋ]	Seilklettern
3	to suit somebody's needs [suːt]	jds. Bedürfnissen entsprechen
	on-site	vor Ort
	clay shooting	Tontaubenschießen
	archery [ˈɑːtʃəri]	Bogenschießen
	raft building	Floßbau
	well-earned	wohlverdient
	weather-dependent	wetterabhängig
	team-orientated	teamorientiert
	descent [dɪˈsent]	Abstieg
	riddle	Rätsel
	en route *Our adventure park offers many surprises en-route.*	auf dem Weg, unterwegs
4	carbon footprint	CO_2 Fußabdruck, CO_2 Bilanz
	energy efficiency	Energieeffizienz
	to generate energy	Energie erzeugen

Unit 3

	custom [ˈkʌstəm]	Brauch
	habit [ˈhæbɪt] *What are your bad habits?*	Gewohnheit
	to have a good time *Have a good time!*	Spaß haben
	neighbourhood	Nachbarschaft
	to repeat sth. [rɪˈpiːt]	etw. wiederholen
	to take a message	eine Nachricht annehmen
	space *I need more space in my room.*	Raum, Weltraum
1	mountain *He is climbing a mountain.*	Berg
	news *I'm just watching the news.*	Nachrichten; Neuigkeiten
	to take a photo	ein Foto machen
	to chat with sb. [tʃæt]	mit jmdm. plaudern/ chatten
	special [ˈspeʃəl]	besonders
	to invite sb. to sth. [ɪnˈvaɪt]	jmdn. zu etwas einladen
	free time	Freizeit
	leisure time [ˈleʒə]	Freizeit
	jump	Sprung
	bike racing	Radrennen fahren
	well paid	gut bezahlt
	to be honest	ehrlich gesagt
	exciting [ɪkˈsaɪtɪŋ] *France beat Brazil in an exciting football match.*	aufregend
	parkour *Kids absolutely love parkour.*	Parkour
	newbie	Anfänger/in
	traffic	Verkehr
2	pronoun	Pronomen
3	adverb of frequency	Häufigkeitsadverb
	always	immer
	often	oft
	sometimes	manchmal
	area *My friends all live in the same area.*	Gebiet, Bereich
	board game	Brettspiel
4	guitar [gɪˈtɑː]	Gitarre
6	to find out	herausfinden
	New Year's Eve	Silvester
7	to dance	tanzen
8	to invite sb. out	jmnd. zum Weggehen einladen
9	to sound *That sounds good!*	klingen
	Are you free on …?	Hast du Zeit am …?
	sleepover (AE)	Übernachtungsparty
	That sounds great!	Das klingt gut!
10	dress code	Bekleidungsvorschrift
	date	Datum; Verabredung
12	to visit *Will you visit Moscow when you're in Russia?*	besuchen
	programme [ˈprəʊgræm]	Programm
	delegation	Delegation, Abordnung
	to vote	wählen

Vocabulary

14	UK: (short for) United Kingdom	das Vereinigte Königreich		kitchen	Küche
	apartment	Wohnung		living room	Wohnzimmer
	boarding school	Internatsschule		bedroom	Schlafzimmer
	countryside	Landschaft; ländliche Gegend		study	Arbeitszimmer
	I spent my childhood in the countryside.			bedside table	Nachtkästchen
				bookshelf	Bücherregal
	expensive [ikˈspensɪv]	teuer		chair	Sessel
	to fly	fliegen		desk	Schreibtisch
	Do you like flying?			kitchen bin	Küchenabfalleimer
	forever	(für) immer		tea towel	Geschirrtuch
	mobile [ˈməʊbaɪl]	beweglich, mobil		washing machine	Waschmaschine
	quiet [kwaɪət]	ruhig	25	environmentally friendly	umweltfreundlich
	safe	sicher		balcony	Balkon
	term [tɜːm]	Semester, Trimester		triple glazed window	dreifach verglastes Fenster
	to grow up	aufwachsen		sliding door	Schiebetür
	almost	fast, beinahe		green roof	begrüntes Dach
	to live in the countryside	auf dem Land leben		blinds	Fensterläden, Sichtschutz
	to pollute [pəˈluːt]	verschmutzen		solar panels	Solarkollektoren
	businessman	Geschäftsmann/Geschäftsfrau		conservatory [kənˈsɜːvətəri]	Wintergarten
	cheap	billig		energy efficient [ˈenədʒi]	energieeffizient
	view	Aussicht		bush	Busch, Strauch
	beautiful	schön		pond	Teich
	on	auf		waste separation unit	Mülltrennanlage
	next to	neben		insulation	Isolierung
	near	in der Nähe		access [ˈækses]	Zugang, Zutritt
	twice a week	zweimal pro Woche	26	to house-sit	auf das Haus aufpassen
16	clean [kliːn]	sauber, rein		Is there/Are there …?	Gibt es …?
	dangerous [ˈdeɪndʒərəs]	gefährlich	27	main	hauptsächlich; Haupt-…
	noisy	laut		contact [ˈkɒntækt]	Kontakt
	ugly [ˈʌgli]	hässlich		*We keep in close contact with our grandparents.*	
17	to dislike sb./sth.	jmdn./etw. nicht mögen			
19	river	Fluss		furnished [ˈfɜːnɪʃt]	möbliert
	opinion	Meinung		*The whole place was rented furnished.*	
	city centre	Innenstadt			
	floor	Stockwerk; (Fuß-)Boden		furniture [ˈfɜːnɪtʃə]	Möbel
	ground floor	Erdgeschoß		immediately [ɪˈmiːdiətli]	sofort
	underground line	Ubahn Linie		included	enthalten, inbegriffen
	east of	östlich von		rent	Miete
	west of	westlich von		central heating	Zentralheizung
21	landmark	Sehenswürdigkeit		advert (short for)	Werbung, Inserat
22	bedclothes [ˈbedkləʊðz]	Bettzeug		advertisement [ˈædvɜːt]	
	bunk bed	Stockbett		studio apartment	Einzimmerwohnung
	cooker	Küchenherd		to let sth.	etw. vermieten
	cutlery [ˈkʌtləri]	Essbesteck		available	verfügbar
	drawer	Schublade		heating	Heizung
	fridge: (short for) refrigerator [rɪˈfrɪdʒəreɪtə]	Kühlschrank	30	bus stop	Bushaltestelle
				except	ausgenommen, nicht inkludiert
	mirror	Spiegel	32	mug [mʌg]	Becher, Häferl
	plant	Pflanze	34	on second thoughts	nach nochmaliger Überlegung
	plate	Teller		to be on a budget	sparen müssen
	pots and pans	Töpfe und Pfannen, Kochgeschirr		on principle	prinzipiell
	rug	Teppich(läufer)		on purpose	absichtlich
	shelf (pl. shelves)	Regal		be on duty	im Dienst
	towel [taʊəl]	Handtuch		on condition that	vorausgesetzt dass
	wardrobe [ˈwɔːdrəʊb]	Kleiderschrank	35	to slow down	langsamer werden/sprechen
	to share sth.	etw. teilen	38	amazing [əˈmeɪzɪŋ]	großartig, erstaunlich
	bathroom	Badezimmer		previous	vorhergehend
	dining room	Esszimmer			

Vocabulary

Unit 4

1

	personal music player	tragbares Abspielgerät
	technology [tek'nɒlədʒi]	Technologie; Technik
	Brazilian [brə'zɪliən]	Brasilianer/in; brasilianisch
	cassette [kə'set]	Tonbandkassette
	government ['gʌvənmənt]	Regierung
	headphones	Kopfhörer
	invention [ɪn'venʃən]	Erfindung
	memory *I have a good memory for names.*	Gedächtnis; (Daten-)Speicher
	to wear *I wear jeans all the time.*	tragen
	to believe [bɪ'liːv] *She says she's only thirty but I don't believe it.*	glauben; vermuten
	to develop sth. [dɪ'veləp]	etw. entwickeln
	computer scientist	Computerwissenschaftler/in
	the late 1950s	die späten 1950er Jahre
	electronics	Elektronik
	electronic gadgets	kleines, elektronisches Gerät
	to end up doing sth.	etw. schließlich tun
	later on	später
	television set	Fernsehgerät
	to graduate ['grædjueɪt]	Schule abschließen, einen akademischen Grad erlangen
	software engineer [ˌendʒɪ'nɪə]	Software Ingenieur/in
	CERN: (short for) European Organization for Nuclear Research	Europäische Organisation für Kernforschung
	particle physics	Teilchenphysik
	laboratory	Labor
	scientist	Wissenschaftler/in
	accelerator	Beschleuniger
	to notice sth. ['nəʊtɪs]	etw. bemerken
	technology	Technologie
	hypertext	Hypertext
	fundamental	grundlegend
	to remain	verbleiben
	foundation	Grundlage, Basis
	HTML: Hypertext Markup Language	
	formatting	Formatieren
	URI: Uniform Resource Identifier	
	address [ə'dres]	Adresse
	unique [juː'niːk]	einzigartig
	to identify sth.	etw. identifizieren
	resource	Ressource, Hilfsmittel
	commonly called	allgemein genannt
	URL: (short for) Uniform Resource Locator	
	HTTP: Hypertext Transfer Protocol	
	retrieval	Abfragung (von Daten)
	linked	verbunden
	web community	Web-Community, Web-Gemeinschaft
	to realise sth. ['rɪəlaɪz]	etw. erkennen
	permission	Erlaubnis
	to spark sth.	etw. entfachen, entzünden
	a global wave	eine weltweite Bewegung
	creativity	Kreativität
	collaboration	Kooperation, Zusammenarbeit
	innovation	Innovation
	to commit to sth.	sich etw. verpflichten
	Royalty Free Policy	Strategie der Gebührenfreiheit
	to be devoted to sth.	sich etw. verschreiben, verpflichten
	to found sth.	etw. gründen
	W3C: (short for) World Wide Web Consortium	
	target	Ziel
	to be just	gerecht sein
	successful [sək'sesfəl]	successful
	society	Gesellschaft
	belt	Gürtel
	to support sb./sth. [sə'pɔːt]	jmnd./etw. unterstützen
	participation	Teilnahme, Beteiligung
	decade	Jahrzehnt
	technical ['teknɪkəl]	technisch
	to create sth.	etw. schaffen, erstellen
	European [ˌjʊərə'piːən]	Europäer/in
3	communications company	Telekommunikationsfirma
	complete [kəm'pliːt]	vollständig
	telecommunications	Telekommunikation, Nachrichtentechnik
	type-setting	Schriftsatz
	independent	unabhängig
	contractor	Auftragnehmer/in, Unternehmer/in
4	inventor	Erfinder/in
	mobile phone	Handy, Mobiltelefon
	statement	Aussage
5	by the end of 2005	bis (spätestens) Ende 2005
	transport timetable	Fahrplan (für öffentlichen Verkehr)
6	accidental ['æksɪdentəl]	zufällig
	function	Funktion
	hunting	Jagen
	seeds	Samen
	to publish sth.	etw. veröffentlichen
	to popularize sth.	etw. bekannt machen
	astronaut	Astronaut/in
	equipment [ɪ'kwɪpmənt]	Ausrüstung
7	to present sth. [prɪ'zent]	etw. präsentieren/vorstellen
	to prepare sth.	etw. vorbereiten
10	Nigeria [naɪ'dʒɪəriə]	Nigeria
	Scotland	Schottland
	memories	Erinnerungen
11	column ['kɒləm]	Säule; Textspalte
	strange [streɪndʒ]	sonderbar; fremd
13	accident ['æksɪdənt]	Unfall
14	digital camera	Digitalkamera
	meal	Mahlzeit, Essen
	possession	Besitz

Vocabulary

	activity ['æktɪvəti]	Aktivität
15	tutoring	Nachhilfe
17	length	Länge
	width [wɪtθ]	Breite
	shape	Form
	depth [depθ]	Tiefe
	cube [kju:b]	Würfel
	cubic	würfelig
	rectangle ['rektæŋgəl]	Rechteck
	rectangular [rek'tæŋgjələ]	rechteckig
	cylinder ['sɪlɪndə]	Zylinder
	cylindrical [sə'lɪndrɪkəl]	zylindrisch
	prism ['prɪzəm]	Prisma
	triangle ['traɪæŋgəl]	Dreieck
	triangular [traɪ'æŋgjələ]	dreieckig
	cone [kəʊn]	Kegel
	conical ['kɒnɪkəl]	kegelförmig
	pentagon ['pentəgən]	Fünfeck
	pentagonal [pen'tægənəl]	fünfeckig
	pyramid ['pɪrəmɪd]	Pyramide
	pyramidal [pɪ'ræmɪdəl]	pyramidenförmig
	circle ['sɜ:kəl]	Kreis
	circular ['sɜ:kjələ]	kreisförmig
	spiral ['spaɪərəl]	spiralförmig
	sphere [sfɪə]	Kugel
	spherical ['sferɪkəl]	kugelförmig
	hemisphere ['hemɪsfɪə]	Hemisphäre, Halbkugel
	diagonal [daɪ'ægənəl]	diagonal
	diameter [daɪ'æmɪtə]	Durchmesser
18	scale drawings	maßstabgetreue Zeichnung
	dimension [daɪ'menʃən]	Dimension
20	equilateral [ˌikwɪ'lætərəl]	gleichseitig
	angle	Winkel
	equal ['i:kwəl]	gleich
	diamond-shaped	diamant-/rautenförmig
	central point	(Kreis-)Mittelpunkt
23	even	sogar
	contraction	(Wort-) Verkürzung
	to abbreviate sth.	etw. verkürzen
	trip abroad	Reise ins Ausland
	summer residence	Sommerhaus
	plane	Flugzeug
	window seat	Fenstersitz
	to discover sth.	etw. entdecken
	seafood	Meeresfrüchte
	slope	Hang
	volcano	Vulkan

Unit 5

	to order sth. What can she order?	etw. bestellen
	preference ['prefərəns]	Vorliebe
	reminder Was that a gentle reminder?	Mahnung, Erinnerung
1	cash	Bargeld
	escalator ['eskəleɪtə]	Rolltreppe
	newsagent	Zeitschriftengeschäft
	pharmacy ['fɑ:məsi]	Apotheke

	mall, shopping centre	Einkaufszentrum
	to mention sth.	etw. erwähnen
	sales assistant	Verkäufer/in
	cothes shop	Kleidungsgeschäft
	jewellery ['dʒu:əlri]	Schmuck
	luggage ['lʌgɪdʒ]	Gepäck
	bank/cash machine	Bankomat
	Indian restaurant	indisches Restaurant
2	shopping centre	Einkaufszentrum
	boot [bu:t] I need a pair of boots.	Stiefel
	maps	Landkarten
	trousers	Hose
3	countable ['kaʊntəbəl]	zählbar
	uncountable [ʌn'kaʊntəbəl]	nicht zählbar
	to count	zählen
	cotton	Baumwolle
	pattern ['pætən]	Muster
	suitcase	Koffer
6	rather ['rɑ:ðə]	lieber, eher, ziemlich
	I'd rather …	Ich würde lieber …
	to prefer sth. [prɪ'fɜ:]	etw. vorziehen, lieber tun
7	comedy	Komödie
	classical music	klassische Musik
9	hiking map	Straßenkarte
	outdoor jacket	Regenjacke
	shop assistant	Verkäufer/in
	How much is/are …?	Wie viel kostet/kosten …?
11	customer	Kunde/Kundin
13	lamb [læm]	Lamm
	prawn [prɔ:n] He ordered a prawn cocktail.	Garnele, Krabbe
	salmon ['sæmən]	Lachs
	beef [bi:f]	Rindfleisch
	carbohydrates [ˌkɑ:bəʊ'haɪdreɪts] Potatoes are high in carbohydrates.	Kohlehydrate
	diet ['daɪət] They're good for you if you're on a diet.	Ernährungsweise; Diät
	to be high in sth. Mozzarella is high in calcium.	viel von etw. enthalten
	lettuce ['letɪs]	Salat
	to be low in sth. Their diet is low in fat.	wenig von etw. enthalten
	onion	Zwiebel
	potato (pl. potatoes)	Kartoffel
	skin Now supermarkets sell carrots with purple skins.	Haut; Schale
	to agree I agree with you.	zustimmen, einig sein
	dairy products ['deəri]	Milchprodukte
	chicken	Hühnchen
	lemon	Zitrone
	yoghurt ['jɒgət]	Joghurt
	broccoli	Broccoli
14	low-carb	wenig Kohlenhydrate enthaltend
	naturally ['nætʃərəli]	von Natur aus
	healthy [helθi]	gesund
	weight [weɪt]	Gewicht

177

Vocabulary

	lies	Lügen
	stupidity	Dummheit
	detoxing	entgiften
	weight-loss	Gewichtabnahme
	toxin	Giftstoff
	caveman	Urmensch, Höhlenmensch
	non-scientific	nicht wissenschaftlich
	justification [ˌdʒʌstɪfɪˈkeɪʃən]	Rechtfertigung
	myth	Mythe
	anthropology	Anthropologie, Menschenkunde
	obviously	offensichtlich
	home-cooked meal	hausgemachte Speise
	underlying	zugrunde liegend
	demonisation	Verteufelung
	convenience food [kənˈviːniəns]	Fertiggerichte, Fertigprodukte
	sexism	Sexismus
	building block	Baustein, Grundstein
	nutritional	ernährungs- …
	processed food	verarbeitete Lebensmittel
	ready-meal	Fertiggericht
16	menu [ˈmenjuː]	Speisekarte
	choice	Auswahl
	crisps	Kartoffelchips
	smoked bacon	geräucherter Speck
	smashed	zertrümmert, zerschmettert
	Batavia lettuce	Kopfsalat
	sourdough	Sauerteig
	chargrilled	auf Holzkohle gegrillt
	rump steak	Rumpsteak
	caramelized onions	karamellisierte Zwiebel
	hand-battered	handgeschlagen
	cod goujons	Dorschstücke
	tartare sauce	Tartar Sauce
	savoury	pikant, salzig
	cauliflower	Karfiol
	side salad	Beilagensalat
	spicy [ˈspaɪsi]	würzig, scharf
	vegetarian [ˌvedʒɪˈteəriən]	vegetarisch
	herb oil	Kräuteröl
	marinated	mariniert
17	hungry [ˈhʌŋɡri]	hungrig
	dessert	Dessert, Nachspeise
	tight budget	knappes Budget
	to be allergic to sth. [əˈlɜːdʒɪk] Are you allergic to anything?	allergisch auf etw. sein
	garlic	Knoblauch
18	fruit [fruːt] They like to eat fruit.	Frucht; Obst
	bitter	bitter
	bland	geschmacklos, fad
	crunchy	knusprig, knackig
	greasy	fettig
	juicy	saftig
	mushy	matschig
	pleasant [ˈplezənt]	angenehm
	smoked	geräuchert
	sour	sauer
	creamy	cremig
	tasteless [ˈteɪstləs]	geschmacklos
	mild [maɪld]	mild
	grilled	gegrillt
	roasted	geröstet, gebraten
	stimulating	anregend, stimulierend
	fried Do you like fried potatoes?	gebraten, frittiert
	liquid	flüssig
	acid	sauer
	unripe	unreif
	smooth	glatt, weich, geschmeidig
	oven	Backrohr
	to check attendance	Anwesenheit überprüfen
	announcement	Ankündigung
19	to explain [ɪkˈspleɪn] Let me explain this to you.	erklären
	breadcrumbed and fried veal scallop	Wiener Schnitzel
	veal	Kalbfleisch
	roast pork	Schweinebraten
	pancake	Palatschinke
	raisins	Rosinen
	this	diese/r/s
	that	jene/r/s
	these	diese (Plural)
	those	jene (Plural)
21	suitable	passend
22	bilingual [baɪˈlɪŋɡwəl]	zweisprachig
	monolingual [ˌmɒnəˈlɪŋɡwəl]	einsprachig
23	live [laɪv] There's a bar here that does live music.	live
	performance [pəˈfɔːməns]	Aufführung
	meaning A word may have several meanings.	Bedeutung
	spelling	Schreibweise
26	training It was great training for what I do now.	Ausbildung, Training
	dentist	Zahnarzt
	appointment I've made an appointment with the dentist.	Verabredung; Termin
	to make it I'm stuck in traffic; I won't make it in time.	es schaffen
	to book sth. He booked tickets online.	etw. buchen/reservieren
	to cancel [ˈkænsəl]	etw. absagen/stornieren
	briefing	Briefing, Einweisung
	sales rep	Vertriebsmitarbeiter/in, Vertreter/in
	to postpone sth.	etw. (nach hinten) verschieben
	accounting	Buchhaltung
	agenda	Agenda, Tagesordnung
	asap – as soon as possible	so bald wie möglich
	to finalise sth.	etw. fertig stellen
	brochure	Broschüre
	product sample	Produktmuster

	projector	Projektor, Beamer	
	marker	Filzstift	
	urgently ['ɜːdʒəntli]	dringend	
	to sort sth. out	etw. klären, erledigen	
	tight schedule ['ʃedjuːl]	enger Zeitplan	
	to get back to sb.	jmnd. Bescheid sagen	
	to clarify a situation	eine Situation klären	
28	HR – human resources	Personalabteilung	
29	advantage [əd'vɑːntɪdʒ]	Vorteil	
	disadvantage [ˌdɪsəd'vɑːntɪdʒ]	Nachteil	
30	boiled	gekocht	
	pork	Schweinefleisch	
	lunch	Mittagessen	
	dinner	Abendessen	
	fish	Fisch	
31	instead of sb./sth.	(an)statt einer Person/Sache	
	You can go instead of Simon, if you want.		
	ankle boots	Stiefelette	
	upstairs	oben, die Treppe hinauf	
	shower gel	Duschgel	
	waterproof	wasserdicht	
	entrance	Eingang	
	I guess …	Ich denke/ glaube …	
	takeaway	Essen zum Mitnehmen	
32	cucumber	Gurke	
	to deliver sth.	etw. liefern	
	dietary requirement	Diätvorschrift	
	mustard ['mʌstəd]	Senf	
	spicy	würzig; scharf	
	table linen ['lɪnɪn] tablecloths and napkins	Tischwäsche	
	takeaway (meal)	Essen zum Mitnehmen	
	to place an order	eine Bestellung aufgeben	
	ready for collection	zur Abholung bereit	
	cream cheese	Frischkäse, Rahmkäse	
	pepper	Paprika	
	tuna	Tunfisch	
	fruit salad	Fruchtsalat	
	apple pie	Apfelkuchen	
	cream	Obers	
	fruit juice	Fruchtsaft	
	food intolerance [ɪn'tɒlərəns]	Lebensmittelunverträglichkeit	
	allergy	Allergie	
	to put sth. together	etw. zusammenstellen	
	I'll put together a nice meal for you.		
	to cater for sb.	jmnd. verpflegen, sorgen für, bewirten	

Competence check: Units 3–5

1	meeting point	Treffpunkt
	to mark sth. [mɑːk]	etw. markieren
	outdoor activities	Outdoor Aktivitäten
	lodge [lɒdʒ]	Hütte, Häuschen
	to take sth. in	etw. (mental) aufnehmen, wahrnehmen
	stunning	atemberaubend, beeindruckend

	surroundings	Umgebung
	zip wire	Seilrutsche
	adventure lover	Abenteuerliebhaber
	off-road	gelände-…
	attraction [ə'trækʃən]	Attraktion
	to stretch	sich erstrecken
	to be proud	stolz sein
	state of the art	hochmodern, auf dem Stand der Technik
	take to sth.	sich etw. angewöhnen
	to master sth.	etw. beherrschen
	green technology	umweltfreundliche Technologie
	to whizz through sth.	durch etw. sausen, zischen
	trail	Pfad
	unforgettable	unvergesslich
	to differ	sich unterscheiden
	epic	episch, groß
	to traverse [trə'vɜːs]	durchqueren
	exhilarating experience	spannende, begeisternde Erfahrung
	hike	Wanderung
	to follow signs ['fɒləʊ]	Schildern folgen
	facilities	Einrichtungen, Ausstattung
	to disturb sb./sth.	jmnd./etw. stören
	to climb	klettern
	landscape	Landschaft

Unit 6

	leisure (time)	Freizeit
1	engineer [ˌendʒɪ'nɪə]	Ingenieur/in
	engineering	Technik, Ingenieurwissenschaft
	She wants to study engineering.		
	fashion designer	Modeschöpfer/in
	accountant	Buchhalter/in
	useful	nützlich, praktisch
	cook/chef [ʃef]	Koch/Köchin
	doctor	Arzt/Ärztin
	lawyer ['lɔɪə]	Rechtsanwalt/Rechtsanwältin
2	unemployed [ˌʌnɪm'plɔɪd]	arbeitslos
	dishes	Geschirr
	to earn a living	den Lebensunterhalt verdienen
	car mechanic	Automechaniker/in
	to repair sth.	etw. reparieren
	engine	Motor
	bodywork	Karosserie (Auto)
	collision	Zusammenstoß
	necessary ['nesəseri]	notwendig
	suit	Anzug
	individual [ˌɪndɪ'vɪdʒuəl]	einzeln/e
	client ['klaɪənt]	Kunde/Kundin, Klient/in
	career	Karriere
	to be responsible for sb./sth.	für jmnd./etw. verantwortlich sein
	stressful	stressig
	application	Bewerbung
	CV: (short for) curriculum vitae	Lebenslauf

Vocabulary

	up to date	aktuell, auf dem neuesten Stand
	delicious [dɪˈlɪʃəs]	köstlich
3	permanent	dauerhaft, permanent
	long term	langfristig
	temporary	vorübergehend, temporär
	these days	heutzutage
	angry	wütend, verärgert
6	to perform an action	eine Handlung ausführen
7	a speech	eine Rede
	decision [dɪˈsɪʒən] *It can be difficult to make decisions.*	Entscheidung
8	housework	Hausarbeit
	to be asleep	schlafen
	kettle	Wasserkocher
9	oil rig	Ölplattform
	work hours	Arbeitszeit
	accommodation	Unterbringung
	me time	Zeit für mich
	time off	Freizeit, Auszeit
	catering assistant	Catering Assistent/in
	daily life	tägliches Leben
	balance	Balance, Ausgleich
10	part-time job	Teilzeitstelle
	travel agency [ˈeɪdʒənsi]	Reisebüro
	advice [ədˈvaɪs]	Rat
	to arrange sth.	etw. arrangieren, zusammenstellen
	visa	Visum
	complaint [kəmˈpleɪnt]	Beschwerde
	refund	Rückzahlung, Vergütung
	specialised	spezialisiert
	trekking	Trekking
	to expect sb./sth.	jmnd./etw. erwarten
	to earn sth.	etw. verdienen
	seasoned [ˈsiːzənd] *My dad is a seasoned project manager; he has a lot of experience.*	erfahren, reif
	payment	Zahlung
	bonus	Bonuszahlung, Prämie
	incentive	Anreiz
	to organise sth.	etw. organisieren
	dream holiday	Traumurlaub
	customer service	Kundenservice
	passion	Begeisterung
	quality	Qualität
	competent	kompetent
	irregular	unregelmäßig
	attention to detail	Detailgenauigkeit
	tour operator	Reiseveranstalter/in
11	presentation [ˌprezənˈteɪʃən]	Referat
	package deal [ˈpækɪdʒ]	Pauschalangebot
12	client *someone who pays for services or advice*	Klient/in, Kunde/Kundin
13	character trait [ˈkærəktə]	Charaktereigenschaft
15	market researcher [ˈmɑːkɪt]	Marktforscher/in

	various	verschieden(e)
	employer	Arbeitgeber/in
16	to be awfully sorry	einem furchtbar leid tun
	give sb. a ring	jmnd. anrufen
	no idea	keine Ahnung
	actually *Well, actually, I'm busy tonight.*	eigentlich
	quite busy [kwaɪt ˈbɪzi]	ziemlich beschäftigt
17	to relax	(sich) entspannen
	tired [taɪəd]	müde
	to feel well	sich gut/gesund fühlen
	salesperson	Verkäufer/in
	trainers	Sportschuhe
	study group	Lerngruppe
18	to carry	tragen; dabei haben
	library [ˈlaɪbrəri]	Bibliothek
	salesperson	Verkäufer/in
	trainers [ˈtreɪnəz]	Turnschuhe
19	platform	Bahnsteig
	sweets	Süßigkeiten
	culture	Kultur
20	co-ed school: (short for) co-educational [ˌedʒʊˈkeɪʃənəl] school	gemischtgeschlechtliche Schule
	digit [ˈdɪdʒɪt] *any number from 0 to 9*	einstellige Zahl
	grade	Note
	language lab(oratory): *a room in which students can use equipment to help them practise listening to and speaking a foreign language*	Sprachlabor
	locker	Spind
	nerdy [ˈnɜːdi] *Not everyone shares my nerdy love of science.*	doof; streberhaft, langweilig
	otherwise *You should write it down, otherwise you'll forget it.*	ansonst(en)
	textile [ˈtekstaɪl]	textil; Textil-...
	to call sb. by his/her first name	jmdn. Beim Vornamen nennen/duzen
	surprised [səˈpraɪzd] *I'm surprised to see you here.*	überrascht
	service	Serviceorganisation und Servieren (Schulfach); Dienst(leistung)
	uncertainty [ʌnˈsɜːtənti]	Unsicherheit
	to attend school	in eine Schule gehen, eine Schule besuchen
	three-digit	dreistellig
	stuff	Zeugs, Sachen
	private college	Privatcollege
	business administration	Betriebswirtschaftslehre
	business-related	geschäftsbezogen
	office management	Büroleitung
	assignment [əˈsaɪnmənt] *When I come home from school, I still have to do the assignments for the next day.*	(Arbeits-) Auftrag

Vocabulary

	relaxed	entspannt
	high school	Gymnasium (American), Highschool
21	division [dɪˈvɪʒən]	Division
	multiplication [ˌmʌltɪplɪˈkeɪʒən]	Multiplikation
	subtraction [səbˈtrækʃən]	Substraktion
	fraction [ˈfrækʃən]	Bruch
	addition [əˈdɪʃən]	Addition
	to subtract sth. from sth. [səbˈtrækt]	etw. von etw. Abziehen
	to add	addieren
	to add up to sth.	etw. ergeben
	to multiply sth. by sth. [ˈmʌltɪplaɪ]	etw. mit etw. multiplizieren
	to divide sth. by sth. [dɪˈvaɪd]	etw. durch etw. teilen/dividieren
	numerator: the number above the line in fractions [ˈnjuːməreɪtə]	Zähler
	denominator: the number below the line in fractions [dɪˈɒmɪneɪtə]	Nenner
	power [paʊə]	Kraft, Macht; Potenz (in der Mathematik)
	square [skweə]	quadratisch, Quadrat; Platz
	squared	quadriert
	square root	Quadratwurzel
	cubed 4 cubed is 64.	hoch drei
	cube root The cube root of 8 is 2.	Kubikwurzel
	square bracket	eckige Klammer
	to equal One plus one equals two.	gleich sein, gleichsetzen
	equal sign	Gleichheitszeichen
	equation [ɪˈkweɪʒən]	Gleichung
	SI unit: SI stands for Systeme International	SI-Einheit
25	exchange student	Austauschstudent/in
	homeroom	engl. Schulsystem: Klassenzimmer in dem Klassenvorstand jeden Morgen die Anwesenheit überprüft
	dress code	Kleidungsvorschriften
	to cheer	anfeuern, zujubeln, aufmuntern
	sweatshirts	Trainingspullover
	sweatpants	Trainingshose, Jogginghose
26	to spend time	Zeit verbringen
27	to depend on sth. The city largely depends on the car industry.	von etw. abhängig sein
	probably	wahrscheinlich
	public transport	öffentliche(s) Verkehrsmittel

Unit 7

	to board He boarded the train.	besteigen, einsteigen
	to check in We have to check in two hours before departure.	einchecken
	timetable	Fahrplan
	to give directions [dɪˈrekʃənz]	den Weg erklären
1	Habal-Habal	Habal-Habal – Motorrad mit Fahrer
	suspension railway	Schwebebahn
	hydrofoil	Tragflügelboot
	sled	Schlitten
	trolley bus	Oberleitungsbus, Obus
	Maglev train	Magnetschwebebahn
	unusual [ʌnˈjuːʒuəl]	ungewöhnlich
2	to get to How do I get to Paris?	hinkommen
	luggage	Gepäck
	ride Thanks for the ride.	Fahrt
	to catch Catch the number 42 bus.	nehmen; kriegen; fangen
	reindeer	Renntier
	to be cramped	eng, zusammengepfercht sein
	monorail	Einschienenbahn
	to approach sth.	etw. näher kommen, sich nähern
	to pick someone up	jmnd. abholen
	Philippines	Philippinen
	seating	Sitzgelegenheit
	glacier	Gletscher
	refuelling	Auftanken
	snow-covered	schneebedeckt
4	dental practice	Zahnarztpraxis
5	to cycle [ˈsaɪkəl]	Rad fahren
6	to ride He rides a motorbike.	fahren; reiten
	traffic jam Turn left at the traffic lights.	Verkehrsstau
	traffic light	Ampel
	to turn	drehen, sich wenden; umdrehen
	unicycle [ˈjuːnɪˌsaɪkəl]	Einrad
	wonder No wonder he is happy.	Wunder
	exercise [ˈeksəsaɪz]	Bewegung, Betätigung
8	suntan lotion	Sonnencreme
	address book	Adressbuch
	guide book	Reiseführer (Buch)
	tissue [ˈtɪʃuː]	Taschentuch
	passport	Reisepass
	toothbrush	Zahnbürste
	comb	Kamm
	pen	Füllfeder
	to go away on a trip	verreisen, wegfahren
13	front door	Haustür, Vordereingang
	riverside	Flussufer, Ufergegend
	preposition [ˌprepəˈzɪʃən]	Präposition, Vorwort
15	departure [dɪˈpaːtʃə]	Abfahrt, Abflug
	passenger [ˈpæsəndʒə]	Passagier/in
	express coach [kəʊtʃ]	Expressbus
	direct bus	direkte Busverbindung
	to change	umsteigen
	single ticket	Einzelfahrschein
	return ticket	Retourfahrkarte
16	day return (ticket)	Tagesrückfahrkarte

Vocabulary

	open return (ticket)	offene Rückfahrt		to pay attention	Acht geben
19	baggage collection ['bægɪdʒ]	Gepäckausgabe		insects	Insekten
	customs He was stopped going through customs.	Zoll	45	Cambodia [kæm'bəʊdiə]	Kambodscha
				scooter He rides around on a scooter.	(Motor-)Roller
	gate	Tor; Flugsteig		per cent, percent	Prozent
	passport control	Passkontrolle			
	security [sɪ'kjʊərəti]	Sicherheit		**Unit 8**	
	to arrive [ə'raɪv] We arrived at the station around 4 o'clock.	ankommen		to arrange sth. Why don't we arrange a surprise party?	etw. organisieren/planen
	boarding gate	Flugsteig		suggestion [sə'dʒestʃən] Philip made a few suggestions.	Vorschlag
	check-in	Einchecken, Check-in			
20	boarding pass	Bordkarte		arrangement [ə'reɪndʒmənt]	Vereinbarung, Plan; Anordnung
	delayed [dɪ'leɪd] The flight was delayed.	verspätet		to respond	antworten
	to schedule sth.	etw. planen, festlegen		imagination	Vorstellungskraft
	cancelled	storniert		thank-you note	Dankesschreiben
	boarding	an Bord gehen, einsteigen	1	animated film They've made an animated film of the book.	Zeichentrickfilm
	on time	pünktlich			
22	wallet ['wɒlɪt]	Brieftasche		extract ['ekstrækt]	Auszug
	to come forward	vortreten, sich melden		documentary [ˌdɒkjə'mentəri]	Dokumentation, Dokumentarfilm
24	to link sth.	etw. verbinden		drama	Drama
25	to be frightened ['fraɪtənd]	Angst haben		science fiction	Science Fiction
	receptionist [rɪ'sepʃənɪst]	Rezeptionist/in		romantic	romantisch
26	funny	lustig		abortion	Abtreibung
	to mix sth. up	etw. verwechseln	2	adoption [ə'dɒpʃən]	Adoption
	storytelling	Geschichten erzählen		box office	Kartenkasse
27	huge [hju:dʒ]	riesig		Malian ['mɑ:liən] from Mali, a country in West Africa	malisch
	spider	Spinne			
29	art gallery	Kunstgalerie			
30	bear cub	Bärenjunges		pregnant	schwanger
32	to miss sth. I missed the train by three minutes.	etw. verpassen		to realise sth. I immediately realised he was wrong.	etw. begreifen/realisieren
34	to obtain sth. [əb'teɪn]	etw. erhalten; etw. erlangen		to be set in The story is set in a school.	spielen in
	to receive sth. [rɪ'si:v]	etw. erhalten		fantasy	Fantasy-...
36	to get home	heimkommen		incredible	unglaublich
39	to apologise [ə'pɒlədʒaɪz] He apologised to her for losing the book.	sich entschuldigen		prequel	Prequel, Vorläufer, Vorgeschichte
				series	Serie
	to complain [kəm'pleɪn] People have complained about the noise.	sich beschweren		the pond (AW: slang for the Atlantic Ocean)	Slang für Atlantischer Ozean
40	to bump into sb. I bumped into someone, so I said, "I'm sorry!"	mit jmdm. zusammenstoßen		to be amazed	erstaunt/verblüfft sein
				gradually	allmählich, schrittweise
				complicated	kompliziert
41	convention	Tagung, Konferenz		directed by	unter der Regie von, inszeniert von
	station	Bahnhof		century	Jahrhundert
	underground station	Ubahn Haltestelle		magic	magisch
44	ancient ['eɪnʃənt]	alt, antik		powerful ['paʊəfəl]	machtvoll
	climate ['klaɪmət]	Klima		stranger	Fremde/r
	cricket	Grille; Kricket		league	Liga
	entire [ɪn'taɪə]	ganz		tail	Schwanz
	to ignore sb./sth. [ɪg'nɔ:]	jmdn./etw. ignorieren		mastermind	Kopf, Drahtzieher
	to suppose [sə'pəʊz]	vermuten		hilarious	urkomisch, lustig
	volunteer [ˌvɒlən'tɪə]	Freiwillige/r		minions (animated characters)	
	volunteer work	Freiwilligenarbeit, ehrenamtliche Tätigkeit			

Vocabulary

	to capture sth.	etw. erfassen, einfangen
	The film beautifully captures 19th century life in London.	
4	superlative [suːˈpɜːlətɪv]	Superlativ
	syllable [ˈsɪləbəl]	Silbe
	careful	vorsichtig
	further [ˈfɜːðə]	weiter
	furthest	am weitesten
7	to emphasise sth.	etw. betonen
9	unnecessary	unnötig, nicht erforderlich
	process	Prozess, Ablauf
	keyword	Stichwort
	draft	Entwurf
	script	Skriptum, Drehbuch
	actor, actress	Schauspieler, Schauspielerin
	storyboard	Storyboard, Szenenbuch
	rehearsal [rəˈhɜːsəl]	Probe
	to edit sth.	etw. bearbeiten, (Film) schneiden
10	some time	einige Zeit; irgendwann
	I'll text you some time.	
	Why don't we …?	Warum machen wir nicht …?
11	Fine with me.	Einverstanden.
	Shall we …?	Sollen wir …?
	How about …?	Wie wärs mit …?
14	to text sb.	jmdm. SMS schicken
15	to be stuck in traffic	im Stau stecken
17	supremacy [suːˈpreməsi]	Übermacht
	labyrinth [ˈlæbərɪnθ]	Irrgarten
20	latest project	neuestes Projekt
	to shoot a film	einen Film drehen
	distributor	Vertreiber/in, Händler/in
	regarding	betreffend
	to host sth. [həʊst]	Gastgeber sein, etw. veranstalten
	in the pipeline	in Vorbereitung
	to keep one's fingers crossed	Daumen halten
	to pursue a career	eine Karriere verfolgen
	to focus on sth.	sich auf etw. konzentrieren
	support	Unterstützung
	challenging	herausfordernd
	carpet	Teppichboden
23	career counsellor	Berufsberater
24	camping	Zelten, Kampieren
	They go camping a lot.	
	instructor	Lehrer/in,
	How do you become a driving instructor?	
	inn	Gasthaus
	a pub or small hotel where you can stay for the night, usually in the countryside	
	art gallery	Kunstgalerie
	chalet	Chalet, Hütte, Ferienhaus
	canoeing	Kanufahren
26	uncomfortable	unbequem
29	driving test	Fahrprüfung
	stressed	gestresst
	slightly	ein bisschen, leicht
	game console	Spielkonsole

30	guess	Vermutung
31	face	Gesicht
	to get together	sich treffen
32	hiking [ˈhaɪkɪŋ]	Wandern
35	ellipsis [ɪˈlɪpsɪs]	Auslassung
	ice cream	Eiscreme
36	graduation [ˌɡrædʒuˈeɪʃən]	Ausbildungsabschluss
37	apparently [əˈpærəntli]	anscheinend
	Apparently it's going to rain today.	
	cast	Besetzung
	character	Charakter, Figur
	to recommend sth. (to sb.) [ˌrekəˈmend]	(jmdm.) etw. empfehlen
	Can you recommend a place to stay?	
38	production [prəˈdʌkʃən]	Produktion, Aufführung
	storyline	Handlung
39	to feature [ˈfiːtʃə]	aufweisen, beinhalten
	folk music [fəʊk]	Folk (Musikrichtung)
40	piano [piˈænəʊ]	Klavier
	approximately	ungefähr
	to inspire sb./sth.	jmnd./etw. inspirieren
	kid	(kleines) Kind
	sleep under the stars	im Freien übernachten
	courtyard	(Innen-)hof

Competence check: Units 6–8

1	to pretend	etw. vortäuschen
	to be bossed around	herumkommandiert werden
	monastery	Kloster
	to argue with sb. [ˈɑːɡjuː]	sich mit jmdm. streiten
	faded	verblasst
3	likeable	sympathisch, liebenswert, nett
	annoyed	verärgert, genervt
	grumpy	grantig, mürrisch

Unit 9

	advice	Rat(schlag)
	headache [ˈhedeɪk]	Kopfschmerzen
	I've got a bad headache.	
	health [helθ]	Gesundheit
	to give advice	Rat geben
	pharmacy	Apotheker/in, Drogist/in
	to apologise	sich entschuldigen
	instructions [ɪnˈstrʌkʃənz]	Anleitung
1	grain [ɡreɪn]	Korn
	to grow	wachsen
	muscle [ˈmʌsəl]	Muskel
	stomach [ˈstʌmək]	Magen
	thumb [θʌm]	Daumen
	bone	Knochen
	to weigh	wiegen
	sore throat [sɔː ˈθrəʊt]	Halsschmerzen
	to have a temperature [ˈtemprətʃə]	Fieber haben
	knee	Knie

Vocabulary

	sick, ill	krank
	a bit	ein bisschen
3	cold *I've got a cold.*	Erkältung; kalt
	to feel sick *I'm feeling a bit sick.*	sich schlecht fühlen (es ist einem übel)
	pain	Schmerz
	sore [sɔː] *I have a sore throat.*	weh, wund
	temperature	Temperatur; Fieber
	throat	Hals, Kehle, Rachen
4	symptom ['sɪmptəm]	Symptom
6	dairy products	Milchprodukte
7	ache [eɪk]	Schmerz
	to continue [kən'tɪnjuː]	fortsetzen; andauern
	dose [dəʊs] *What is the recommended dose?*	Dosis
	package	Packung
	painkiller	Schmerzmittel
	paracetamol [ˌpærə'siːtəmɒl]	Paracetamol (Schmerzmittel)
	sachet ['sæʃeɪ]	(kleiner) Beutel, Säckchen
	tablet ['tæblət]	Tablette; Tablet(-PC)
	toothache ['tuːθeɪk] *I've got terrible toothache.*	Zahnweh
	to contain sth.	etw. beinhalten
	powder	Puder
	relief	Linderung, Erleichterung
	aches and pains	Schmerzen, Wehwehchen
8	remedy ['remədi]	Heilmittel, Arzneimittel
	pharmacist	Apotheker/in
9	energy ['enədʒi] *I have a lot of energy.*	Energie
	to have no energy	sich schlapp fühlen
10	teabag	Teebeutel
	bottom	Unterseite; Gesäß
	bottom of a foot	Fußsohle
	drop	Tropfen
	Egypt ['iːdʒɪpt]	Ägypten
	garlic clove	Knoblauchzehe
	site	Stelle, Ort; Website
	to tie *Your hair needs tying back.*	binden
	tooth	Zahn
	salt water	Salzwasser
15	to hurt *My eyes really hurt.*	schmerzen, wehtun
	mustard	Senf
16	to inhale [ɪn'heɪl]	einatmen, inhalieren
	steam	Dampf
17	bowl	Schüssel
18	to improve sth. [ɪm'pruːv]	etw. verbessern
	level *Hang photos at eye level.*	Niveau, Höhe
	proper	ordentlich, richtig
	air-conditioner	Klimaanlage
	bright [braɪt]	grell, hell
	environment	Umwelt; Umgebung
	mood	Stimmung
	natural light	Tageslicht
	lift	Lift
20	to entertain [ˌentə'teɪn]	unterhalten, bewirten
	effectively	wirksam, effektiv
21	container	Behälter
	quantity	Menge
22	a couple of	ein paar, einige
24	pocket money	Taschengeld
26	scales	Maßstab; Skala
	tape measure	Maßband
	ounce (= a unit for measuring weight) [aʊns]	Unze (28,35 kg)
	pound [paʊnd]	Pfund (0,453 kg)
	inch (pl. inches)	Zoll (2,54 cm)
	foot (pl. feet)	Fuß (0,3048 m)
	yard: three feet	Yard (0,914 m)
	mile	Meile (1,6 km)
	pint [paɪnt]	Pint (0,568 l bzw. 0,473 l in den USA)
	gallon ['gælən]	Gallone (4,55 l bzw. 3,79 l in den USA)
	barrel	Fass
	calibrated jug: measuring jug	Messbecher
	vessel	Gefäß
	to measure ['meʒə]	messen
	beaker ['biːkə]	Becher(glas)
28	appliance [ə'plaɪəns]	Gerät
30	barometer [bə'rɒmɪtə]	Barometer
	mercury	Quecksilber
31	milometer [maɪ'lɒmɪtə]	Meilen-/Kilometerzähler
	altimeter ['æltɪmiːtə]	Höhenmesser
	laser range finder	Laserentfernungsmesser
	vernier callipers ['vɜːniə 'kælɪpəs]	Schublehre, Messschieber
	(tyre) pressure gauge [geɪdʒ]	(Reifen-)Druckmesser, Manometer
	analogue ['ænəlɒg] *A video camera can use analogue and digital technology.*	analog
	drawing compass	Zirkel
	stopwatch	Stoppuhr
32	reschedule	verschieben, neu planen
	computerised	computerbasiert
	unavailable	nicht verfügbar
	grateful	dankbar
	inconvenience	Unannehmlichkeit
	to catch up	aufholen
	to get one's act together	etwas in den Griff kriegen
	acceptable	akzeptable
	to let sb. down	jmnd. enttäuschen, im Stich lassen
33	wrong *I was wrong.*	falsch; im Unrecht
	to give a presentation	ein Referat halten
	a potential client	ein/e potentielle/r Kunde/Kundin
	reserved	reserviert
	valued customer	ein/e geschätzte/r Kunde/Kundin
	replacement	Ersatz, Umtausch
39	to be able to afford sth.	sich etw. leisten können
	ginger ['dʒɪndʒə]	Ingwer

Vocabulary

	organic food [ɔːˈgænɪk]	Naturkost
	taste [teɪst]	Geschmack
	to bake sth.	etw. backen
	sleeping pattern	Schlafgewohnheit
	to lose weight [luːz]	abnehmen (Gewicht)

Unit 10

1	wild animal	wildes Tier
	instrument	Musikinstrument
	charity	Hilfsorganisation, Wohltätigkeitsverein
	to be retired	pensioniert sein
	suburb	Vorort
	continent	Kontinent
	to explore sth.	etw. erkunden, erforschen
	cruiser	Kreuzfahrtschiff
	pretty annoying	ziemlich ärgerlich
	to stroke sth.	etw. streicheln
	army	Militär
	Latvia	Lettland
	Romania	Rumänien
	to spoil sth.	etw. verderben
	Scandinavian countries	skandinavische Länder
	to brew beer	Bier brauen
3	clam chowder	Muschelsuppe
10	informative [ɪnˈfɔːmətɪv]	informativ
	to research [rɪˈsɜːtʃ]	nach-/ erforschen
	to submit	einreichen
	Did you submit your article to the magazine?	
11	dolphin	Delphin
13	cave [keɪv]	Höhle
	cemetery [ˈsemətri]	Friedhof
	church steeple	Kirchturm
	fountain [ˈfaʊntɪn]	Springbrunnen
	palace [ˈpælɪs]	Palast, Schloss
	ruins [ruːɪnz]	Ruine/n
	sculpture [ˈskʌlptʃə]	Skulptur
	statue [ˈstætʃuː]	Statue
	tomb [tuːm]	Grabmal
	town hall	Rathaus
	city walls	Stadtmauern
	skyscraper	Wolkenkratzer
	waterfall	Wasserfall
15	reef	Riff
	beloved [bɪˈlʌvɪd]	geliebt
	childbirth	Geburt, Entbindung
	emperor	Kaiser
	to enter sth.	etw. betreten; an etw. teilnehmen
	He can enter the competition again.	
	generally	im Allgemeinen
	historical [hɪˈstɒrɪkəl]	historisch, geschichtlich
	immigrant [ˈɪmɪgrənt]	Einwanderer/Einwanderin
	off the coast	vor der Küste
	scuba diving [ˈskuːbə ˌdaɪvɪŋ]	Sporttauchen
	tourist destination	Urlaubsziel

	World Heritage Site [ˈherɪtɪdʒ]	Weltkulturerbe
	criminal background	krimineller Hintergrund
	billion	Milliarde
	snorkelling	Schnorcheln
	tourism	Tourismus
	fascinating	faszinierend
	to be impressed	beeindruckt sein
	corals	Korallen
20	recommendation	Empfehlung
21	day trip	Tagesausflug
24	mandatory	verpflichtend
	caution	Vorsicht
	prohibition	Verbot
	hazard	Gefahr, Risiko, Gefährdung
25	surface [ˈsɜːfɪs]	Oberfläche
	electricity	Elektrizität
	protective gloves	Schutzhandschuhe
	life jacket	Schwimmweste
26	to suspect sth.	etw. vermuten
	to shut sth.	etw. schließen, zumachen
	personal belongings	persönliche Gegenstände
	assembly	Versammlung
27	to be good at sth.	etw. gut können
28	recently [ˈriːsəntli]	vor Kurzem
31	It takes one hour to …	Es dauert eine Stunde um …
32	Brazil [brəˈzɪl]	Brasilien
36	chips	Pommes frites
	colourful	farbenprächtig
	diversity [daɪˈvɜːsəti]	Vielfalt
	Indonesia	Indonesien
	potato chips (AE)	Kartoffelchips
	tile [taɪl]	Fliese, Kachel
	guesthouse	Pension, Gästehaus
37	to display [dɪˈspleɪ]	ausstellen
	to feature sth.	etw. darstellen
	The painting features a snow-covered mountain.	
38	Take care.	Mach's gut!, Pass gut auf dich auf!
	How are things …?	Wie geht's …? Wie läufts …?
42	a former teacher	ein/e frühere/r Lehrer/in

Competence check: Units 9–10

1	stock	Lager, Lagerbestand
	leprosy	Lepra
	infectious	ansteckend
3	to drop in	vorbeikommen, reinschauen
	gore	gestocktes Blut

Competence check: Units 1–2

Reading, exercise 2: 1 T, I hope you're doing; 2 F, You enjoy cycling, don't; 3 T, Somehow, I remember that; 4 F, She tried to avoid; 5 F, I'm fine with both

Reading, exercise 3: 1 I, 2 G, 3 B, 4 A, 5 D, 6 F

Writing, exercise 4, model email on p. 46

Writing, exercise 5, sample text

Username: Deborah
E-Mail: deborah@zmail.com

"Sleep like a bird in a tree"

29 July 2019

As soon as we arrived at the tree house hotel, we knew we were somewhere very special. The forest itself is just stunning – it's like something from a film! – but it's the hotel that is really extraordinary. The main part of the hotel, where the reception and restaurant are, is in a beautiful old castle. But the rooms are in wooden cabins in the forest. They are so cute and really comfortable!

Pedro and Rita, the owners, are very friendly and welcoming. They also prepare the food, which is excellent. The hotel offers lots of activities and trips, such as guided forest walks, rock climbing and mountain biking. You can even hire the bikes and equipment if you want. We tried everything and had loads of fun.

I had a brilliant holiday in Scotland – I felt free as a bird. Heartily recommended!

Listening, exercise 6: 1 the building's and people's; 2 recycled wood, straw, clay; 3 good insulation; 4 triple glazed windows; 5 solar panels; 6 sunshine; 7 stop dripping taps / new, water-efficient devices; 8 40% more efficient

Language, exercise 7

1. I really miss my sister when I am away from home.
2. I'm from Madrid but I live in Barcelona now.
3. We both do in-line skating in our free time.
4. My name's Andrew and I'm from a small town in Wales.
5. I go to dance classes with my friends every Saturday.
6. I can see the famous Opera House from my bedroom.

Competence check: Units 3–5

Reading, exercise 1: 1 C, 2 A, 3 B, 4 C, 5 B
Listening, exercise 2: 1 F, 2 I, 3 A, 4 J, 5 C, 6 B, 7 G, 8 D

Key Competence check

Writing, exercise 3, sample text

From: Vince
To: Liam

Hi Liam,

Last Saturday was incredible. Mum and Dad took me and my sister to Lakeside, a huge shopping mall near London. Obviously, the first shop we went to was the game shop. I used all the vouchers I had and bought three new games – hopefully you'll be online at the weekend and we can play.

Then we went to the sports shop to get some new football boots for me and my sister – we both need them for school this semester. I can't believe how expensive they were, but they are really good quality.

Before we went home, we had burger and chips, and then an ice cream. I can't remember the last time I enjoyed shopping so much. Do you want to come next time we go?

See you soon,

Vince

Language, exercise 4

1 How (much) / many luggage do you want to check in?
2 Would you like a / (some) basmati rice with your steak?
3 I prefer teas / (tea) to fruit juice in the morning.
4 I'd like some / (an) orange, please.
5 My dad drinks many / (a lot of) milk every day.
6 She always puts a / (some) lettuce into her sandwich.
7 My little banana tree needs (a lot of) / a light.
8 Eating (a lot of) / a sugar is not good for your body.

Competence check: Units 6–8

Reading, exercise 1: 1 F, It was written by; 2 T, Francis is a rich; 3 F, After the brothers argue; 4 F, Because of this, they; 5 F, Finally, a journey that; 6 T, Slowly, a new kind

Writing, exercise 2, sample text

From: Ines
To: Nehir

Hey Nehir, great to hear from you!

Of course, I'll come to your party, I wouldn't miss it for the world. Can't wait to see everybody! Is there anything you want me to bring?

Glad to hear you had a great time in Andalusia, even if it was too hot. On our last holiday we had the opposite – we went to Norway, so it was beautiful but also quite cold. We went on a cruise up and down the fjords which were just incredible, and one night we saw the Northern Lights. Oh my god, they are amazing!

We also spent some time in Oslo, which is nice but a bit boring if I'm honest. There isn't much to do apart from museums and stuff. By that time, I was looking forward to getting home and getting online …

Well, see you soon, can't wait for the party,

Ines

Listening, exercise 3: 1 B, 2 D, 3 C, 4A, 5D
Language, exercise 4: 1 were you doing, 2 was raining, 3 were waiting, 4 was playing, 5 were you driving
Language, exercise 5: 1 was released, 2 was played, 3 are followed, 4 are thrown
Language, exercise 6: 1 starts, 2 am meeting, 3 leave, 4 are you going, 5 am going

Key Competence check

Competence check: Units 9–10

Reading, exercise 1: 1 A, 2 D, 3 E, 4 J, 5 C, 6 F, 7 G, 8 I

Writing, exercise 2, sample text

> From: Ava Smith
> To: Stephanie Miller
>
> Dear Stephanie,
>
> I'm really sorry, but my flight has been cancelled. There is a snowstorm here and unfortunately it's not safe for the plane to take off, so I'm afraid I won't be there tomorrow. It's terribly frustrating and I'm sorry to let you down at such short notice.
>
> Weather permitting, I will be on the next available flight, which leaves on Monday next week. I'm sorry that there will be such a long delay, but I can't get there any other way. I'm incredibly disappointed – I was really looking forward to getting there and joining up with the team.
>
> Again, apologies, and I will see you as soon as possible.
>
> Kind regards,
>
> Ava Smith

Listening, exercise 3: 1 C, 2 B, 3 A, 4 B, 5 D, 6 D
Language, exercise 4: 1 symptoms, 2 sachet, 3 allergic, 4 sore, 5 painkiller, 6 dentist
Language, exercise 5: 1 am hoping to, 2 are going to, 3 is hoping to, 4 I'd like to, 5 would like
Language, exercise 6: 1 C, 2 D, 3 G, 4 A, 5 E

Maps

The British Isles

Maps

The United States of America

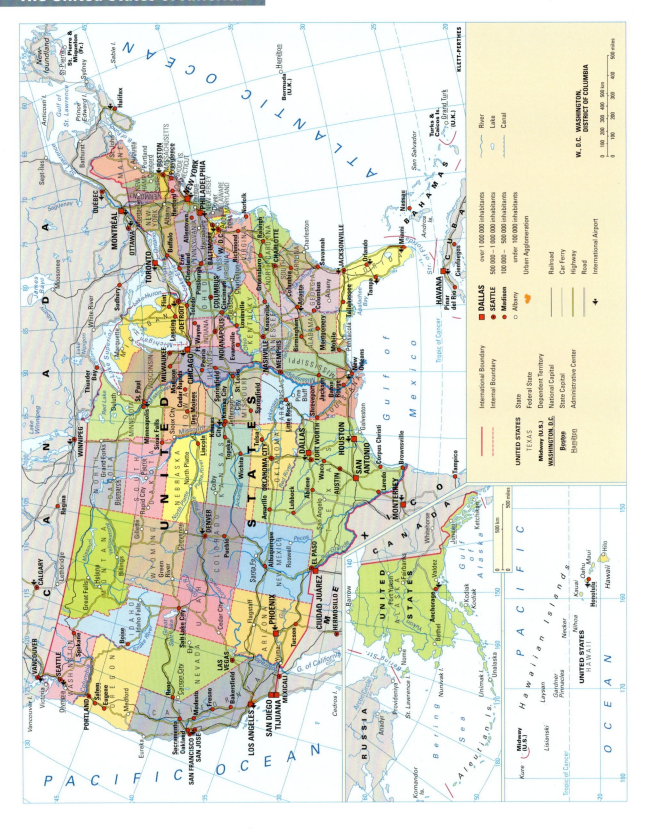

Australia & New Zealand

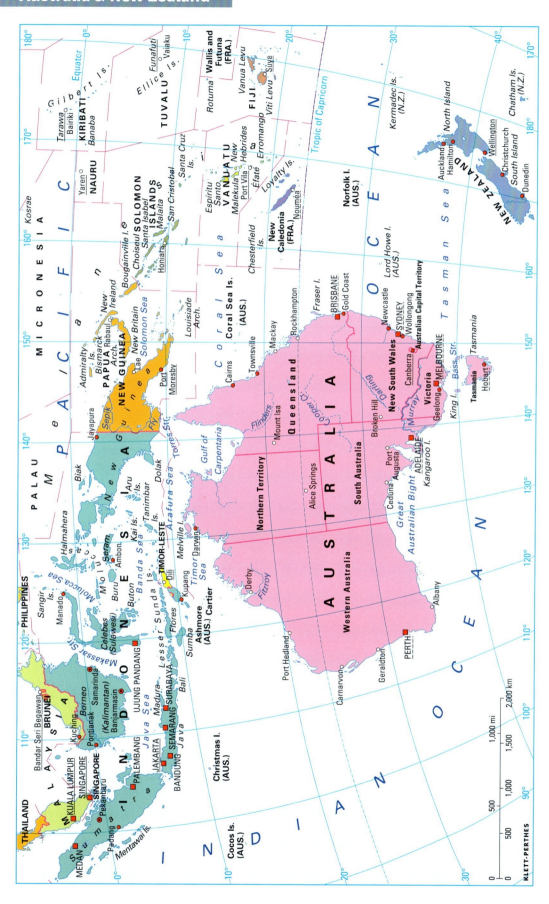

Acknowledgements

The authors and publishers acknowledge the following sources of copyright material and are grateful for the permissions granted. While every effort has been made, it has not always been possible to identify the sources of all the material used, or to trace all copyright holders. If any omissions are brought to our notice, we will be happy to include the appropriate acknowledgements on reprinting.

Texts

29.1: adapted and abridged from Elaine Lemm, "Full Breakfast in England", https://www.thespruce.com/what-is-a-full-breakfast-435324, 12 April 2018; **29.2:** adapted abridged from *Sous Chef*, "Egyptian Breakfast Recipe: Ful Medames ", https://www.souschef.co.uk/bureau-of-taste/egyptian-breakfast-recipe-ful-medames/, 17 November 2017; **35:** adapted and abridged from *ASHCOMBE ADVENTURE CENTRE* www.ashcombeadventure.co.uk; **50:** adapted and abridged from *Word Wide Web Foundation*, "History of the web. Sir Tim Berners-Lee", https://webfoundation.org/about/vision/history-of-the-web/; **63:** adapted and abridged from Tim Lewis, "Meet the chef who's debunking detox, diets and wellness", 18 June 2017, https://www.theguardian.com/lifeandstyle/2017/jun/18/angry-chef-debunking-detox-diets-wellness-nutrition-alternative-facts; **70:** adapted and abridged from *GoApe*, "HIGH ROPES ADVENTURES IN SCOTLAND", https://goape.co.uk/days-out/scotland/aberfoyle; **77:** adapted and abridged from *totaljobs*, "Travel agent job description", https://www.totaljobs.com/careers-advice/job-profile/travel-leisure-jobs/travel-agent-job-description; **88:** adapted from Forward Ltd, "One-Wheeled Wonder", AA Magazine, February 2004; **104:** adapted and abridged from "Interview: Jo Weil talks acting, hosting and plans for 2017 SPECIAL" by MARKOS PAPADATOS, Entertainment, 14 October 2014; **112:** adapted and abridged from Philip French, "The Darjeeling Limited", 25 November 2007, https://www.theguardian.com/film/2007/nov/25/comedy.drama1; **140:** adapted and abridged from "Fast-Paced Education in the Field", http://blogs.msf.org/en/staff/blogs/msf-in-south-sudan/fast-paced-education-in-the-field

Pictures

7.1: Edyta Pawlowska / Fotolia; **7.2:** John Krajewski / iStockphoto; **7.3:** jane / iStockphoto; **7.4:** dawn liljenquist / iStockphoto; **7.5:** Chris Schmidt / iStockphoto; **7.6:** Riorita / iStockphoto; **8.1:** fotomorgana / Fotolia; **9.1:** Goldmund Lukic / iStockphoto; **9.2:** JBryson / iStockphoto; **9.3:** Jani Bryson / iStockphoto; **13.1:** Yobro10 / Getty Images – iStockphoto; **14.1:** FatCamera / Getty Images – iStockphoto; **14.2:** Anchiy / Getty Images – iStockphoto; **15.1:** Carmen Martínez Banús / iStockphoto; **15.2:** Peter Baxter / Fotolia; **15.3:** søren Sielemann / iStockphoto; **15.4:** drbimages / iStockphoto; **16.1:** kevron2001 / Getty Images – iStockphoto; **16.2:** Nataniil / Getty Images – iStockphoto; **17.1:** Justin Horrocks / iStockphoto; **17.2:** Leslie Banks / iStockphoto; **19.1:** Suprijono Suharjoto / iStockphoto; **20.1:** Chris Schmidt / iStockphoto; **21.1:** kate_sept2004 / iStockphoto; **22.1:** AntonioGuillem / Getty Images – iStockphoto; **22.2:** Jodi Matthews / iStockphoto; **22.3:** drbimages / iStockphoto; **22.4:** Tom Fullum / iStockphoto; **24.1:** martin-dm / iStockphoto; **24.2:** jacoblund / Getty Images – iStockphoto; **24.3:** Mark Bowden / Thinkstock; **25.1:** Felix Alim / iStockphoto; **25.2:** meshaphoto / iStockphoto; **26.1:** AntonioGuillem / Getty Images – iStockphoto; **26.2:** GrapeImages / Getty Images – iStockphoto; **26.3:** Andyd / iStockphoto; **26.4:** BrianAJackson / iStockphoto; **26.5:** womue / Fotolia; **26.6:** Markus Mainka / Fotolia; **26.7:** blackwaterimages / Getty Images – iStockphoto; **26.8:** Daniel Cole / Thinkstock; **26.9:** Zerbor / Getty Images – iStockphoto; **26.10:** anna1311/ Thinkstock; **26.11:** chengyuzheng / Thinkstock; **26.12:** urfinguss / Getty Images – iStockphoto; **27.1:** kyletperry / Getty Images – iStockphoto; **27.2:** Pawel Gaul / Getty Images – iStockphoto; **28.1:** Kutlu / TopFoto / picturedesk.com; **28.2:** golubovy / Getty Images – iStockphoto; **29.1:** amoklv / Getty Images – iStockphoto; **29.2:** Adam Khaled / Getty Images – iStockphoto; **30.1:** benstevens / Getty Images – iStockphoto; **30.2:** anzeletti / iStockphoto; **30.3:** Mlenny Photography / iStockphoto; **31.1:** pixelfit / Getty Images – iStockphoto; **32.1:** fderib / Fotolia; **34.1:** pressmaster / Fotolia; **36.1:** Shutterstock / Procyk Radek; **36.2:** mbbirdy / iStockphoto; **36.3:** auremar / Fotolia; **36.4:** Chalabala / Getty Images – iStockphoto; **37.1:** DiyanaDimitrova / Getty Images – iStockphoto; **38.1:** ake1150 – stock.adobe.com / Fotolia; **38.2:** gpointstudio – stock.adobe.com / Fotolia; **38.3:** zelenka68 – stock.adobe.com / Fotolia; **38.4:** olish – stock.adobe.com / Fotolia; **38.5:** one – stock.adobe.com / Fotolia; **38.6:** Kara – stock.adobe.com / Fotolia; **39.1:** DGLimages / Getty Images – iStockphoto; **40.1:** mr.markin / Fotolia; **40.2:** George Dolgikh – stock.adobe.com / Fotolia; **41.1:** Sean Locke / iStockphoto; **41.2:** mediaphotos / iStockphoto; **41.3:** hobo_018 / Getty Images – iStockphoto; **41.4:** FamVeld / Getty Images – iStockphoto; **41.5:** lenta / iStockphoto; **42.1:** pictarena – stock.adobe.com / Fotolia; **42.2:** s4svisuals – stock.adobe.com / Fotolia; **42.3:** trekandshoot / Getty Images – iStockphoto; **43.1:** Herve Champollion / akg-images / picturedesk.com; **43.2:** cjp / iStockphoto; **43.3:** microgen / Getty Images – iStockphoto; **44.1:** Christina Anzenberger-Fink, Wien / öbv; **44.2:** Christina Anzenberger-Fink, Wien / öbv; **44.3:** Christina Anzenberger-Fink, Wien / öbv; **44.4:** Waltraud Donath, Wien / öbv; **44.5:** Christina Anzenberger-Fink, Wien / öbv; **44.6:** AntonioGuillem / Getty Images – iStockphoto; **46.1:** Margaret Cooper / iStockphoto; **46.2:** Marc Dufresne / Getty Images – iStockphoto; **46.3:** mustafa6noz / Getty Images – iStockphoto; **49.1:** Artush / Getty Images – iStockphoto; **50.1:** Hartmut Reeh / dpa / picturedesk.com; **51.1:** xenotar / Getty Images – iStockphoto; **51.2:** Anthony Anex / EPA / picturedesk.com; **52.1:** Brent Bossom / iStockphoto; **53.1:** Maksud_kr / iStockphoto; **53.2:** ugibugi / Fotolia; **53.3:** Stuart Franklin / Magnum Photos / picturedesk.com; **53.4:** Eileen Hart / iStockphoto; **54.1:** Lise Gagne / iStockphoto; **55.1:** Denis Raev / iStockphoto; **55.2:** Ernst Klett Sprachen; **55.3:** mbtphotos / iStockphoto; **55.4:** Retroman / Fotolia; **55.5:** Crusitu Robert / iStockphoto; **56.1:** Ryan Balderas / iStockphoto; **56.2:** Tatiana Popova / iStockphoto; **56.3:** Marcos Moreno García / iStockphoto; **56.4:** -M-I-S-H-A- / iStockphoto; **56.6:** Barbara Henry / iStockphoto; **56.7:** Valerie Loiseleux / iStockphoto; **56.8:** Merih Unal Ozmen / iStockphoto; **56.9:** M / iStockphoto; **56.10:** JLGutierrez / Getty Images – iStockphoto; **56.12:** remar / Fotolia; **56.13:** Christopher Steer / iStockphoto; **56.14:** Jan Rysavy / iStockphoto; **58.1:** Roman Babakin / Getty Images – iStockphoto; **58.2:** RyanJLane / Getty Images – iStockphoto; **59.1:** alvarez / Getty Images – iStockphoto; S. **59.2:** FamVeld / Getty Images – iStockphoto; **59.3:** Nikada / Getty Images – iStockphoto; **60.1:** AndreaAste / Getty